Origami Symphony No. 7

Musical Monkeys

Books by John Montroll
www.johnmontroll.com
Instagram: @montrollorigami

Origami Symphonies

Origami Symphony No. 1: The Elephant's Trumpet Call
Origami Symphony No. 2: Trio of Sharks & Playful Prehistoric Mammals
Origami Symphony No. 3: Duet of Majestic Dragons & Dinosaurs
Origami Symphony No. 4: Capturing Vibrant Coral Reef Fish
Origami Symphony No. 5: Woodwinds, Horns, and a Moose
Origami Symphony No. 6: Striped Snakes Changing Scales
Origami Symphony No. 7: Musical Monkeys

General Origami

Origami Fold-by-Fold
DC Super Heroes Origami
Origami Worldwide
Teach Yourself Origami: Third Edition
Christmas Origami: Second Edition
Storytime Origami
Origami Inside-Out: Third Edition

Animal Origami

Dogs in Origami
Perfect Pets Origami
Dragons and Other Fantastic Creatures in Origami
Bugs in Origami
Horses in Origami
Origami Birds
Origami Gone Wild
Dinosaur Origami
Origami Dinosaurs for Beginners
Prehistoric Origami: Dinosaurs and other Creatures: Third Edition
Mythological Creatures and the Chinese Zodiac Origami
Origami Sea Life: Third Edition
Bringing Origami to Life: Second Edition
Origami Sculptures: Fourth Edition
African Animals in Origami: Third Edition
North American Animals in Origami: Third Edition
Origami for the Enthusiast: Second Edition

Geometric Origami

Origami Stars
Galaxy of Origami Stars: Second Edition
Origami and Math: Simple to Complex: Second Edition
Origami & Geometry
3D Origami Platonic Solids & More: Second Edition
3D Origami Diamonds
3D Origami Antidiamonds
3D Origami Pyramids
A Plethora of Polyhedra in Origami: Third Edition
Classic Polyhedra Origami
A Constellation of Origami Polyhedra
Origami Polyhedra Design

Dollar Bill Origami

Dollar Origami Treasures: Second Edition
Dollar Bill Animals in Origami: Second Revised Edition
Dollar Bill Origami
Easy Dollar Bill Origami

Simple Origami

Fun and Simple Origami: 101 Easy-to-Fold Projects: Second Edition
Origami Twelve Days of Christmas: And Santa, Too!
Super Simple Origami
Easy Dollar Bill Origami
Easy Origami
Easy Origami 2
Easy Origami 3
Easy Origami Animals
Easy Origami Polar Animals
Easy Origami Ocean Animals
Easy Origami Woodland Animals
Easy Origami Jungle Animals
Meditative Origami

To Jon

Origami Symphony No. 7: *Musical Monkeys*

Copyright © 2022 by John Montroll. All rights reserved.
No part of this publication may be copied or reproduced by any
means without the express written permission of the author.

ISBN-10: 1-877656-59-3
ISBN-13: 978-1-877656-59-0

Antroll Publishing Company

Introduction

Welcome to the world premier of the Seventh Origami Symphony! Using parallel ideas from musical symphonies, an origami symphony showcases four movements with varying themes and styles. Detailed and distinct reptiles, farm animals, antiprisms, stars, and monkeys combine to create an origami adventure for this symphony.

Within the four movements are 37 models. Some of the reptiles in the first movement are a Box Turtle, Frilled Lizard, and a Banded Snake. We take a Walk Through the Farm in the peaceful second movement. Fun scenes can be made with the Ducks, Geese, Pigs, and more. From the third movement, Antiprisms show the zany side of origami and can be used as stands for any of the animals in this symphony. Stars from this movement shine through the night. For the fourth movement, the March of Boisterous and Frolicsome Monkeys shows a fun and entertaining side of origami.

Each model can be folded from a single square using standard origami paper. Given the complexity of the subjects, the models are designed to be as simple as possible. A Pig and Sheep, given plenty of detail, are each folded in 18 steps. The detailed Black and White Colobus Monkey is accomplished in 30 steps. Only 20 steps are used for the Baboon. A higher level of origami design is required to allow for fewer steps for the complex subjects, and is more rewarding to the folder.

The diagrams are drawn in the internationally approved Randlett-Yoshizawa style. You can use any kind of square paper for these models, but the best results will be achieved with standard origami paper, which is colored on one side and white on the other (in the diagrams in this book, the shading represents the colored side). Large sheets, such as nine inches squared, are easier to use than small ones.

Origami supplies can be found in arts and craft shops, or at Dover Publications online: www.doverpublications.com. You can also visit OrigamiUSA at www.origamiusa.org for origami supplies and other related information including an extensive list of local, national, and international origami groups.

Please follow me on Instagram @montrollorigami to see posts of my origami.

I give special thanks to Jon Herrity. He folded and took photographs of most of the models. I also thank the folders who continued to encourage me to develop the presentation of origami through an origami symphony.

I hope you enjoy the themes and complexities of Origami Symphony No. 7.

John Montroll
www.johnmontroll.com

Contents

Symbols 9
Origami Symphony 9
Origami Symphony No. 7 10
First Movement 11
Second Movement 45
Third Movement 76
Fourth Movement 99

★ Simple
★★ Intermediate
★★★ Complex
★★★★ Very Complex

First Movement
Adagio, Allegro: Reptiles Picking up Speed

11 Box Turtle ★★★

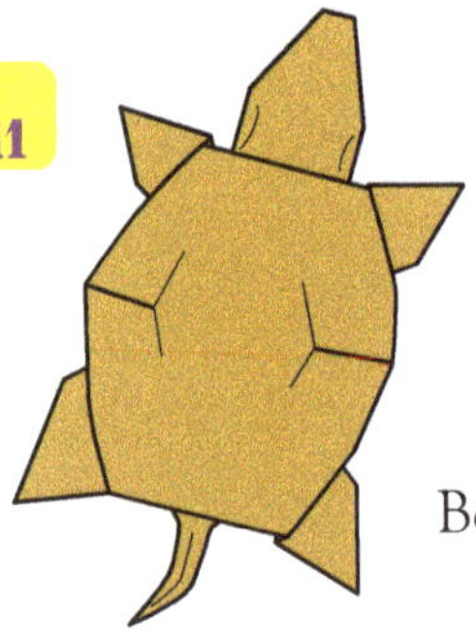

15 Pond Turtle ★★★

19 Green Sea Turtle ★★★

24 Chinese Water Dragon ★★★

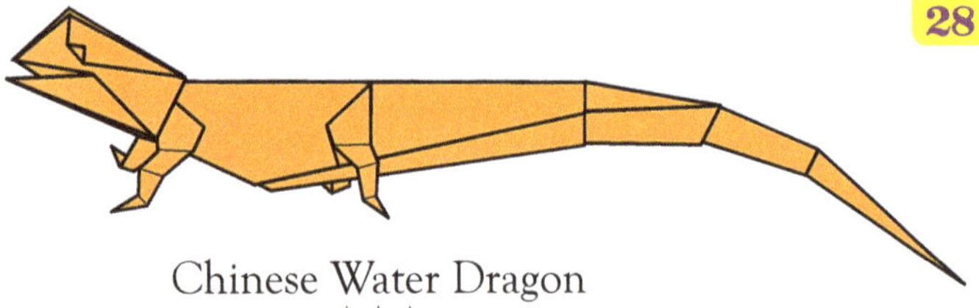

28 Komodo Dragon ★★★

32 Frilled Lizard ★★★

36 Crocodile ★★★

40 Banded Snake ★★★

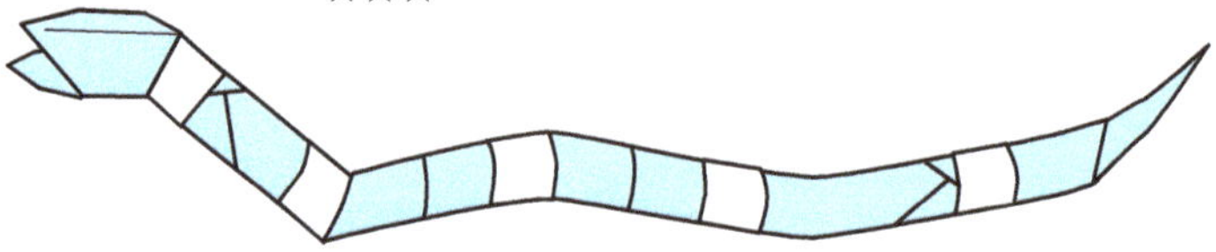

Second Movement
Andante: Walking Through the Farm

45 Swimming Duck ★★

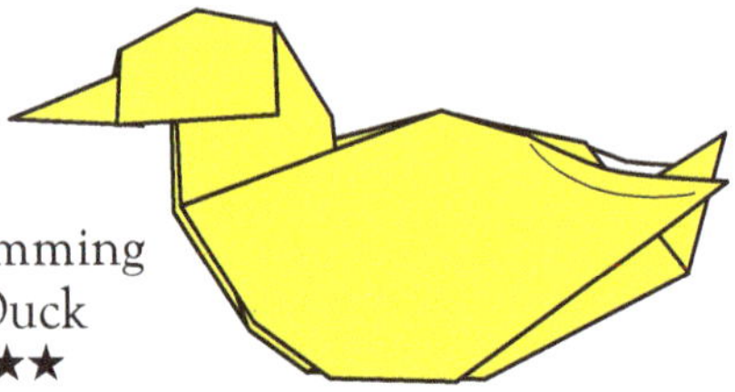

47 Standing Duck ★★

49 Goose ★★

52 Swimming Swan ★★

54 Standing Swan ★★

57 Crow ★★

59 Chick ★★

61 Hen ★★

64 Rooster ★★

67 Pig ★★

69 Sheep ★★

71 Cow ★★★

Third Movement
Minuet of Antiprisms with a Trio of Stars

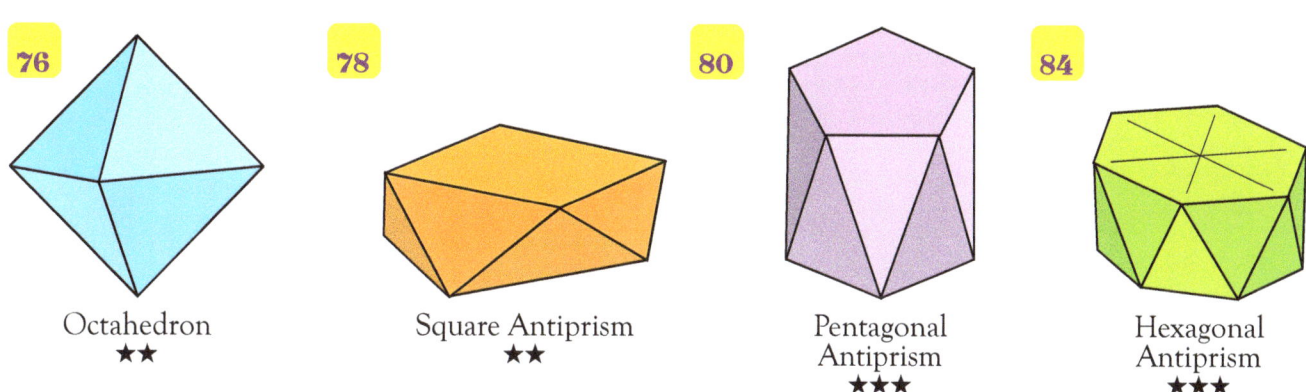

76 Octahedron ★★

78 Square Antiprism ★★

80 Pentagonal Antiprism ★★★

84 Hexagonal Antiprism ★★★

Contents

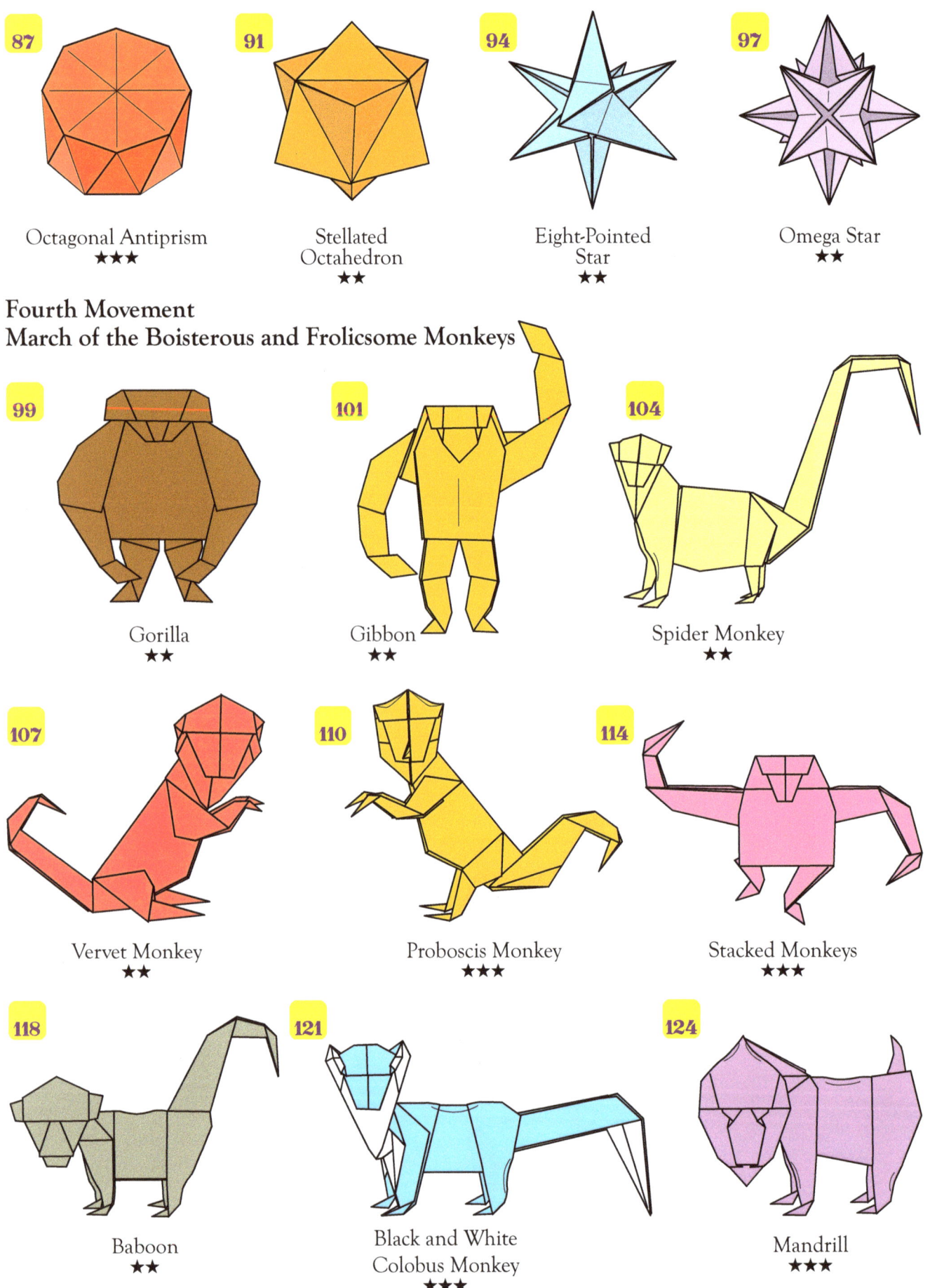

| 87 Octagonal Antiprism ★★★ | 91 Stellated Octahedron ★★ | 94 Eight-Pointed Star ★★ | 97 Omega Star ★★ |

Fourth Movement
March of the Boisterous and Frolicsome Monkeys

| 99 Gorilla ★★ | 101 Gibbon ★★ | 104 Spider Monkey ★★ |

| 107 Vervet Monkey ★★ | 110 Proboscis Monkey ★★★ | 114 Stacked Monkeys ★★★ |

| 118 Baboon ★★ | 121 Black and White Colobus Monkey ★★★ | 124 Mandrill ★★★ |

8 *Origami Symphony No. 7*

Symbols

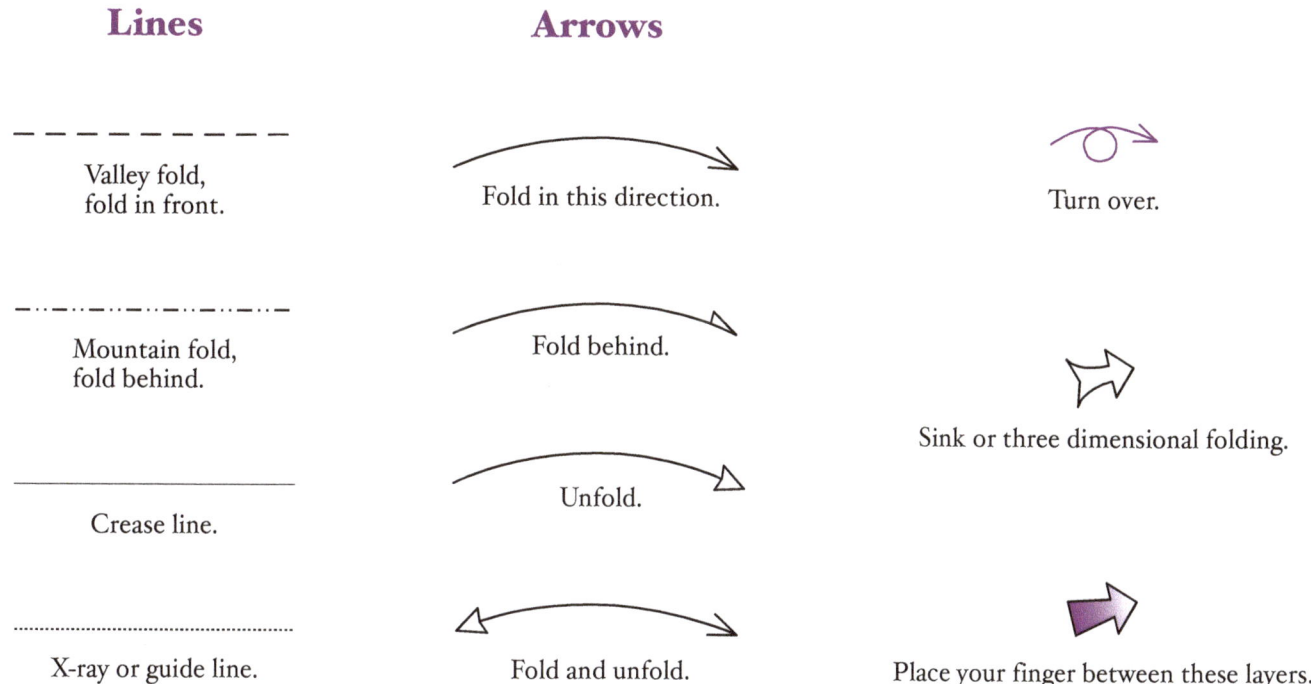

Origami Symphony

I enjoy writing these origami symphonies. This is now the seventh symphony and I wonder if anyone has noticed something in common with all my symphonies versus any other origami book? There are no pages on the basic folds, such as explaining a reverse fold.

Even origami books of complex or super complex work contain several pages explaining the basic folds. I wonder if an experienced folder would need it. Or, for the beginner, would they be ready to fold complex work by learning the basics? Including these pages is at the cost of not showing diagrams for another model.

In piano books, or music books in general, there is no mention of how to read the notes or what the staves mean. It is assumed that the musician is at the appropriate level and ready to enhance their repertoire.

I am treating these origami symphonies in the same manner. By assuming the folder is not a beginner, there is no need for the basic folds. By omitting that and including more models, it brings origami to a higher level.

With that in mind, I hope you are ready for all the adventures this symphony has to offer.

Origami Symphony No. 7

The subjects in Origami Symphony No. 7 are curious reptiles, peaceful farm animals, mind-boggling antiprisms and stars, and playful monkeys. This variety celebrates nature while exploring origami design.

Reptiles fill the first movement as the symphony begins slowly, Adagio, with a trio of turtles. A Box Turtle, Pond Turtle, and Green Sea Turtle walk and swim across the stage. A Chinese Water Dragon picks up the tempo, Allegro, while a Frilled Lizard performs an amusing dance. The first movement ends with a Banded Snake slithering away.

The second movement, Andante, Walking through the Farm, weaves all kinds of melodies from the farm animals. A swimming Duck and standing Duck are represented as two designs. Swans, Geese, Crows, and the Chicken family carry their melodies. Unifying origami structures are used in the designs of these animals. This peaceful movement ends with a Pig, Sheep, and Cow.

The third movement, Minuet of Antiprisms with a Trio of Stars, represents the zany side of origami. The antiprisms make for perfect stands for the reptiles and monkeys. Antiprisms are interesting shapes where the top and bottom are the same polygon and the sides have a band of triangles going around. Triangular (the Octahedron), square, pentagonal, hexagonal, and octagonal antiprisms make for a mind-boggling display. The trio of three-dimensional stars fill the night sky on the farm and elsewhere.

The fun continues with the fourth movement of the March of Boisterous and Frolicsome Monkeys. Upon waking up, Gibbons sing enchanting songs that you must listen to. The Black and White Colobus Monkey swings through the trees. A Gorilla, Baboon, and Spider Monkey all hoot, holler, and bark as they play in the trees. A magnificent Mandrill closes the symphony.

This symphony incorporates many styles and subjects with the hope of challenging the folder. Detailed reptiles, unified structures for the farm animals, elaborate designs for the antiprisms and stars, and distinct monkeys all combine to demonstrate the magic of origami.

First Movement

Adagio, Allegro: Reptiles Picking up Speed

Large and small, found in the water or on rocks and trees, reptiles live all around the world. A box turtle opens the symphony, crawling slowly across the stage. After two more turtles, a Chinese water dragon scampers by and a frilled lizard creates an amusing scene. A hungry crocodile waits patiently and the movement ends with a banded snake slithering away.

Box Turtle

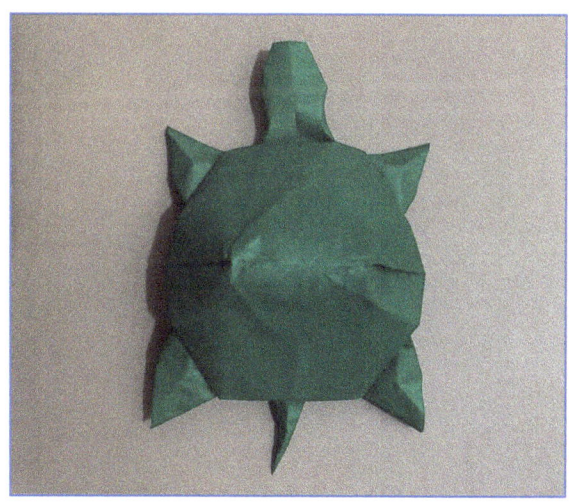

At 5 to 8 inches, box turtles are brightly colored with yellow and orange patterns against a dark brown shell. They are known to live for 30 to 40 years but can reach 100 years. They like to dig in cool mud and bury themselves under leaves in the forest. They feed on berries, mushrooms, insects and other small creatures. A group of turtles is a bale.

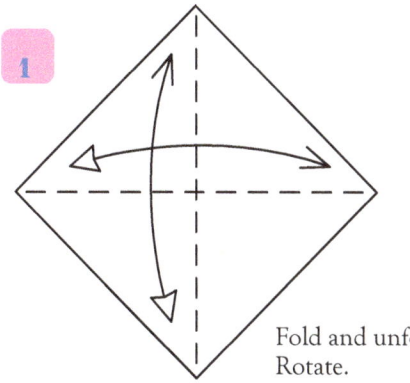

Fold and unfold. Rotate.

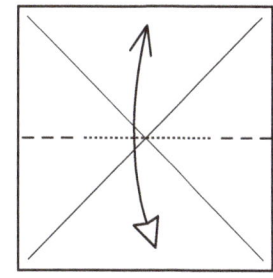

Fold and unfold on the edges.

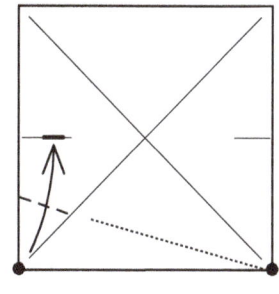

Bring the corner to the crease.

Box Turtle   11

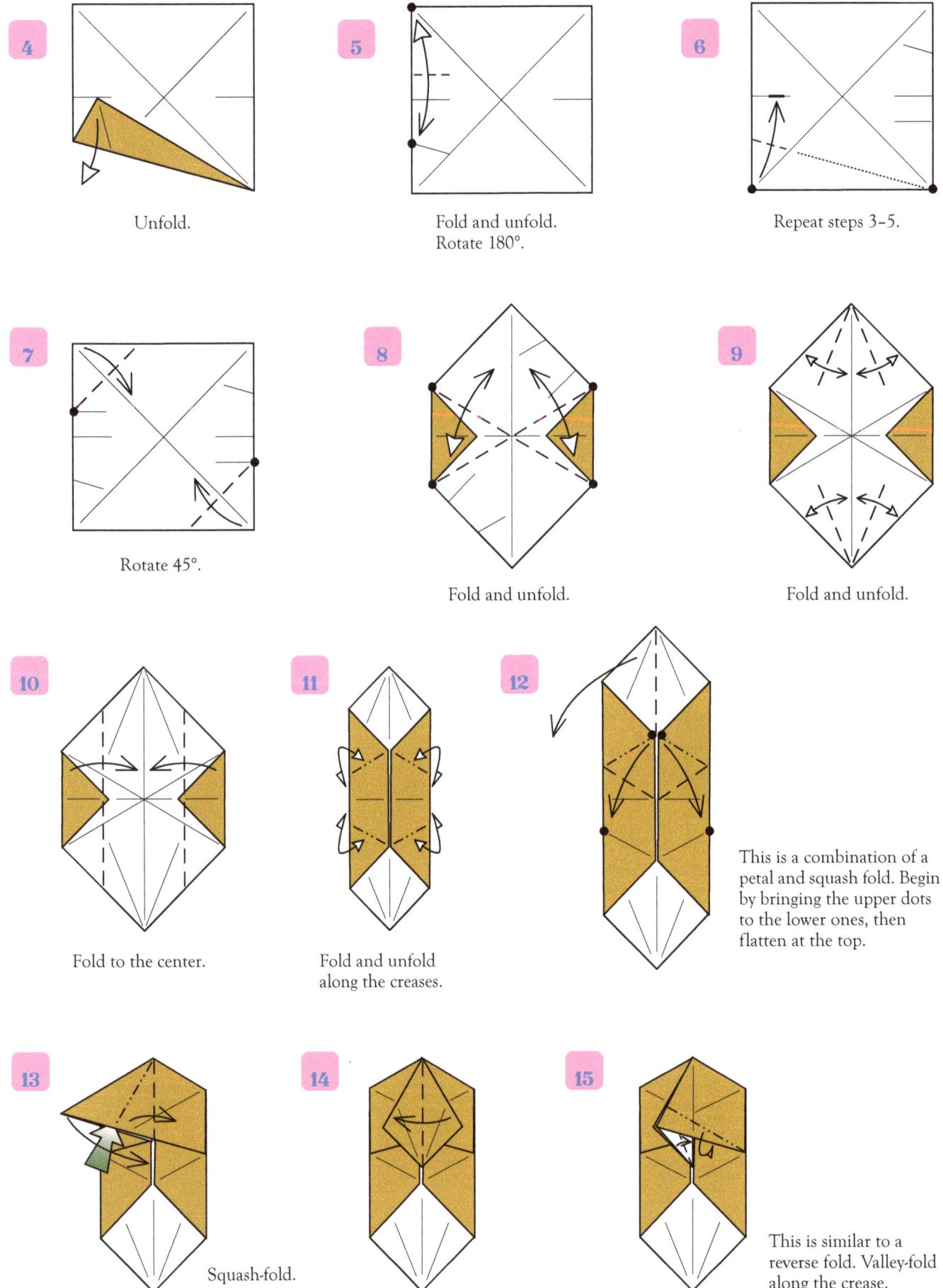

12 *Origami Symphony No. 7*

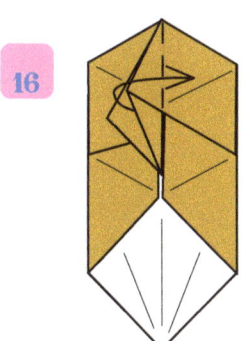

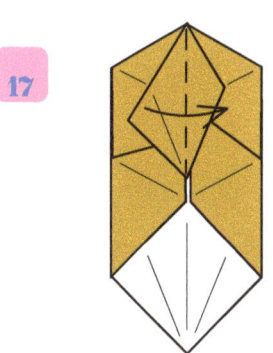

Repeat steps 14–16 on the left.

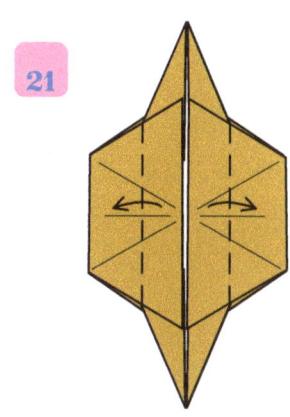

Spread while folding up.

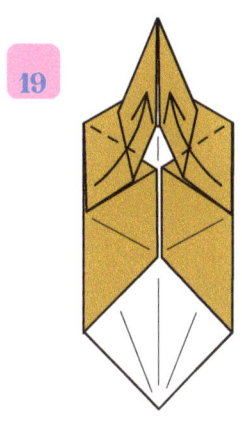

Rotate 180°.

Repeat steps 12–19.

Make squash folds.

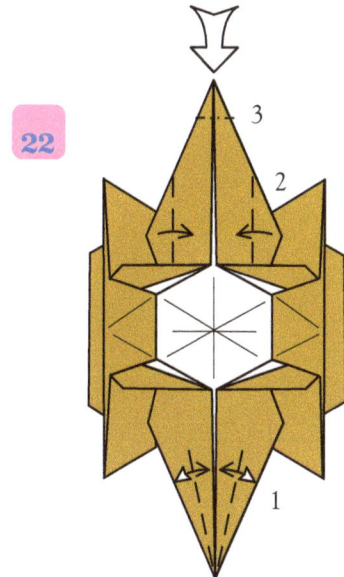

1. Fold and unfold.
2. Fold on the left and right.
3. Sink.

Box Turtle 13

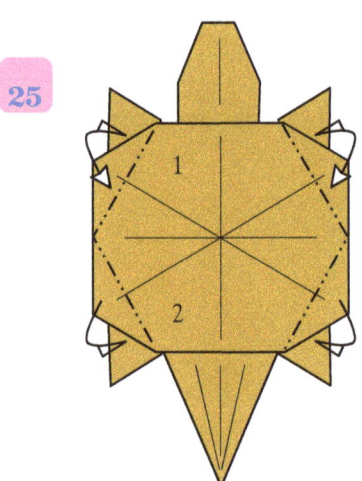
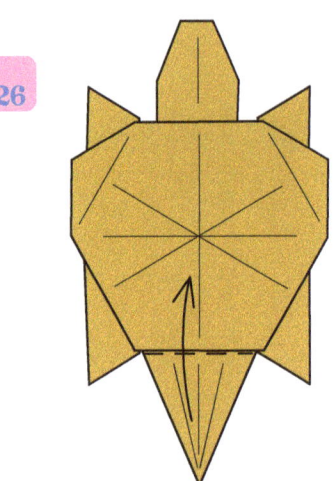
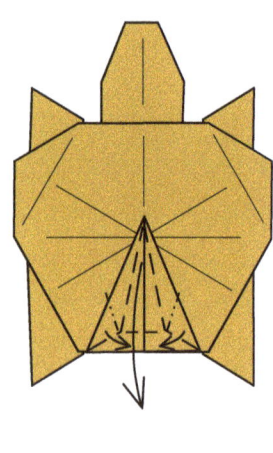

1. Fold and unfold on the top.
2. Fold behind.

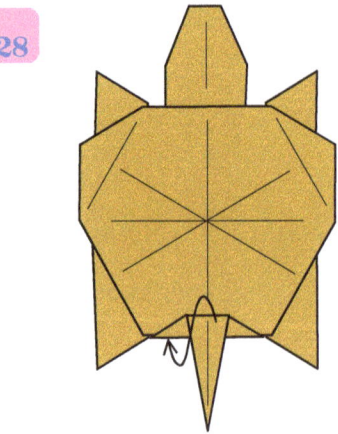

Tuck inside.

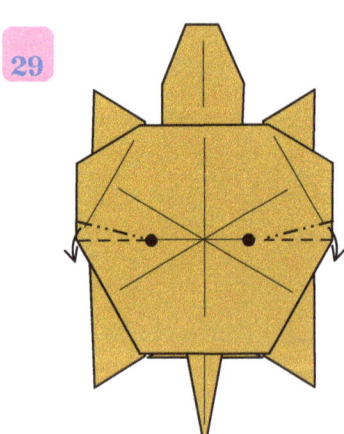

Make pleat folds on the shell. Puff out at the dots.

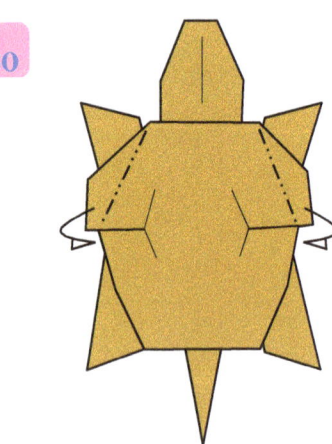

Wrap around.

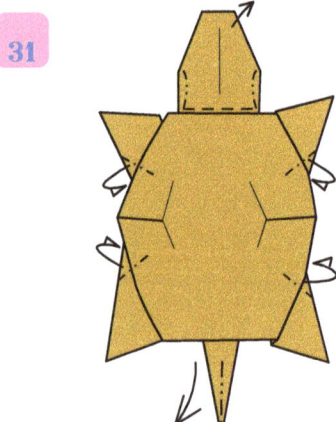

Shape with 3D folding.

Box Turtle

14 *Origami Symphony No. 7*

Pond Turtle

Pond turtles are dark brown or olive colored. This aquatic turtle lives in streams, lakes, marshes and other wetland areas. They feed on fish, tadpoles, aquatic invertebrates, insects, flowers, and algae. At 6 to 10 inches, they bask on logs, branches, boulders, and even stack on each other. They can live to over 50 years. Records have shown turtles to be the oldest reptile, dating back 215 million years ago.

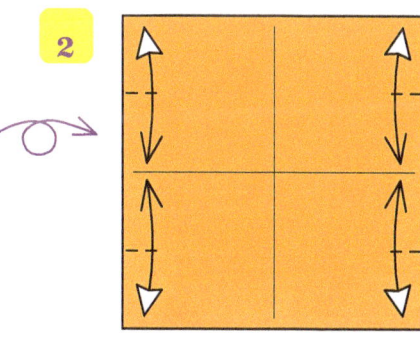

1. Fold and unfold.

2. Fold and unfold on the edges.

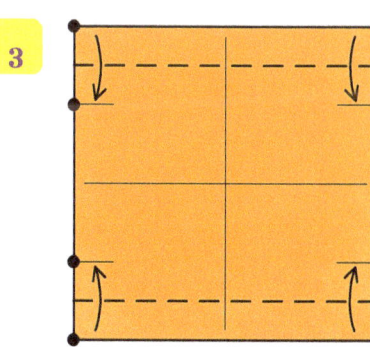

3.

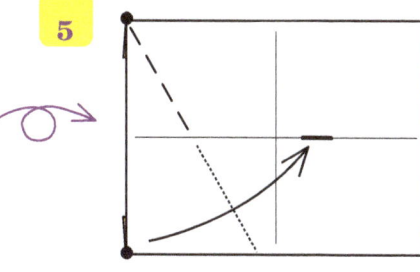

4. Fold and unfold the top layer.

5. Bring the corner to the line.

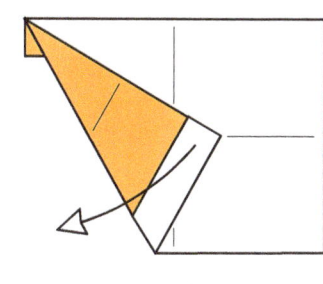

6. Unfold.

Pond Turtle 15

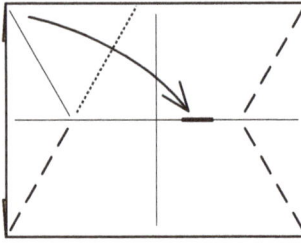

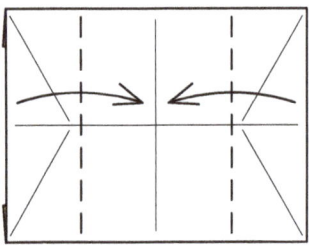
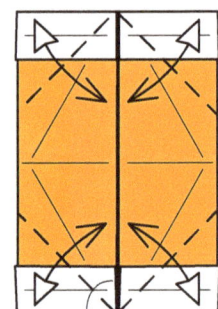

Repeat steps 5–6 three times.

Fold to the center.

Fold to the center and unfold.

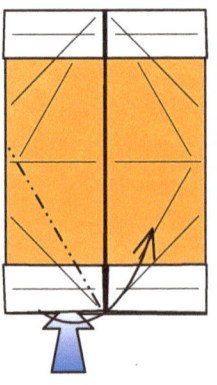
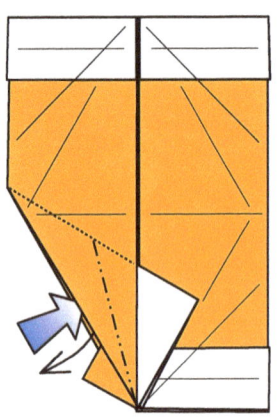
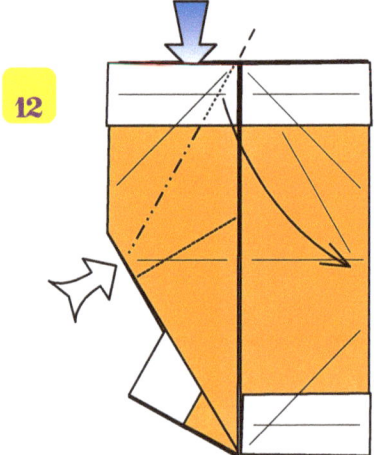

Reverse-fold along the crease.

Reverse-fold along a hidden crease.

Mountain-fold along the crease for this spread squash fold.

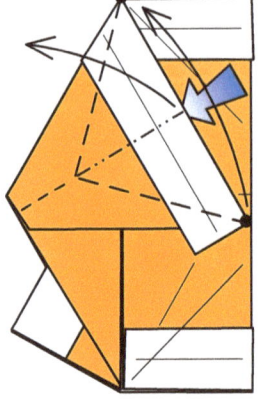

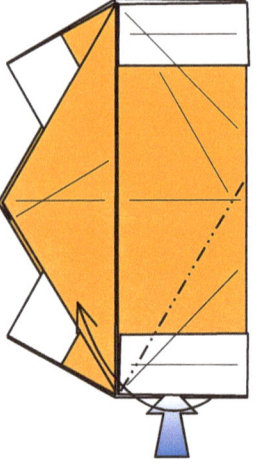
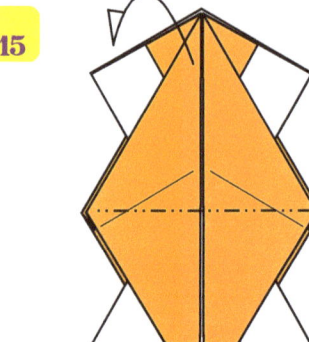

Fold along the creases. The dots will meet.

Repeat steps 10–13 on the right.

16 *Origami Symphony No. 7*

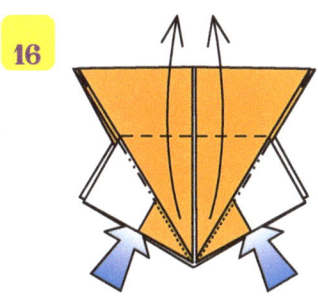

Make squash folds. Repeat behind.

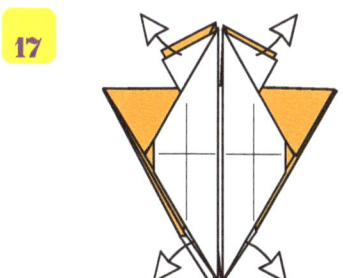

Unfold at the top and bottom. Repeat behind.

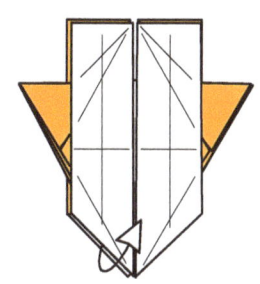

Wrap around, repeat behind.

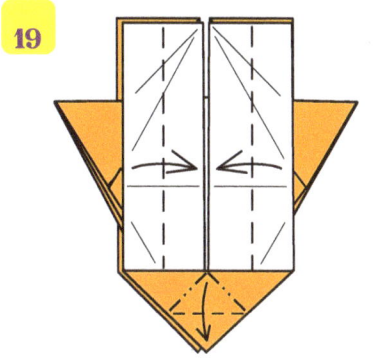

Petal-fold. Do not repeat behind.

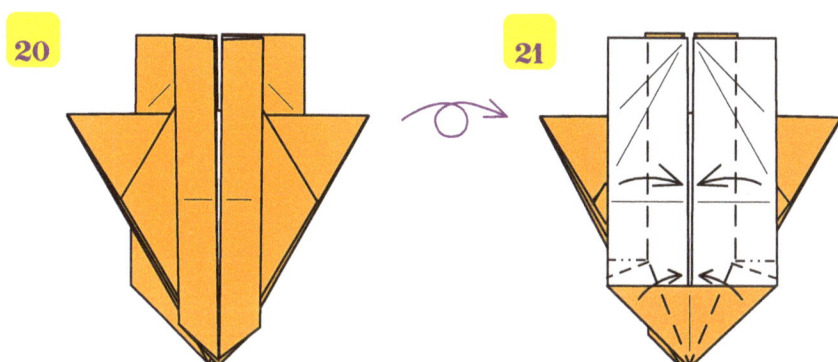

Fold to the center with squash folds.

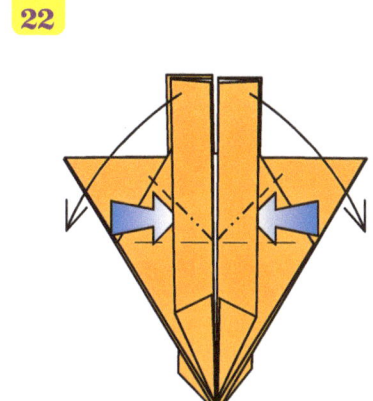

Make reverse folds. Repeat behind.

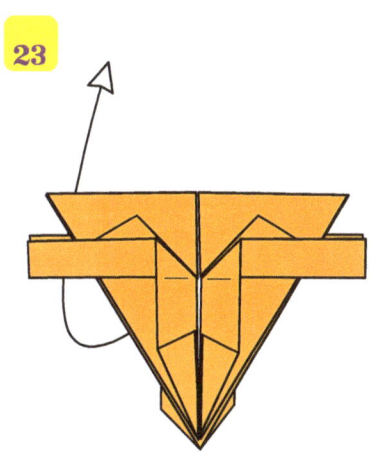

Unfold.

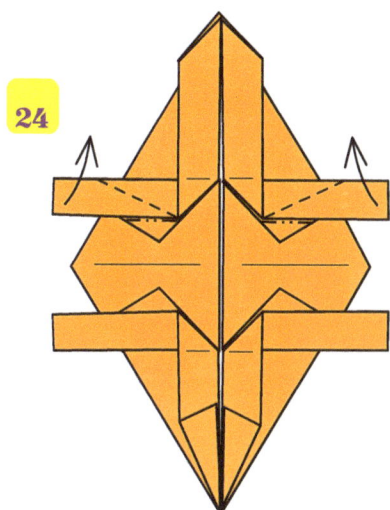

Make squash folds.

Pond Turtle **17**

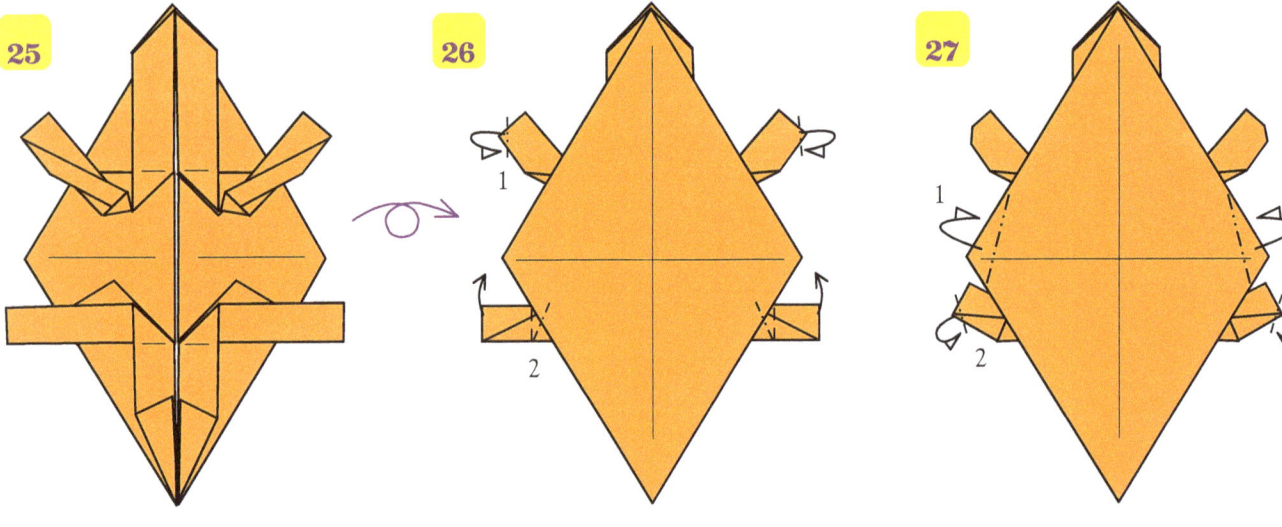

1. Fold behind on the left and right.
2. Make pleat folds on the left and right.

Fold behind on the left and right at 1 and 2.

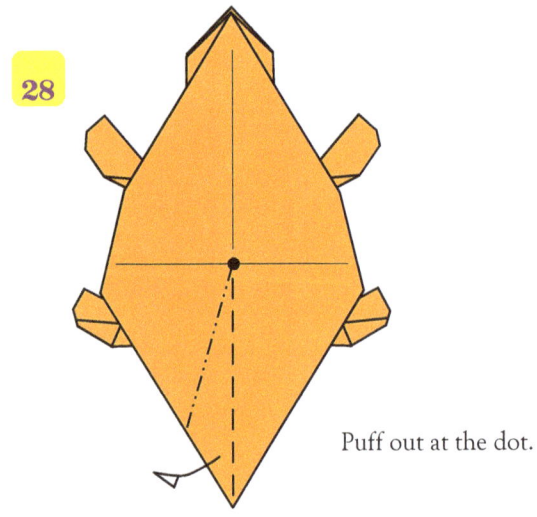

Puff out at the dot.

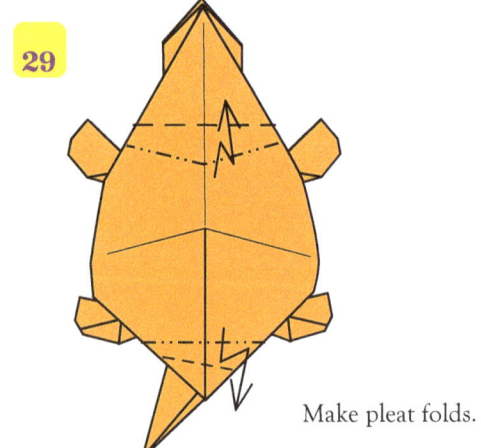

Make pleat folds.

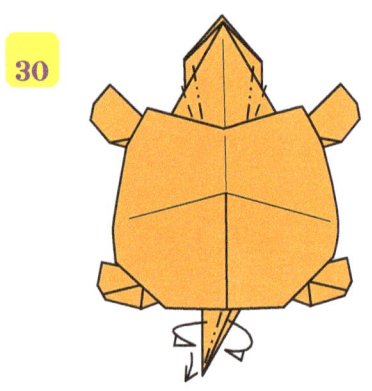

Shape the head and tail with soft folds.

Pond Turtle

Green Sea Turtle

While the green sea turtle is brown or olive, it is named because of the green fat under its skin. Using its powerful flippers, the green sea turtle can swim at 35 miles per hour as it travels across oceans. It can follow earth's magnetic field. As one of the largest species of turtles, it can grow to 3 to 5 feet. The young feed on worms, aquatic insects and other small creatures while the adults are herbivores and feed on algae and seagrass. It can live to over 70 years.

1 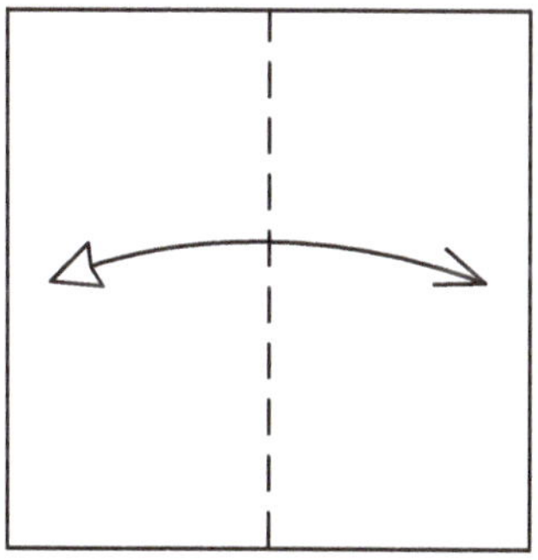
Fold and unfold.

2 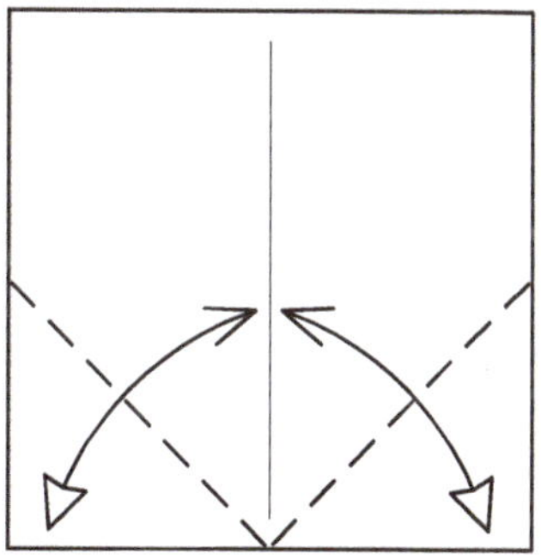
Fold to the center and unfold.

3 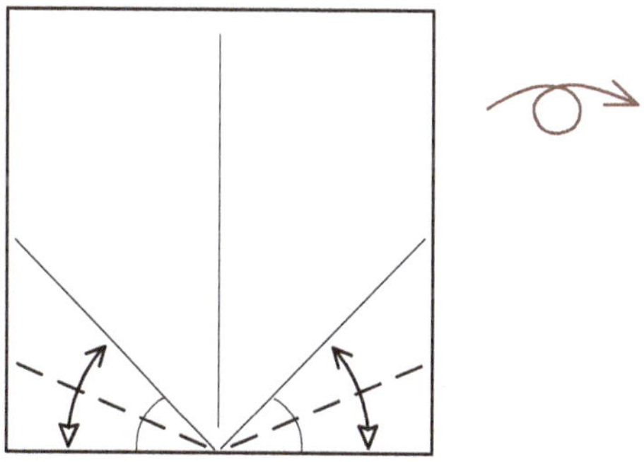
Fold and unfold.

4

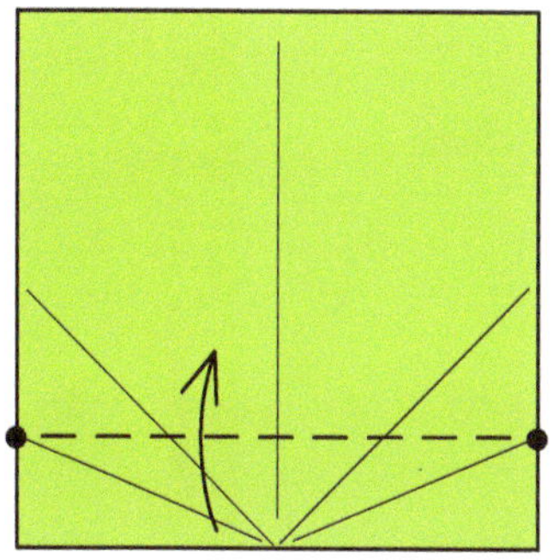

5

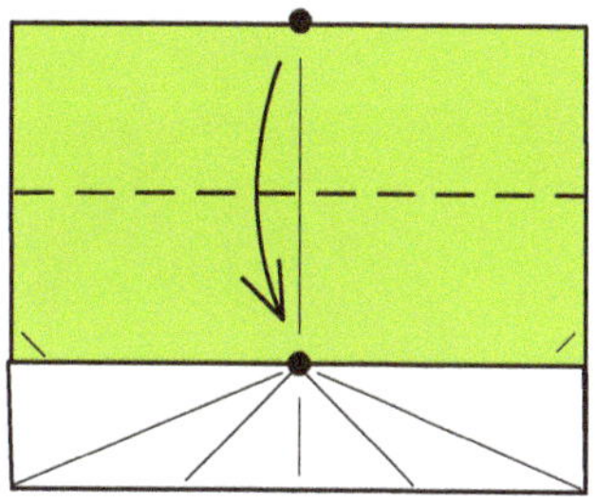

6
1. Fold and unfold the top layer. 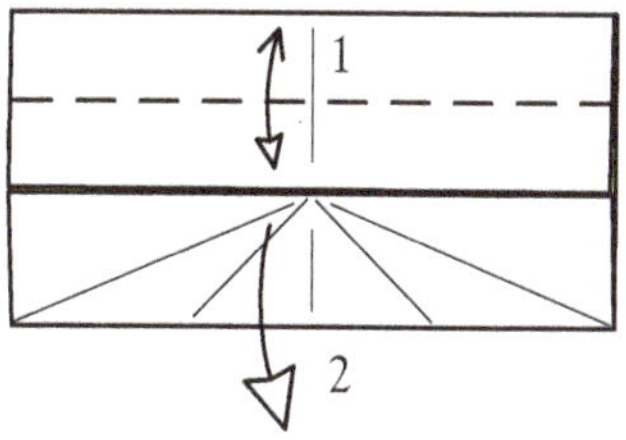
2. Unfold.

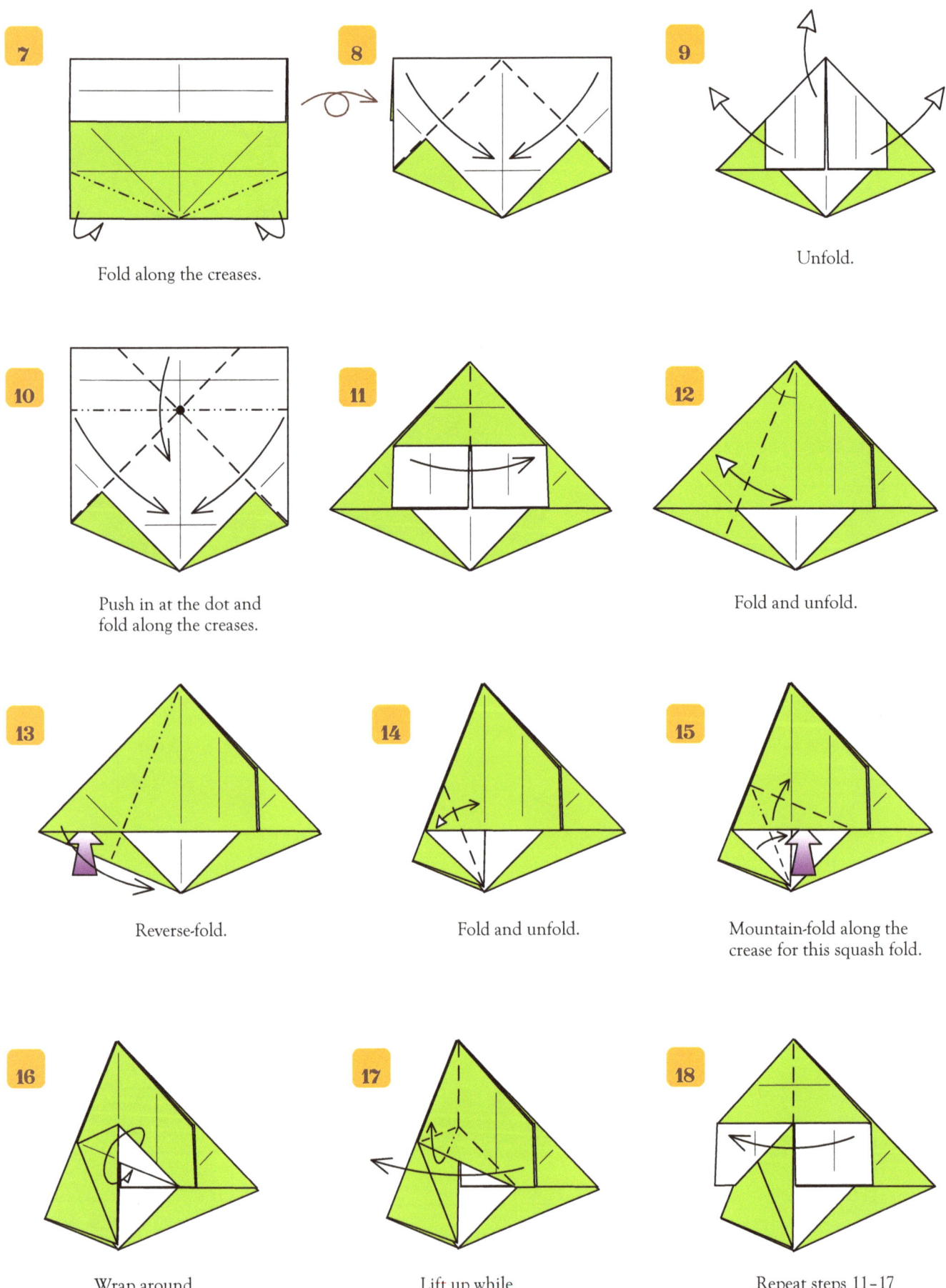

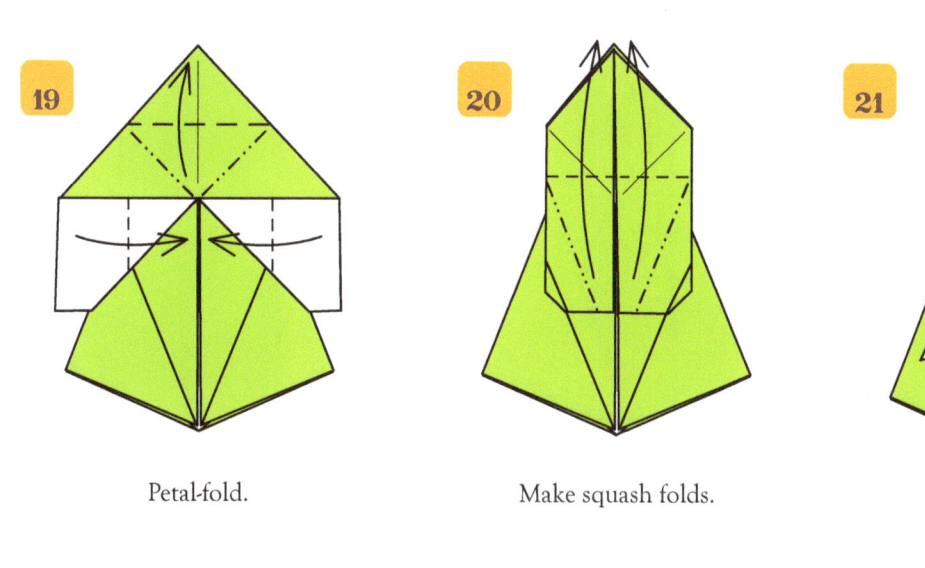
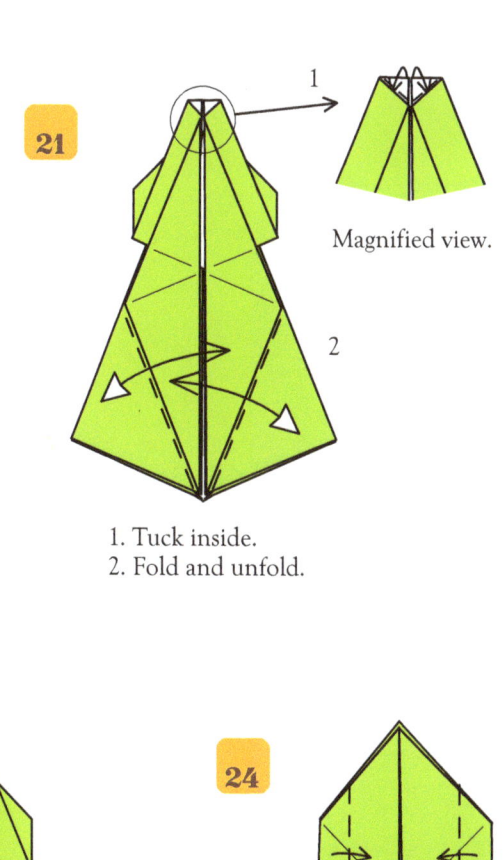

Petal-fold.

Make squash folds.

1. Tuck inside.
2. Fold and unfold.

Magnified view.

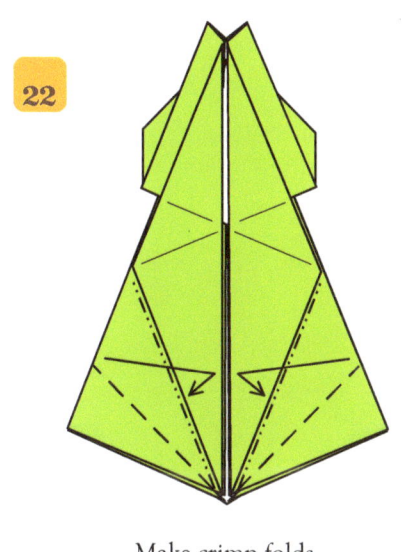
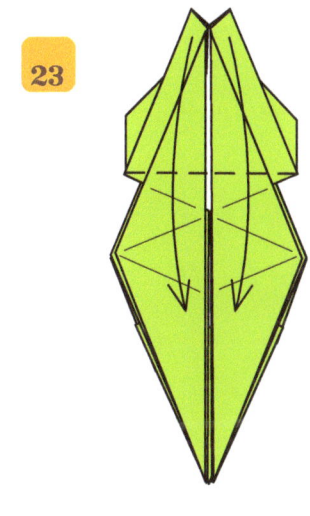
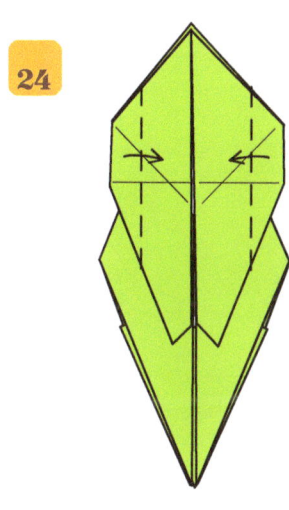

Make crimp folds.

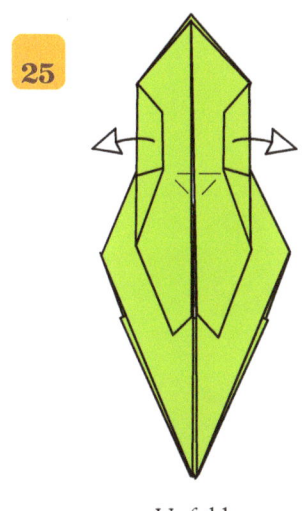
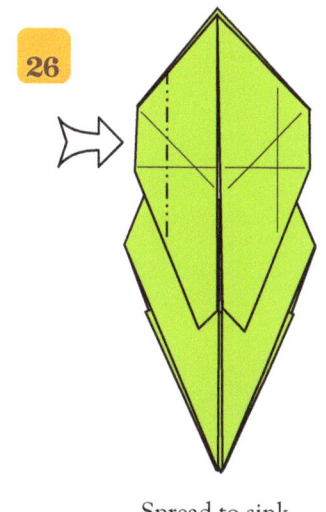
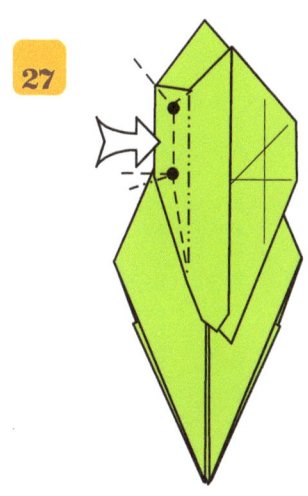

Unfold.

Spread to sink.

This is 3D. Push in at the two dots and flatten.

Green Sea Turtle 21

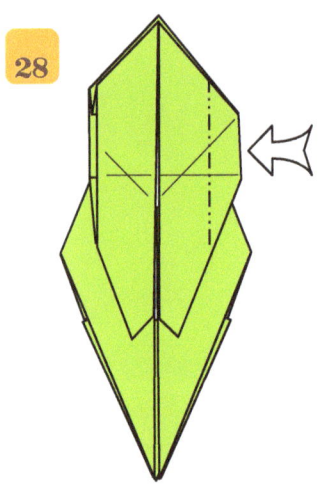

28

Repeat steps 26–27 on the right.

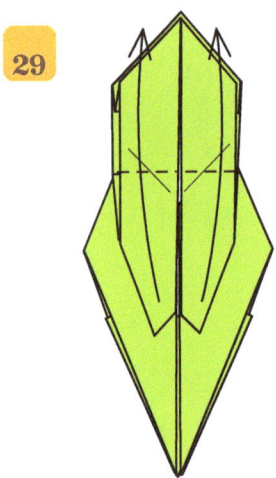

29

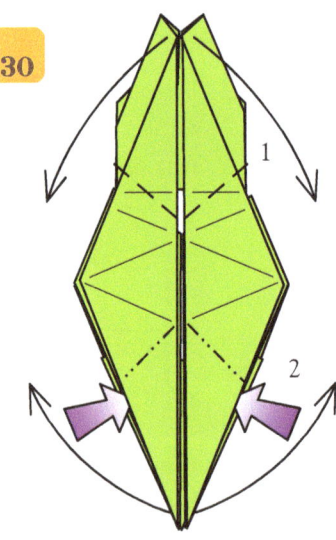

30

1. Make small squash folds.
2. Make reverse folds along the creases.

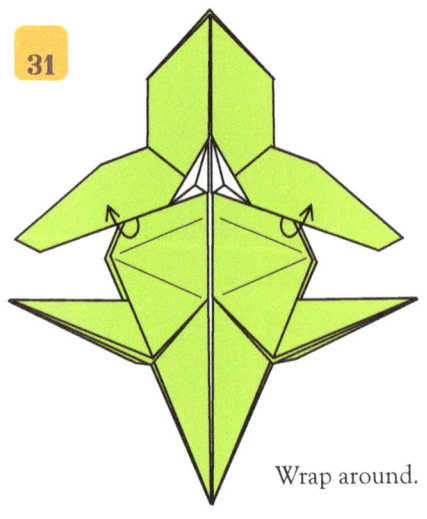

31

Wrap around.

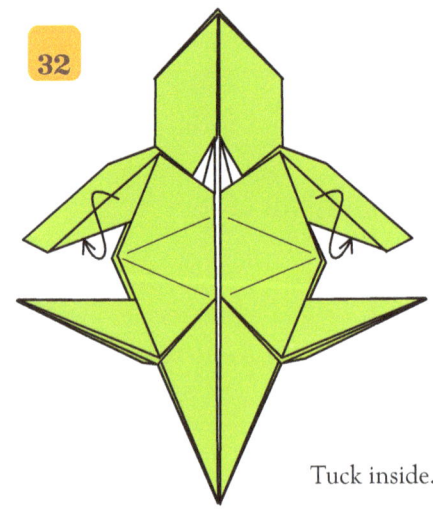

32

Tuck inside.

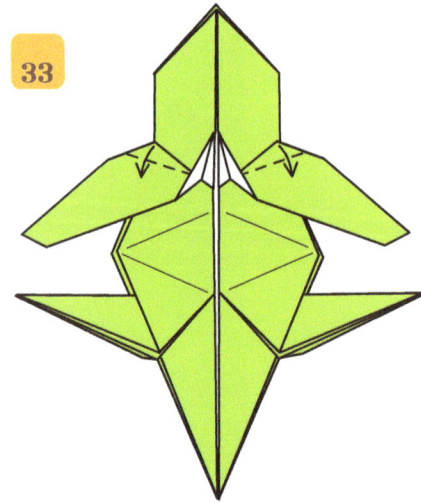

33

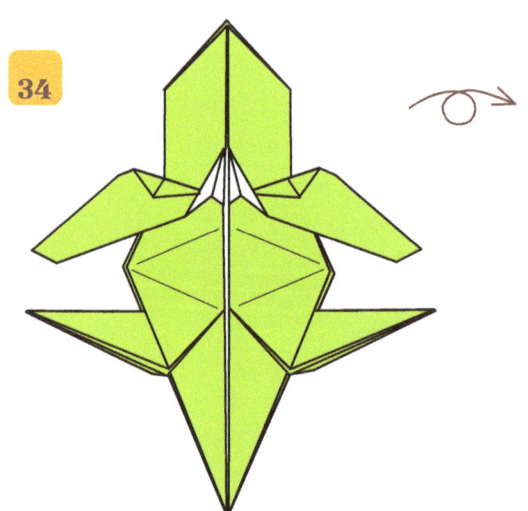

34

22　Origami Symphony No. 7

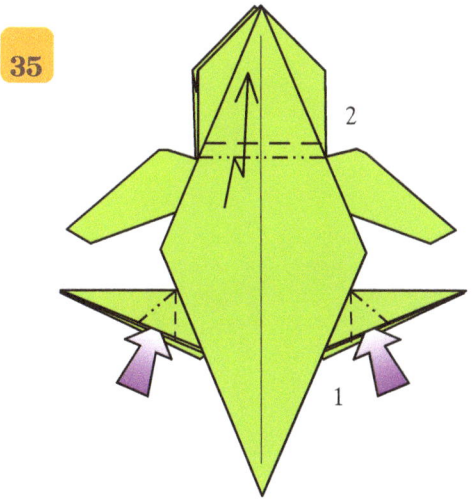

1. Make squash folds.
2. Pleat-fold.

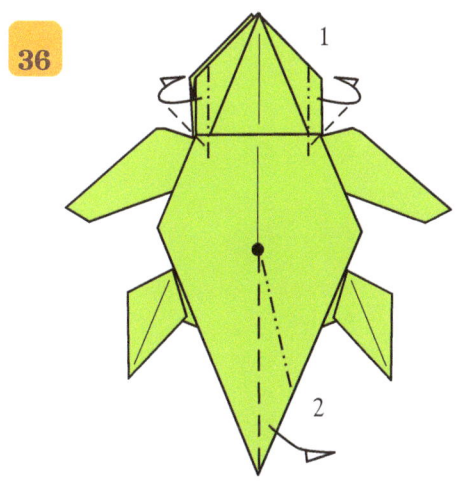

1. Fold behind with small squash folds.
2. Puff out at the dot.

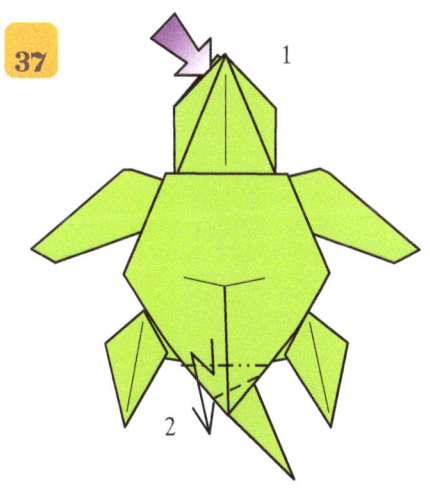

1. Open the mouth.
2. Pleat-fold.

Green Sea Turtle

Green Sea Turtle 23

Chinese Water Dragon

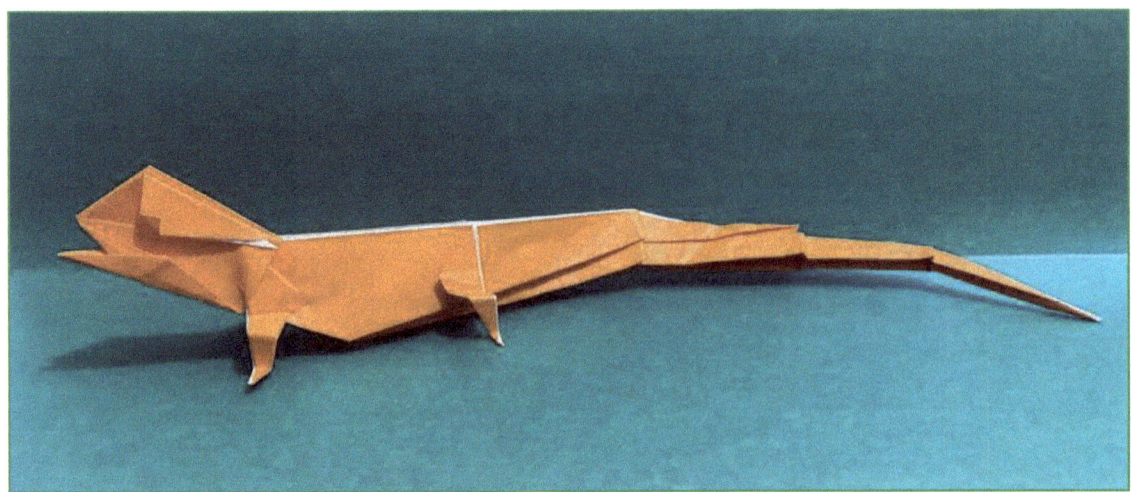

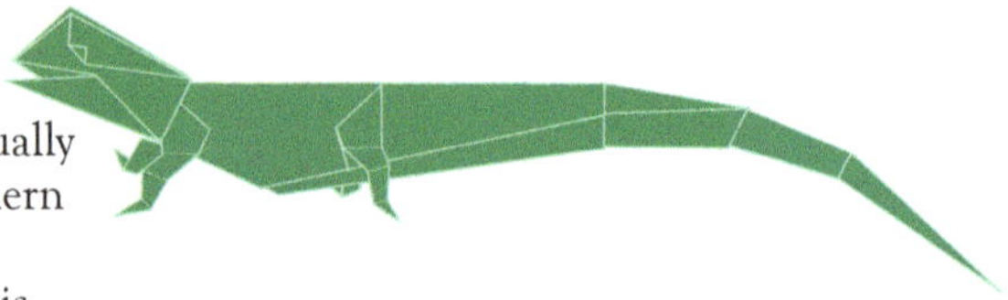

Though not a dragon, the Chinese Water Dragon is a lizard. Usually green or turquoise, they are found in streams and lakes in Southern Asia and Australia. They spend much of their time in trees. At around three feet in length, the tail is 2/3 of its length. The tail is used for balance, swimming, and as a weapon. With strong back legs they can jump and even run on two legs. The young eats crickets, mealworms, ants, and caterpillars while the larger ones feed on birds, mice, and small fish. Many are kept as tame pets.

1. Fold and unfold.

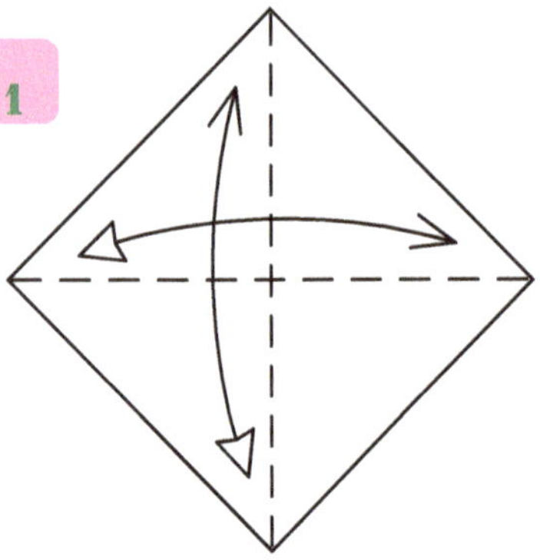

2. Fold and unfold on the edge.

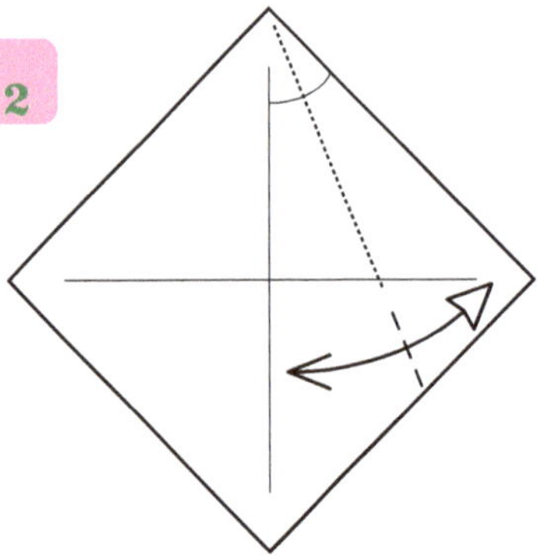

3. Fold and unfold on the edge.

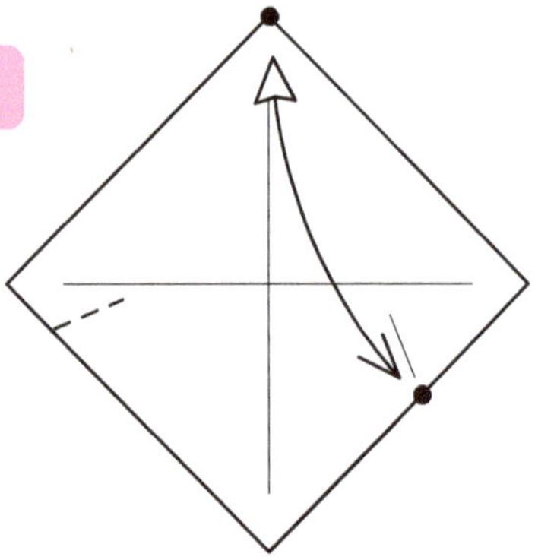

4. Fold and unfold along the diagonal.

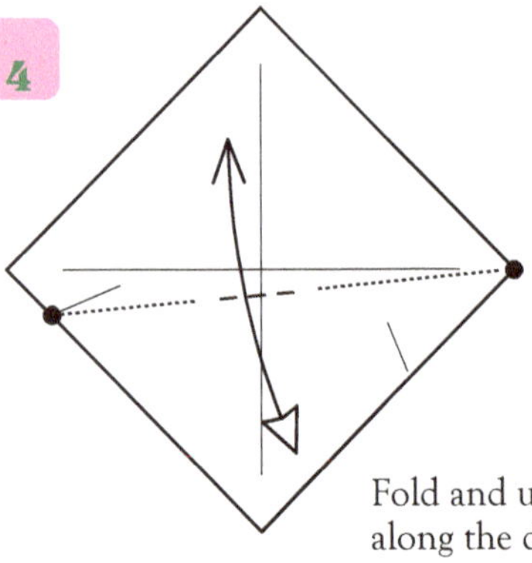

5.

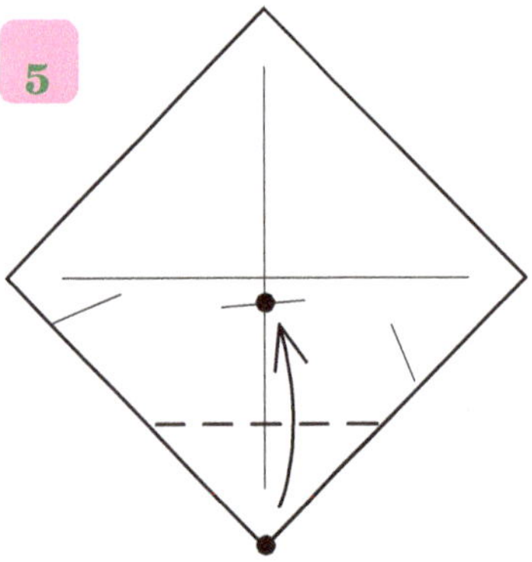

6.

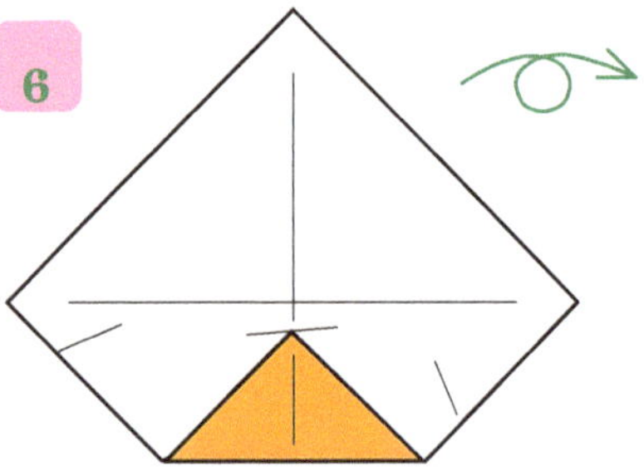

24   Origami Symphony No. 7

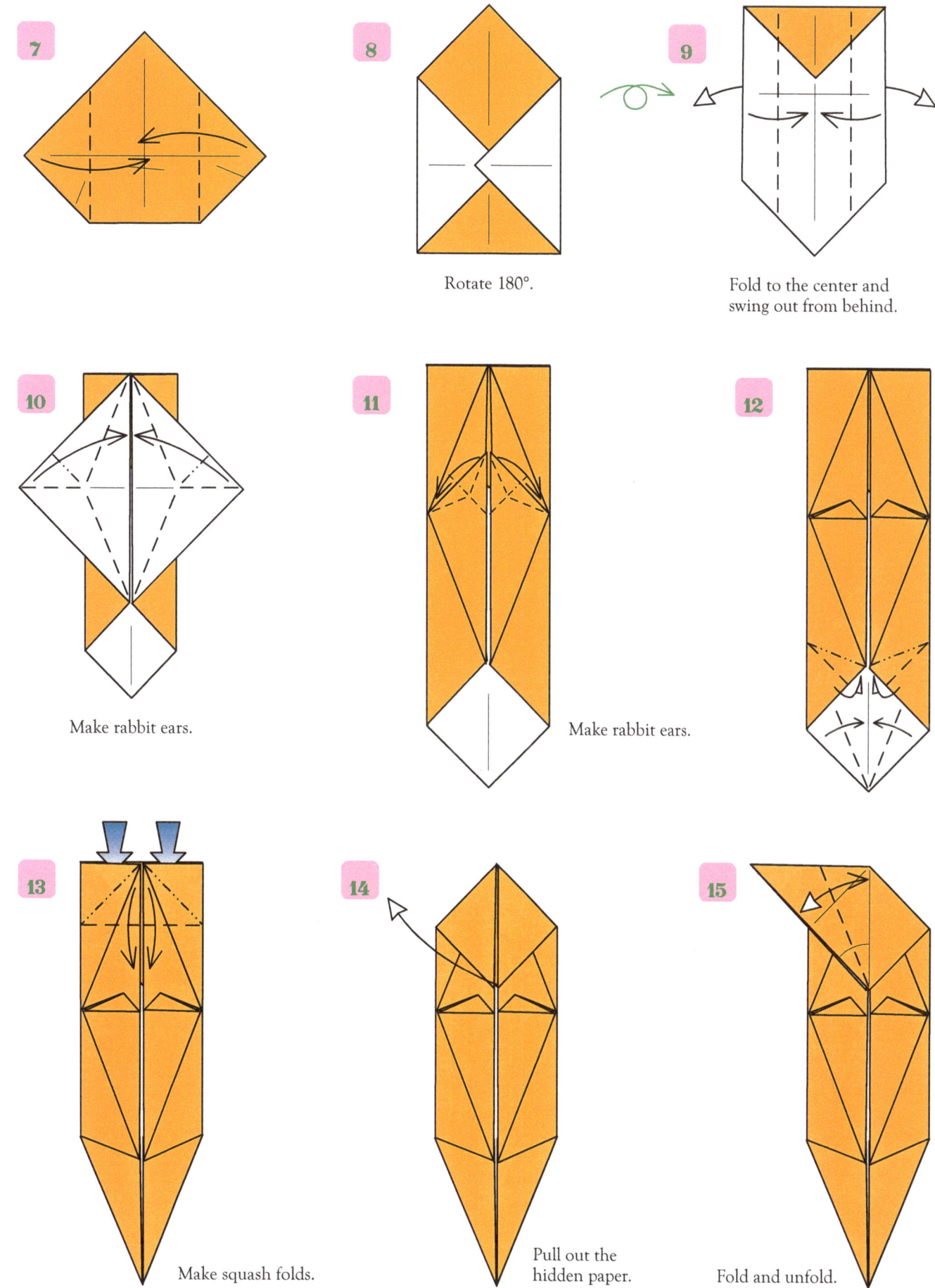

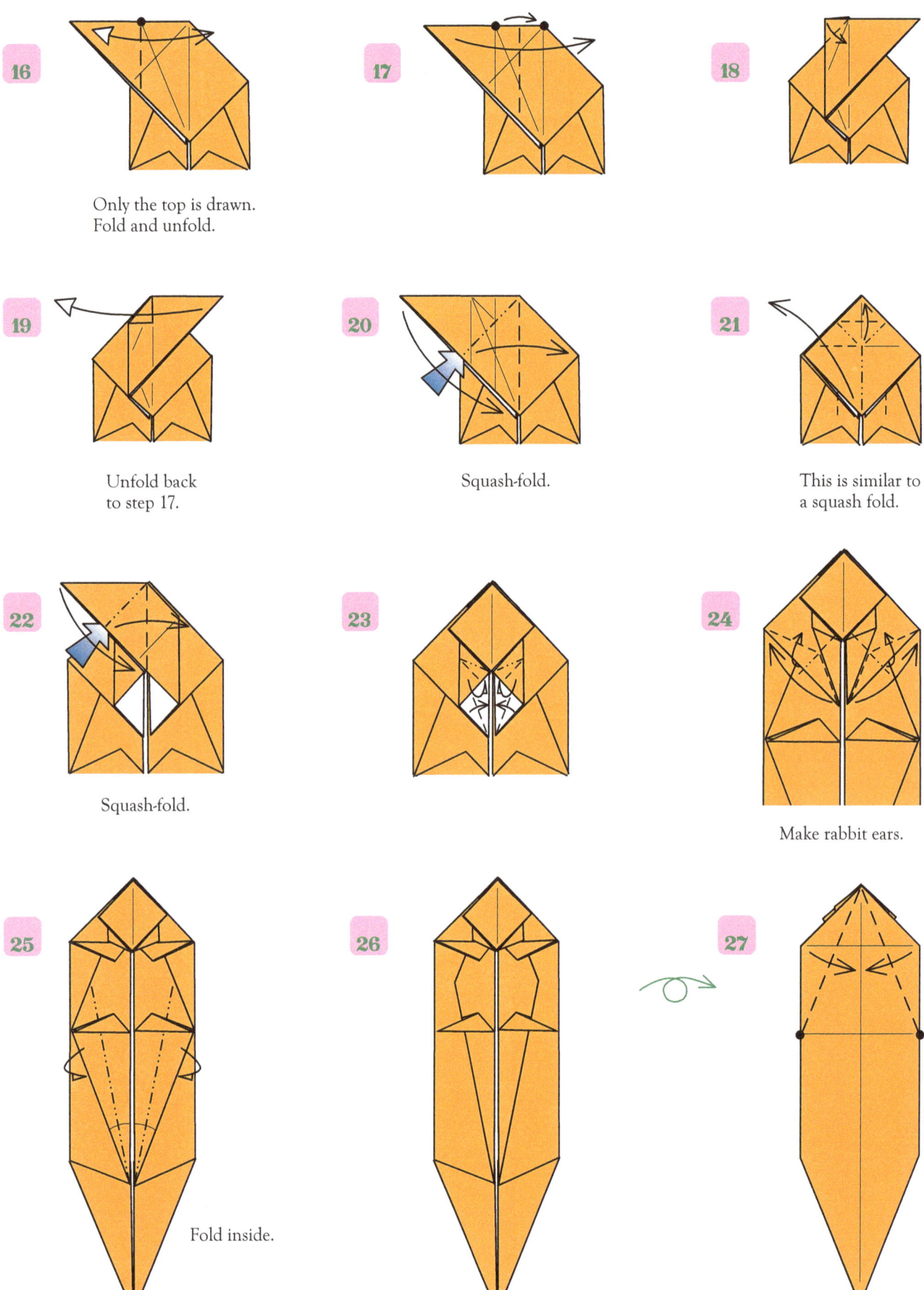

26 Origami Symphony No. 7

28 Fold in thirds.

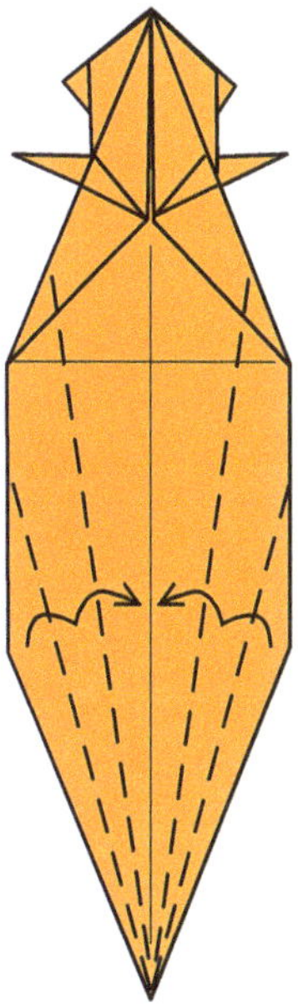

29 Fold in half and rotate 90°.

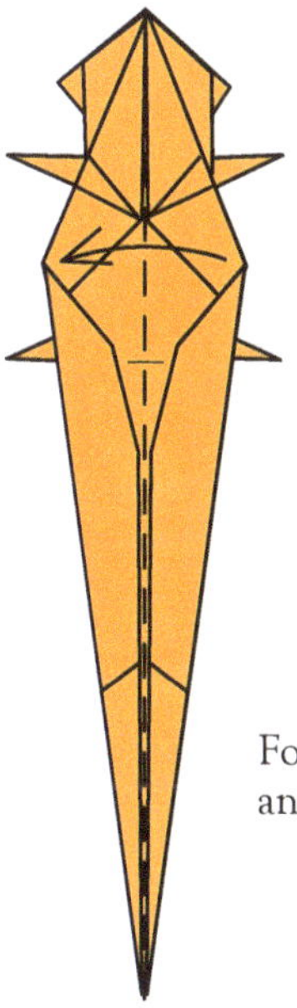

30 Lift up. Repeat behind.

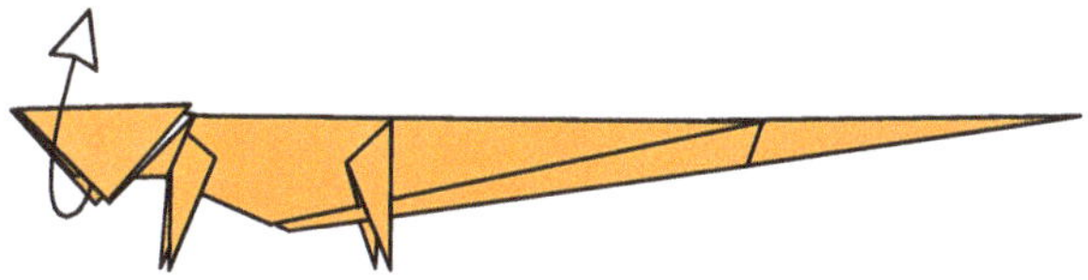

31 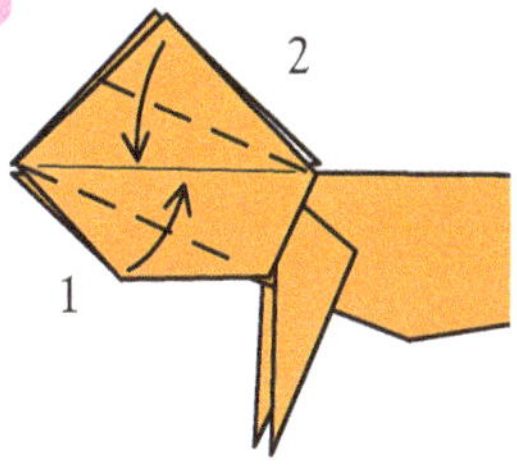
1. Fold up.
2. Fold down.
Repeat behind.

32 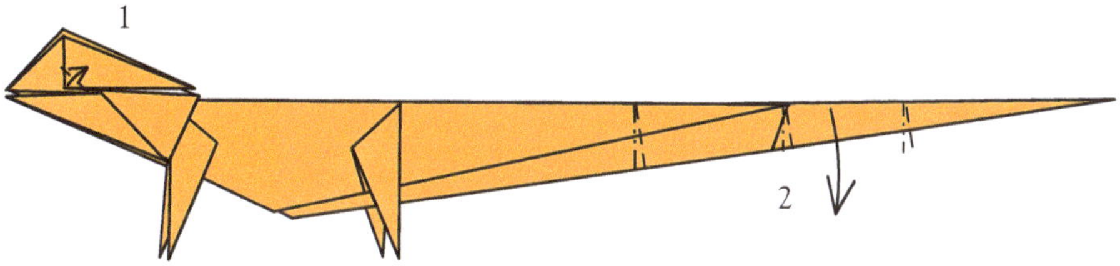
1. Fold the eye, repeat behind.
2. Make crimp folds.

33 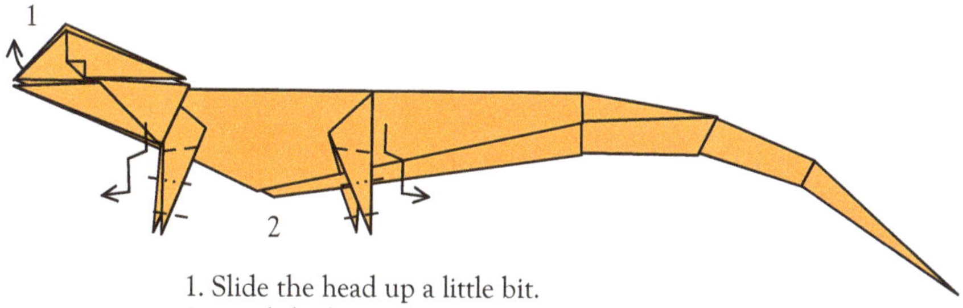
1. Slide the head up a little bit.
2. Bend the legs, repeat behind.

34

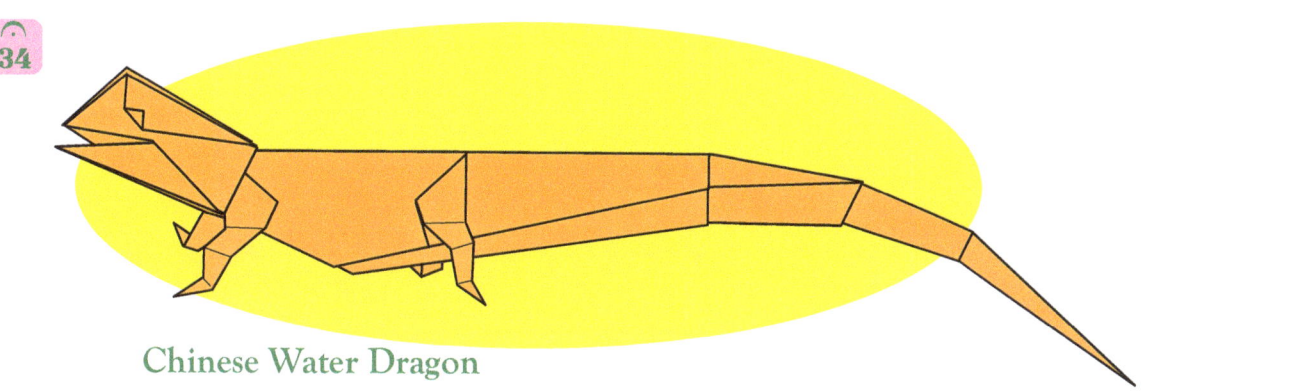

Chinese Water Dragon

Chinese Water Dragon **27**

Komodo Dragon

Weighing 200 to 300 pounds, this 10 foot long creature is the largest lizard. With a life span of 30 years, they are only found on five Indonesian islands. With an excellent sense of smell, they can detect carrion five miles away. They will stalk large prey by hiding in bushes and pouncing on them with strong legs, sharp claws and teeth. They are venomous so even if prey escapes, the animal will not survive long as the komodo dragon will find them. The komodo dragon feeds on deer, pig, water buffalo and even young komodo dragons. Hence the young ones stay in trees. The komodo dragon can eat nearly its entire weight in one meal, and need not dine for a full month. It is a good swimmer and can run as fast as 12 miles per hour. Ferocious as they seem to be, the ones in captivity are playful.

1. Fold and unfold.
2. Fold to the center and unfold.
3. 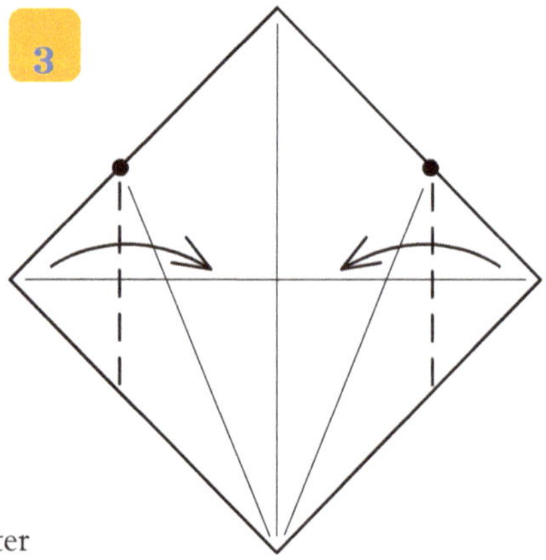
4. 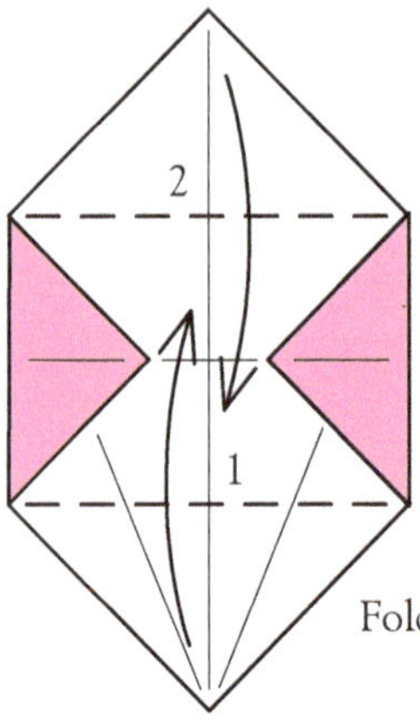 Fold in order.
5. Fold to the center.
6. Make squash folds.

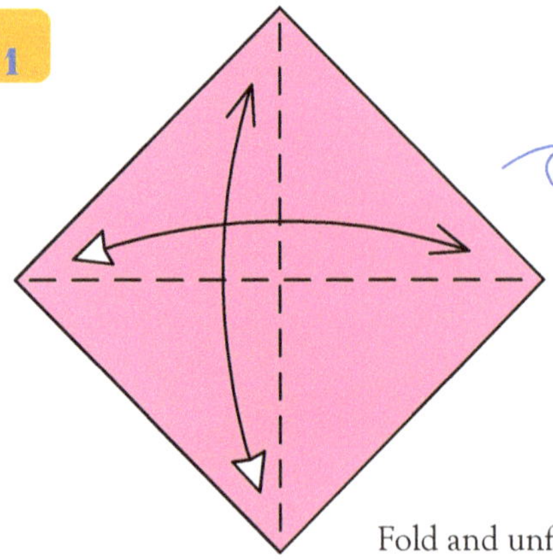

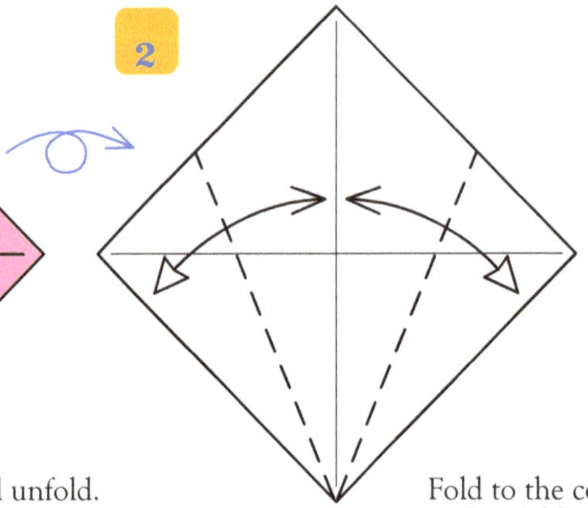

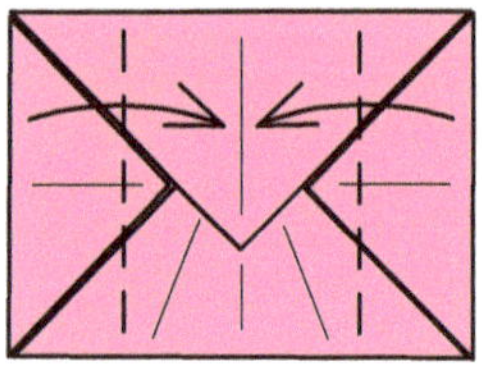

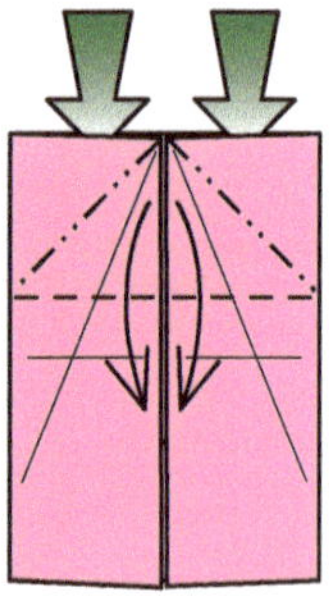

28 Origami Symphony No. 7

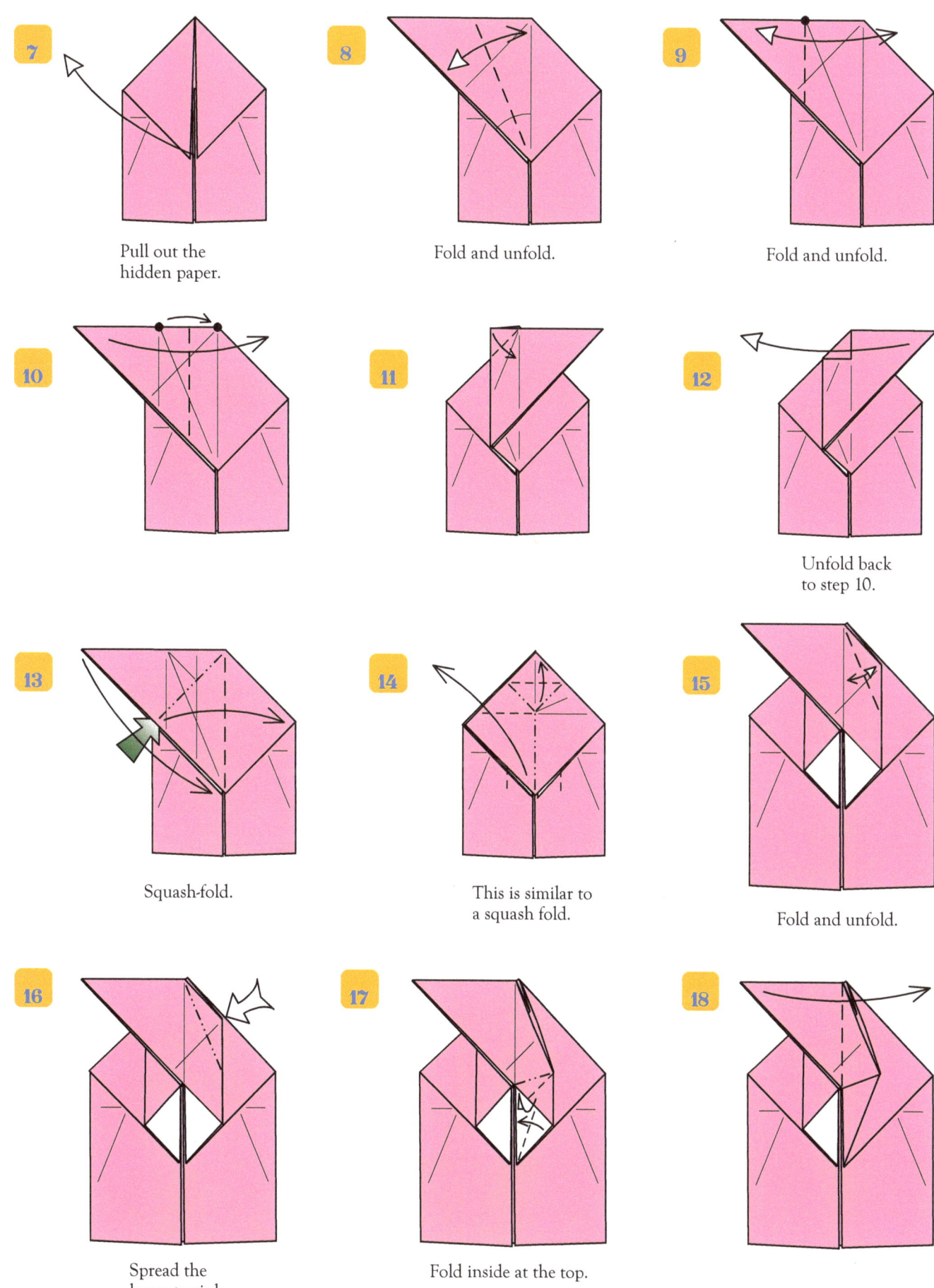

Komodo Dragon 29

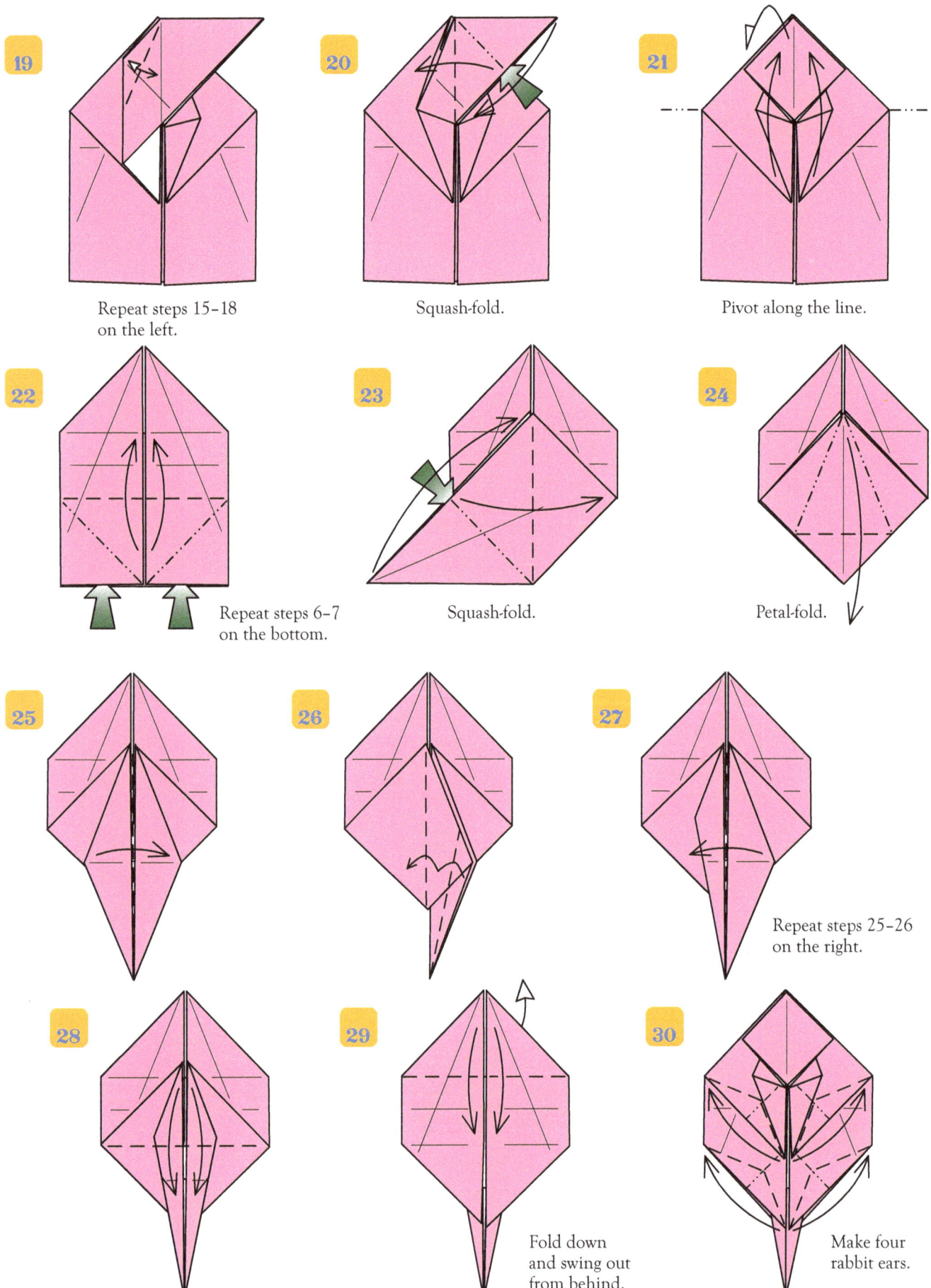

19 Repeat steps 15–18 on the left.
20 Squash-fold.
21 Pivot along the line.
22 Repeat steps 6–7 on the bottom.
23 Squash-fold.
24 Petal-fold.
25
26
27 Repeat steps 25–26 on the right.
28
29 Fold down and swing out from behind.
30 Make four rabbit ears.

30 *Origami Symphony No. 7*

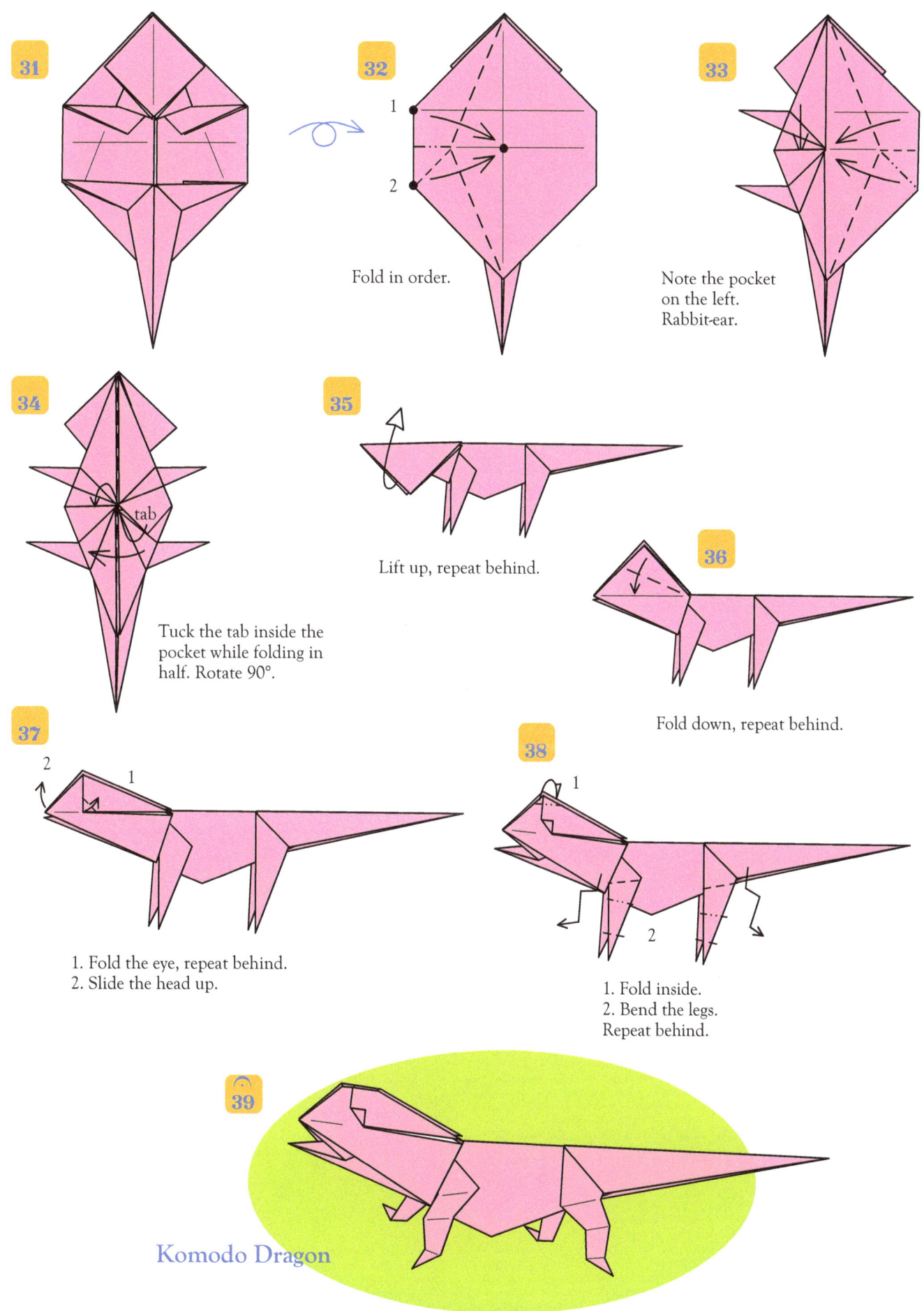

Frilled Lizard

At three feet in length, the frilled lizard is only one or two pounds. Found in Northern Australia and New Guinea, this lizard lives in trees in tropical forests and woodlands. Its brown or reddish-green coloring camouflages with branches and twigs. It feeds on insects, spiders, and small rodents. When threatened, it raises its neck frill with the mouth wide open and hisses. This confuses the predators and gives it time to run quickly, on its hind legs, to the nearest tree. This docile lizard is not venomous.

1

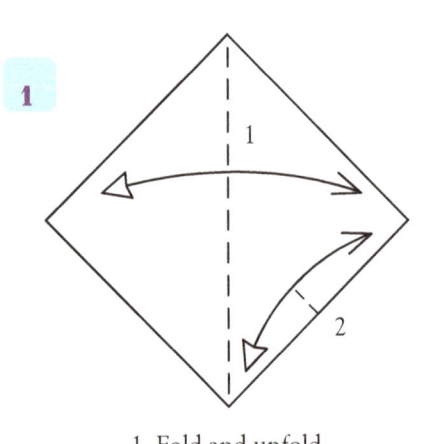

1. Fold and unfold.
2. Fold and unfold on the edge.

2

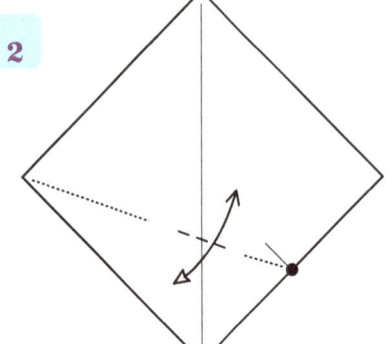

Fold and unfold on the diagonal.

3

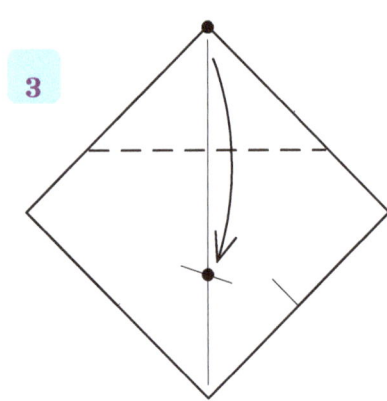

The dots will meet.

4

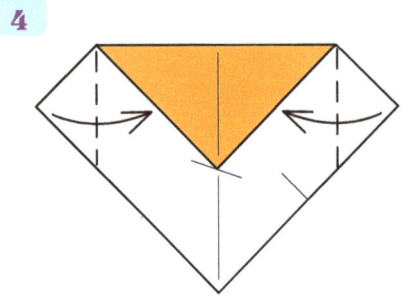

Fold on the left and right.

5

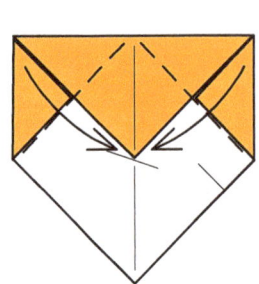

Fold to the center.

6

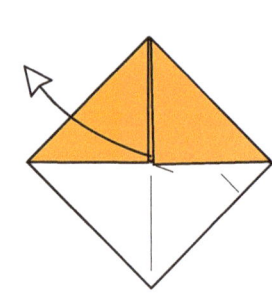

Pull out the hidden flap.

32 Origami Symphony No. 7

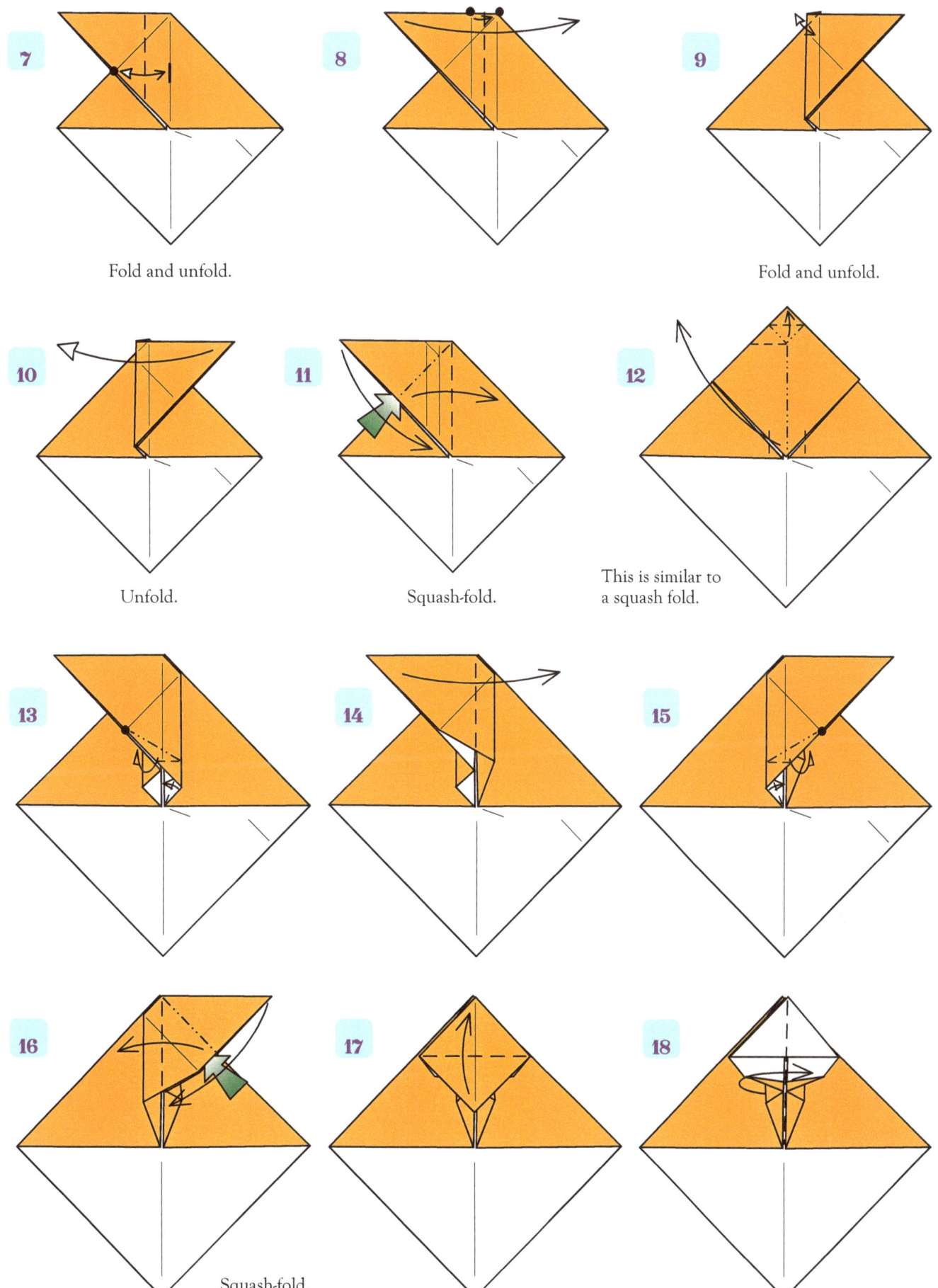

Frilled Lizard 33

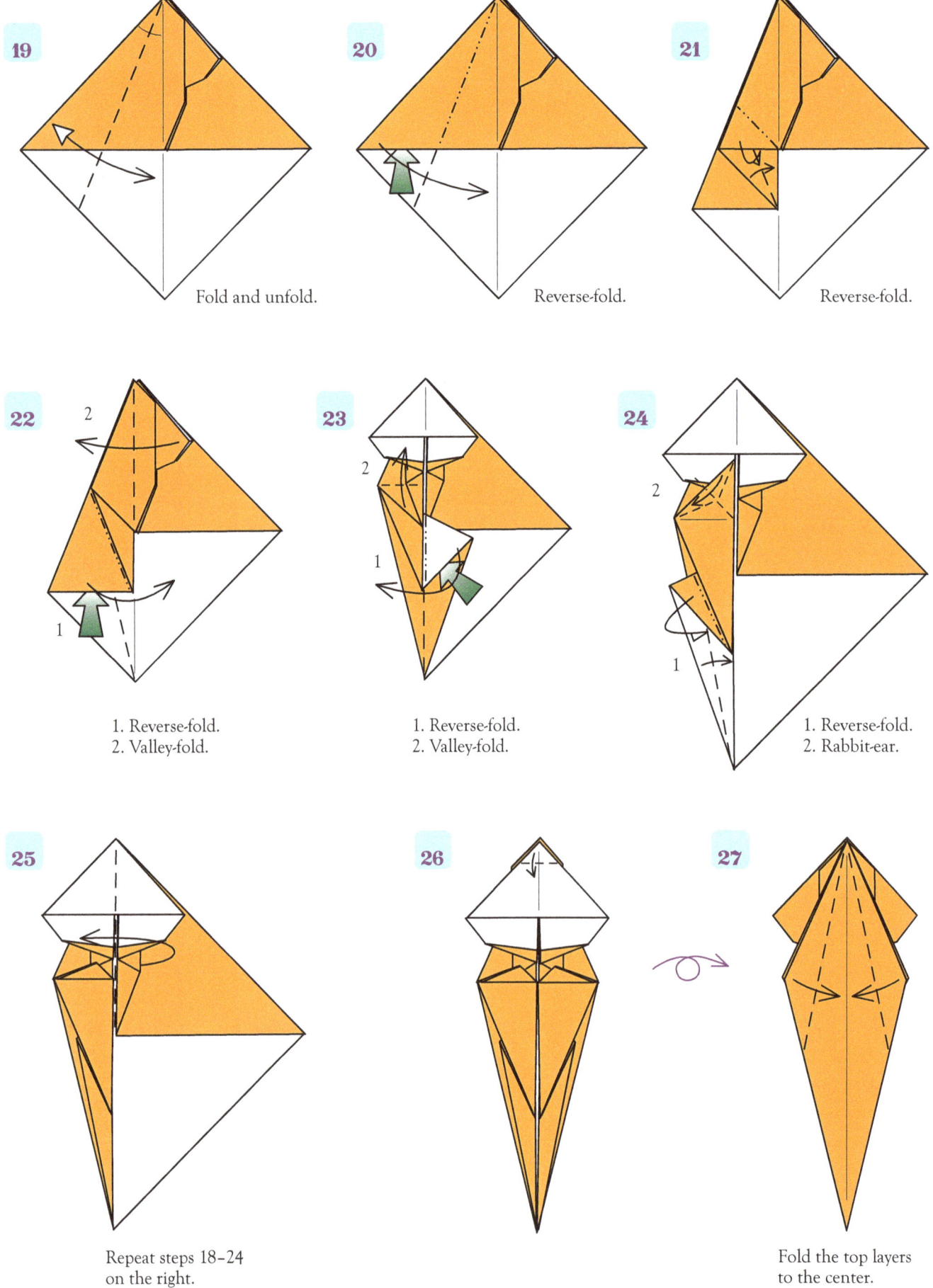

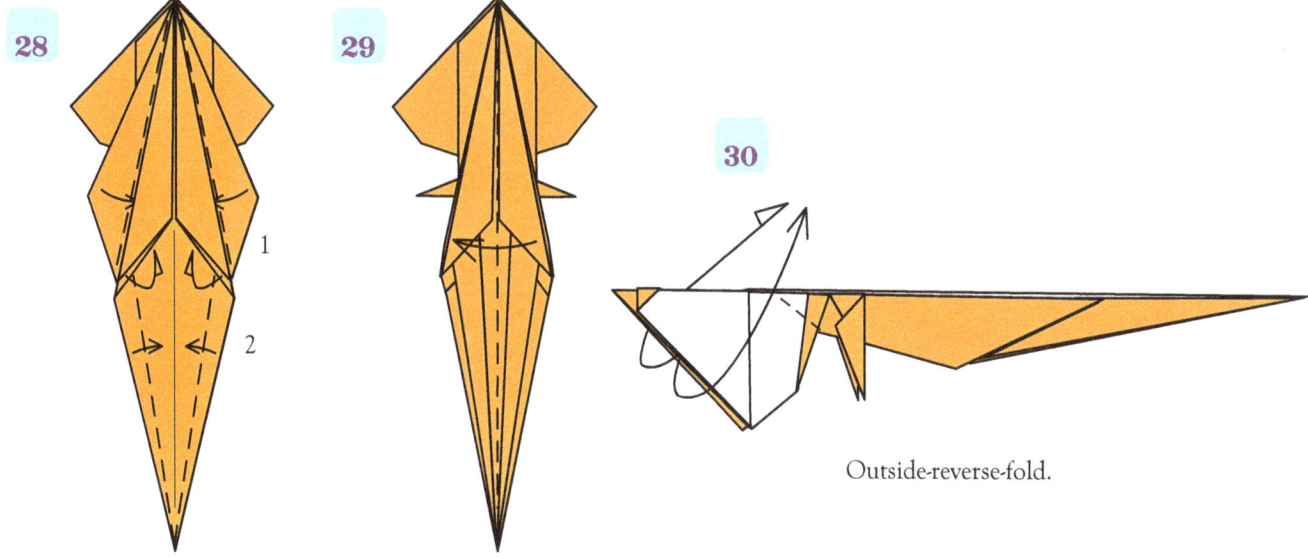

1. Tuck inside.
2. Fold the top part inside.

Fold in half and rotate 90°.

Outside-reverse-fold.

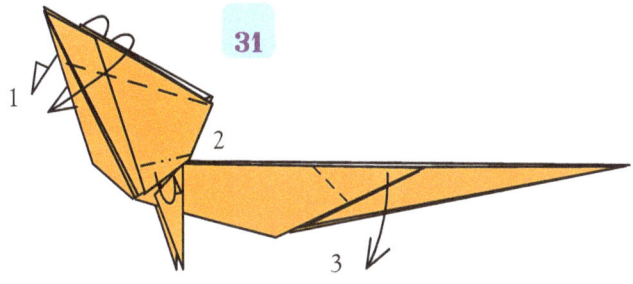

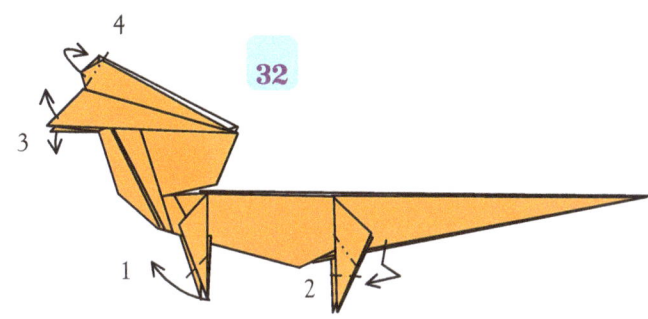

1. Outside-reverse-fold.
2. Reverse-fold, repeat behind.
3. Valley-fold, repeat behind.

1. Outside-reverse-fold, repeat behind.
2. Crimp-fold, repeat behind.
3. Spread the mouth.
4. Reverse-fold.

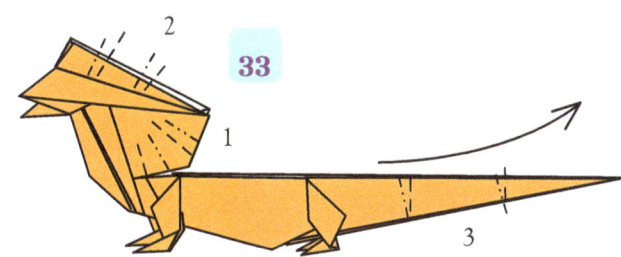

1. Make pleat folds, repeat behind.
2. Make pleat folds, repeat behind.
3. Make crimp folds.

Frilled Lizard

Crocodile

As the largest reptile, the crocodile can grow to 23 feet long and weigh a ton. They can be found in lakes, rivers, and other wetland areas in the tropics. They have 80 teeth and go through 8,000 teeth in their lifetime as they are replaced. Crocodiles have the strongest bite of any animal and dine on fish, birds, reptiles, frogs, and mammals. Unlike the alligator, all the teeth can be seen when a crocodile has its mouth shut. The mouth is often open to release heat and it will sleep with an open mouth. It can hold its breath for over an hour under water and can swim at 22 miles per hour.

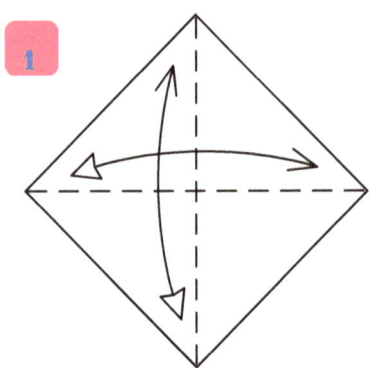

1. Fold and unfold.

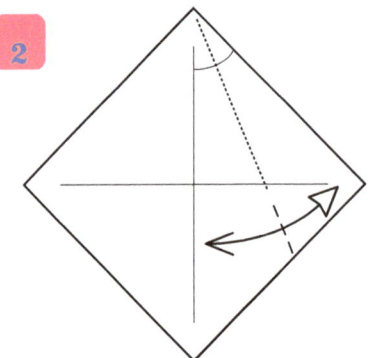

2. Fold and unfold on the edge.

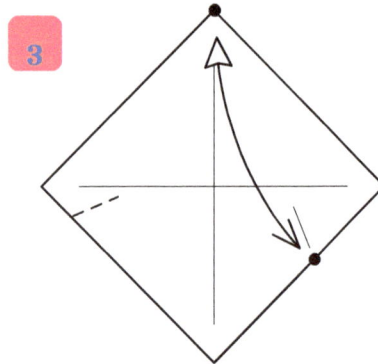

3. Fold and unfold on the edge.

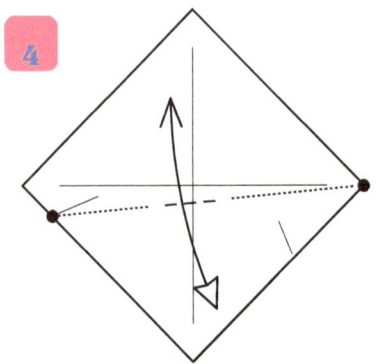

4. Fold and unfold along the diagonal.

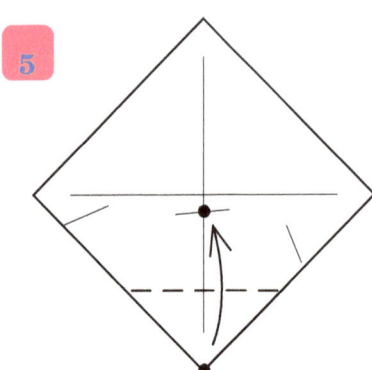

5.

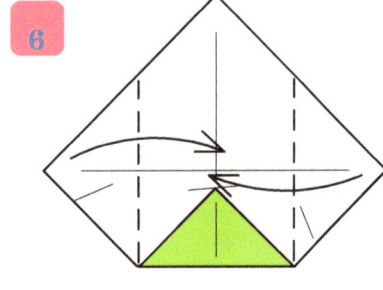

6. Rotate 90°.

36 Origami Symphony No. 7

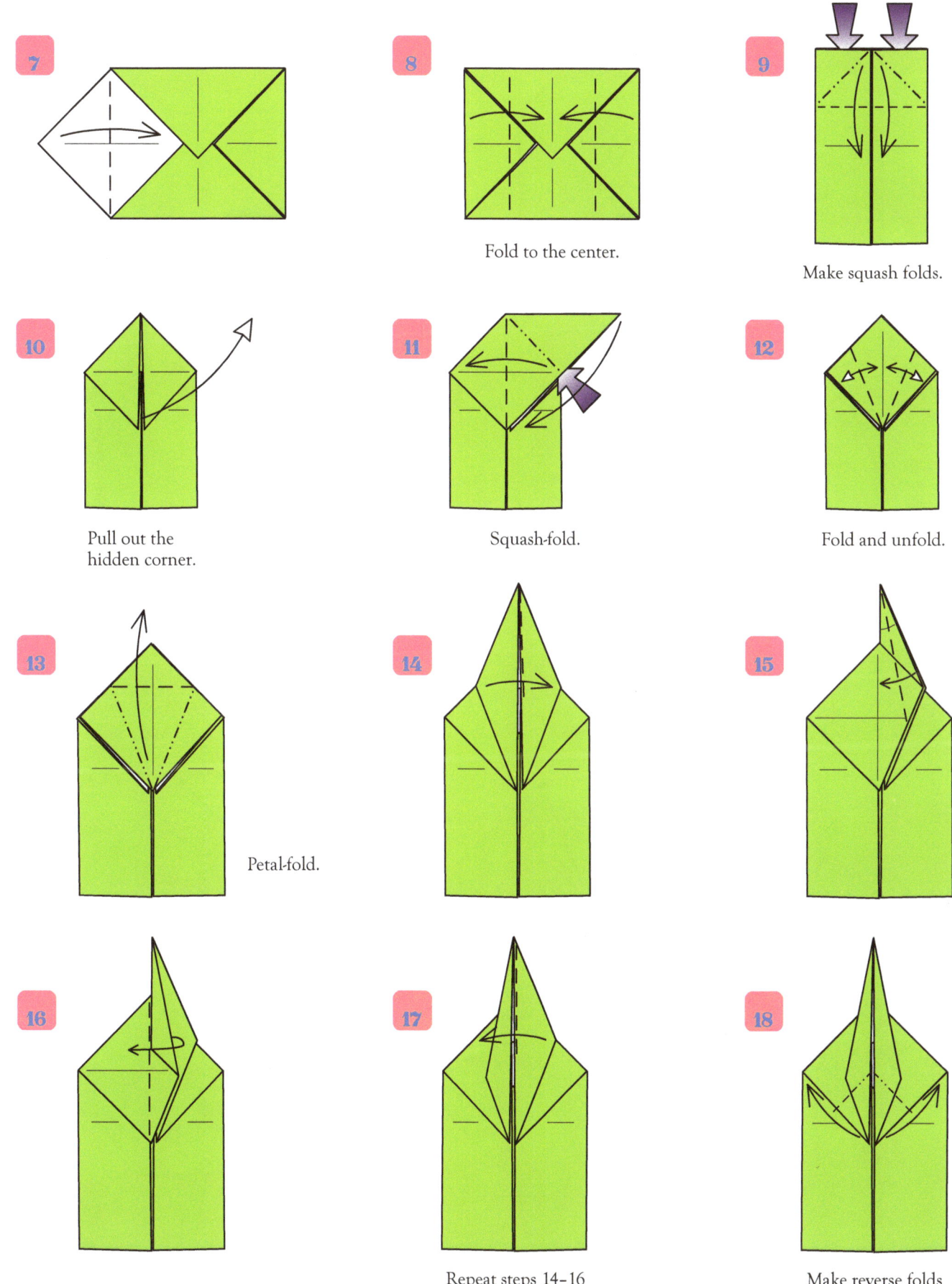

Crocodile 37

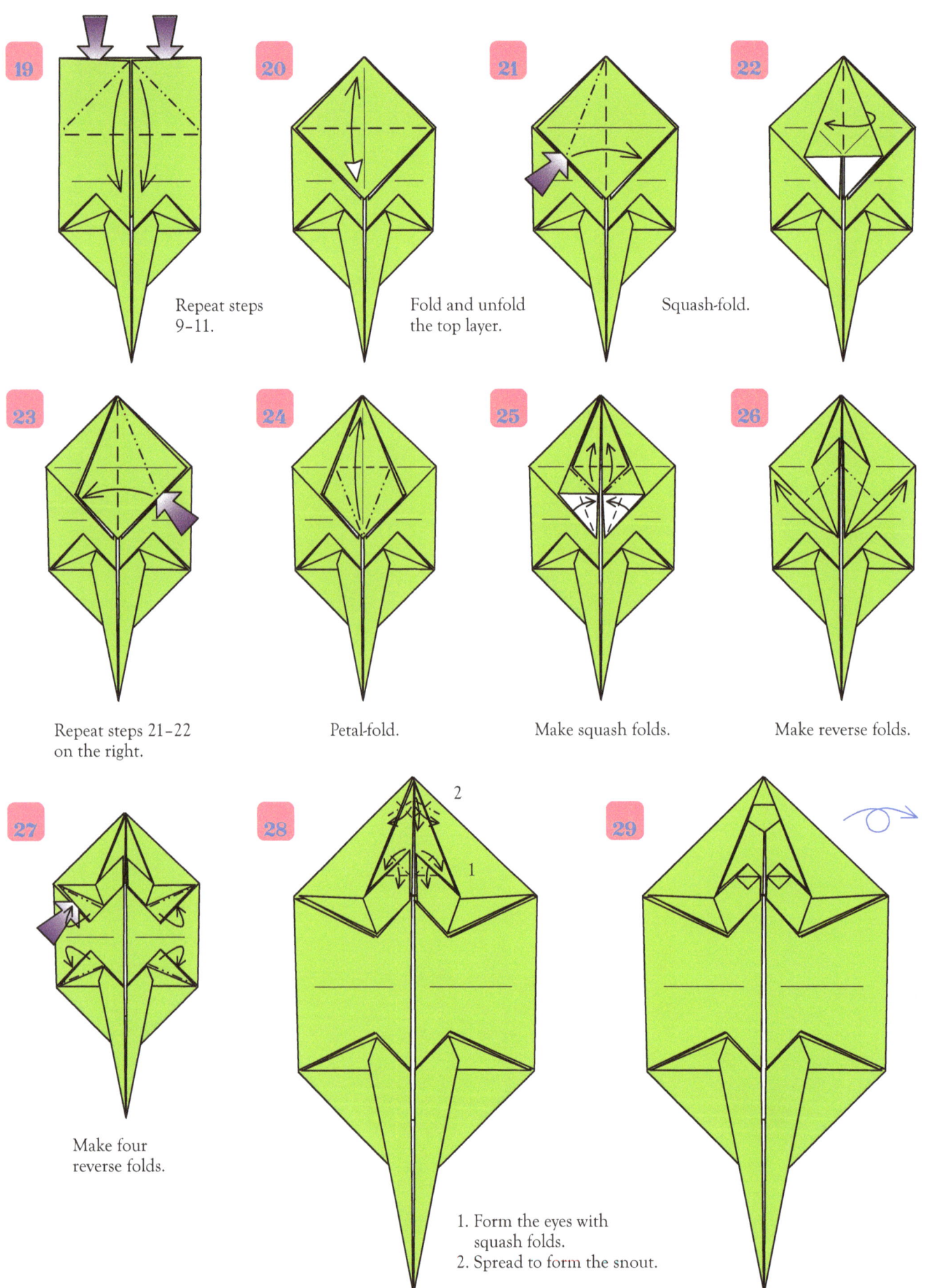

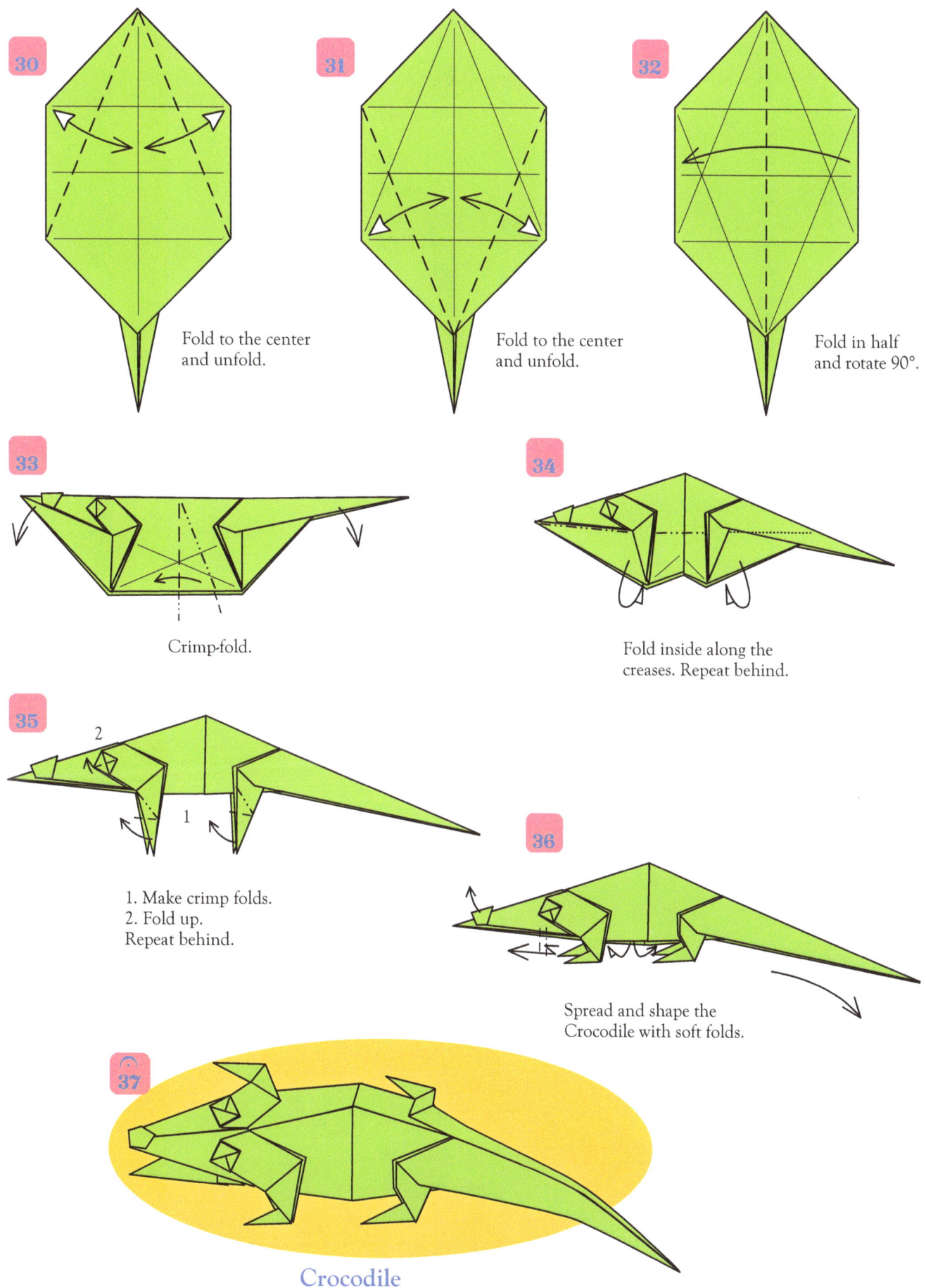

30. Fold to the center and unfold.

31. Fold to the center and unfold.

32. Fold in half and rotate 90°.

33. Crimp-fold.

34. Fold inside along the creases. Repeat behind.

35. 1. Make crimp folds. 2. Fold up. Repeat behind.

36. Spread and shape the Crocodile with soft folds.

37. Crocodile

Crocodile 39

Banded Snake

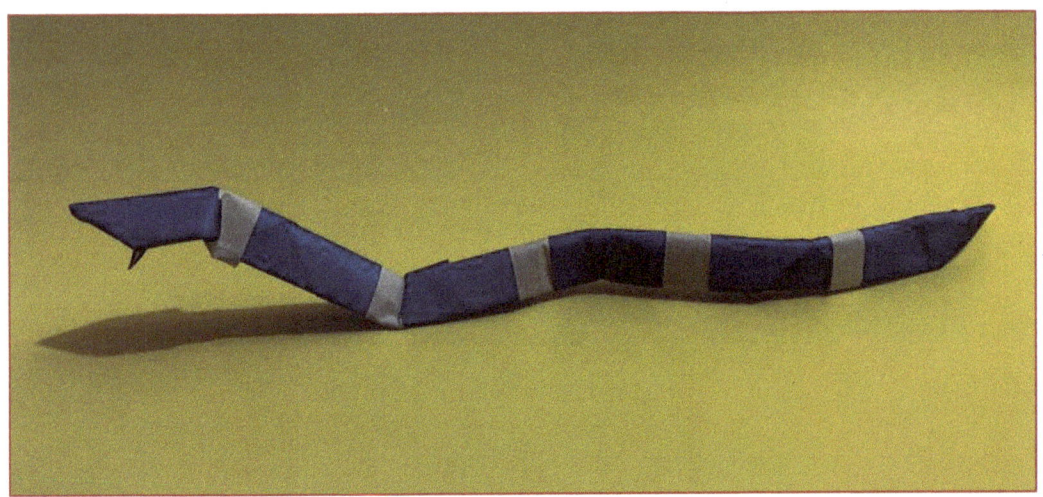

Snakes can live over 100 years. With over 3000 species, they range in size from 4 inches to 20 feet. Snakes continue to grow throughout their lives and shed their skin two to six times a year. Snakes try to avoid other creatures and slither away. If they can't, they will hiss to warn predators that they are ready to strike. They use their forked tongue to smell and feast on lizards, frogs, insects, and mammals. They only have 6 to 30 meals a year. A venomous snake has slit or elliptical pupils while a nonvenomous one has round pupils.

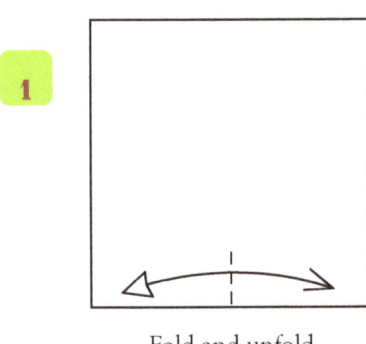

1. Fold and unfold on the bottom.

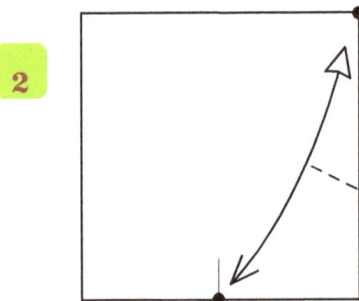

2. Fold and unfold on the right.

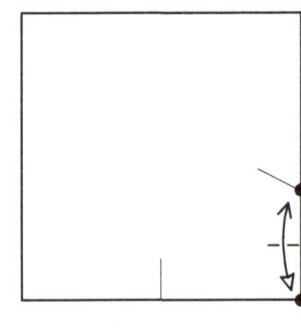

3. Fold and unfold on the right.

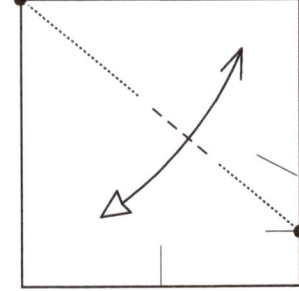

4. Fold and unfold in the center.

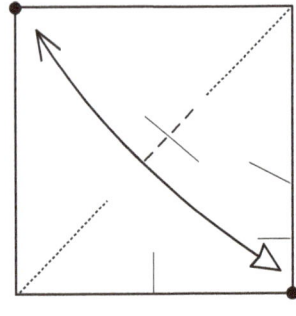

5. Fold and unfold through the intersection.

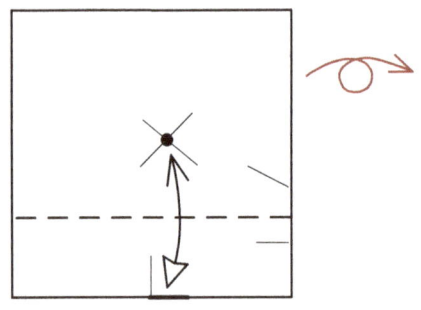

6. Fold and unfold.

40 Origami Symphony No. 7

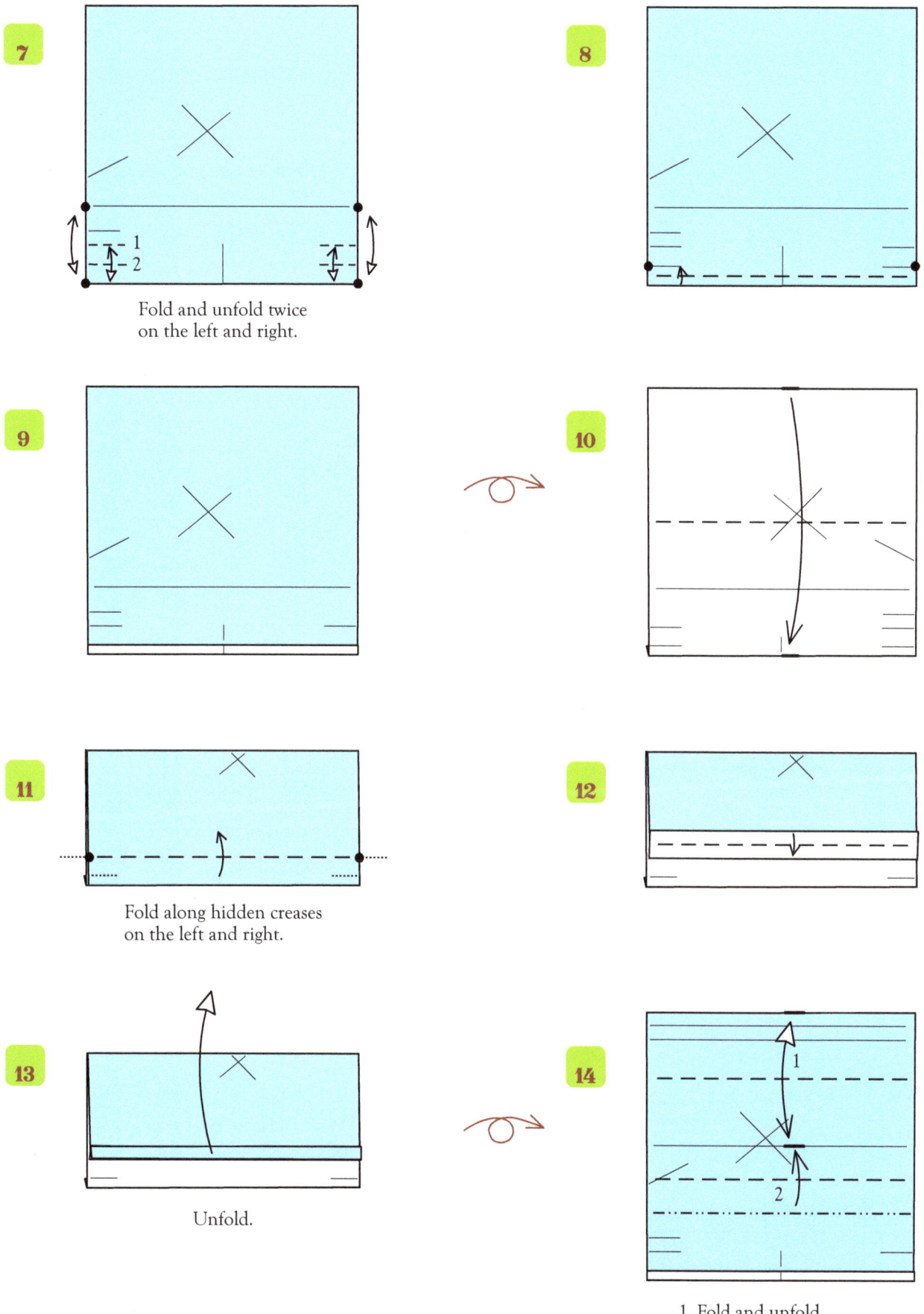

Banded Snake 41

15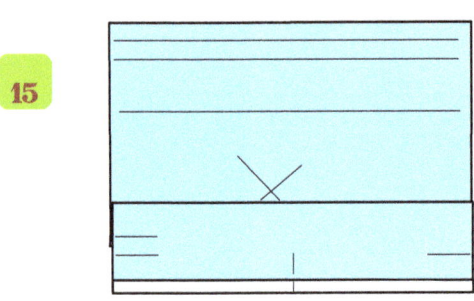

16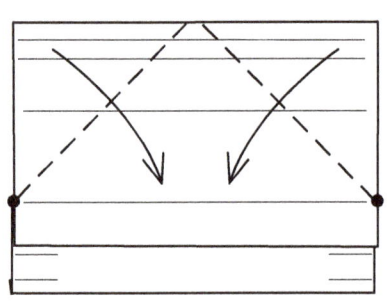

17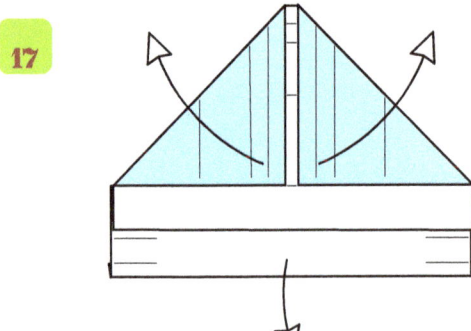

Unfold.

18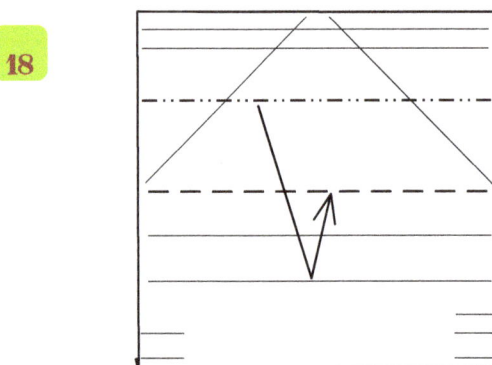

Pleat-fold along the creases.

19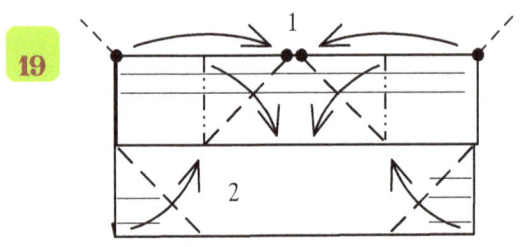

1. Make squash folds.
2. Fold up on the left and right.

20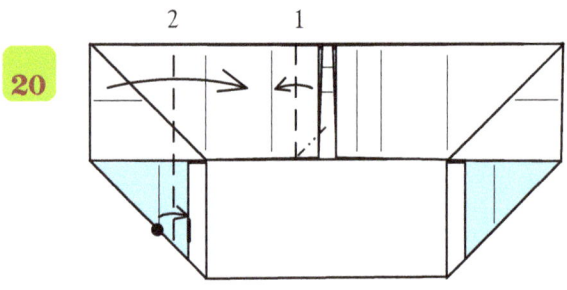

1. Valley-fold along the crease for these squash fold.
2. Bring the dot to the line.

21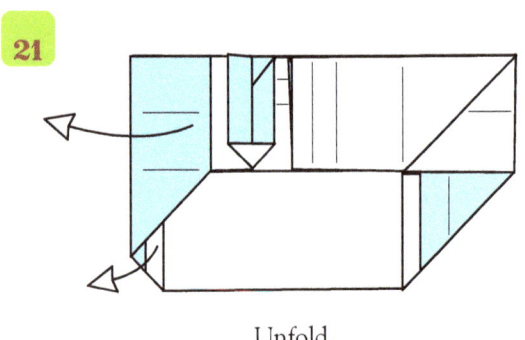

Unfold.

22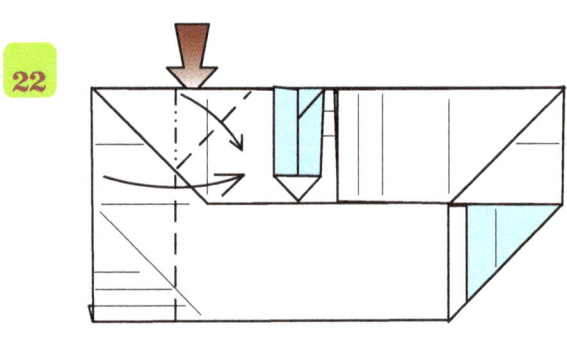

Squash-fold at the top.

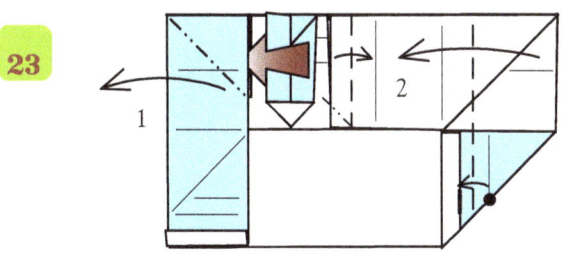

1. Squash-fold.
2. Repeat steps 20–23 on the right.

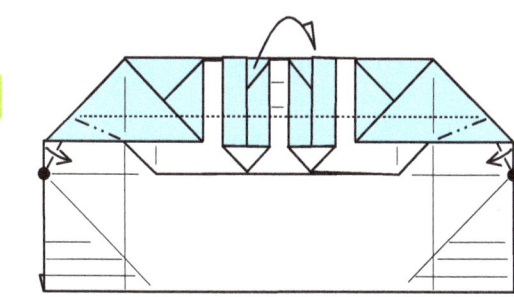

Mountain-fold along a hidden crease. Make small squash folds on the left and right.

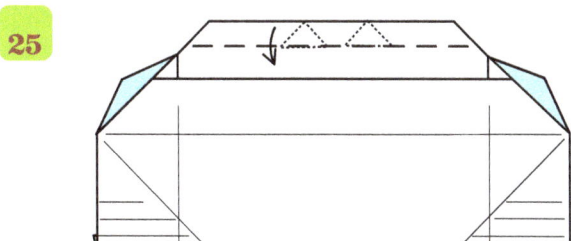

Fold along the hidden triangles.

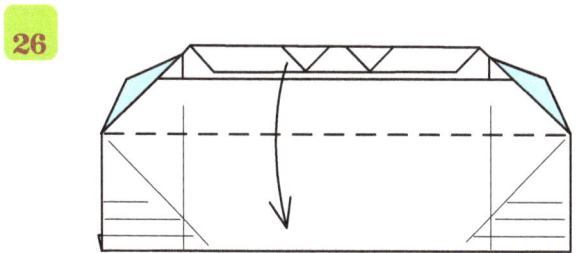

Fold along the crease.

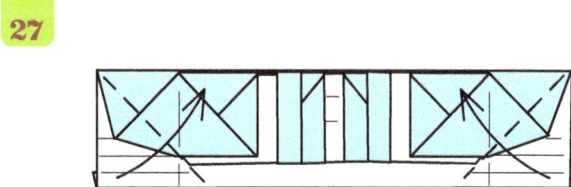

Fold along the crease.

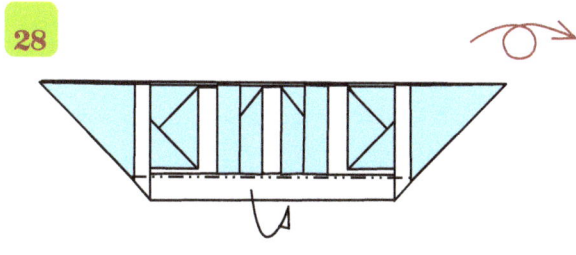

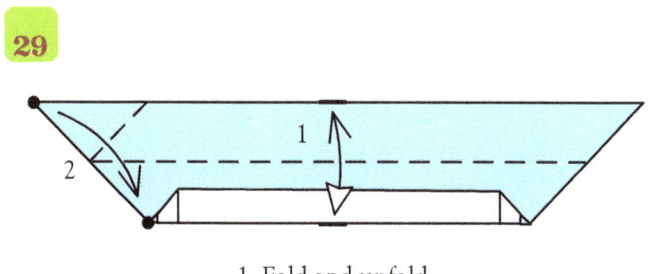

1. Fold and unfold.
2. Valley-fold.

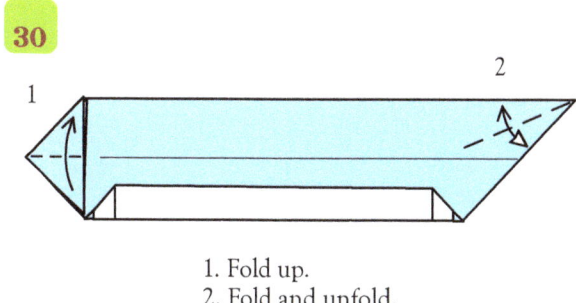

1. Fold up.
2. Fold and unfold.

Banded Snake 43

31 Squash-fold.

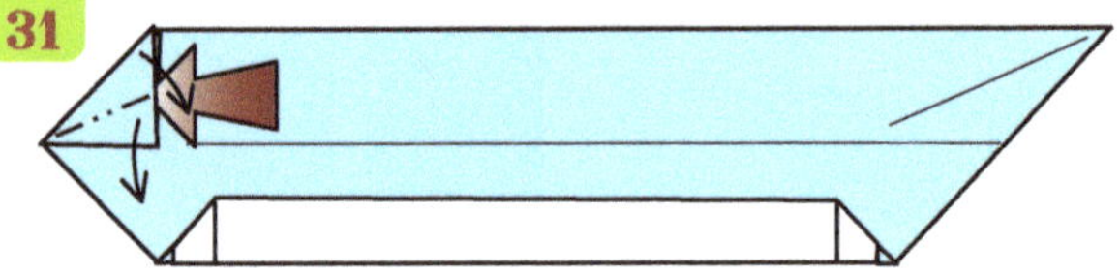

32 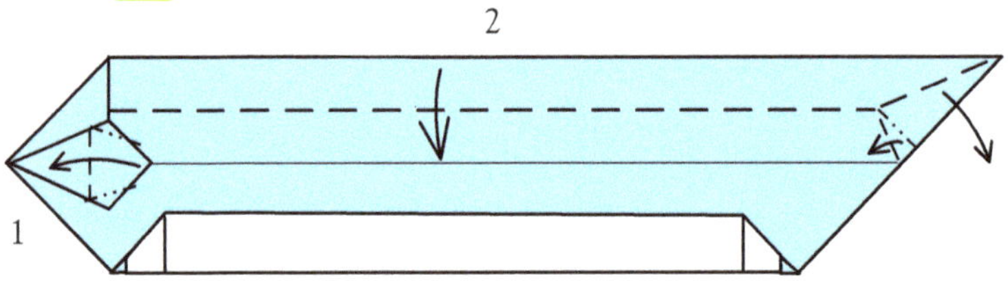
1. Petal-fold.
2. Fold to the center and rabbit-ear on the right.

33 Adjust the layers so it is not too thick.

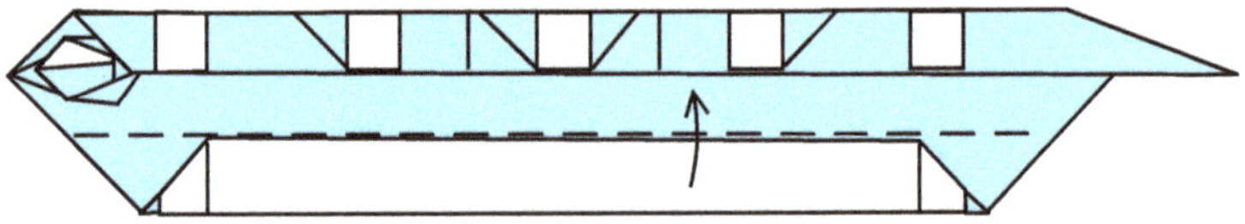

34 Fold in half.

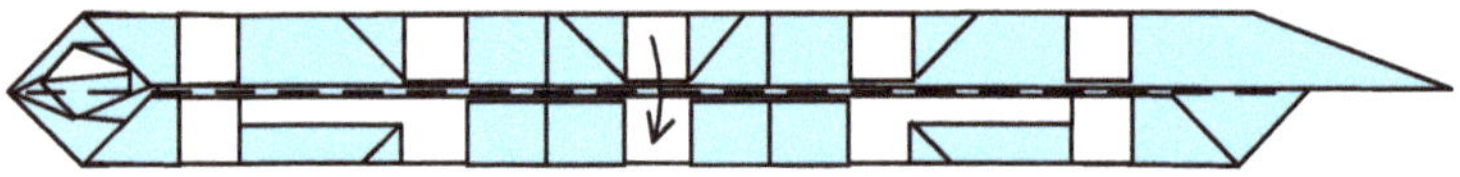

35 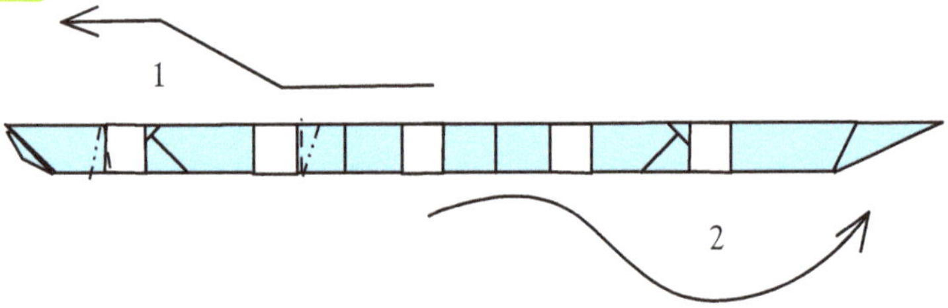
1. Make crimp folds and open the mouth.
2. Curl and shape the snake.
You can shape the snake in many ways.

36 Banded Snake

44 Origami Symphony No. 7

Second Movement

Andante: Walking through the Farm

Walking through the peaceful farm, ducks quack, geese honk, and crows caw. With a family of chickens, a pig, sheep, and cow, the country farm enjoys plenty of noisy company. Swimming and standing ducks and swans are depicted as multiple origami designs. Unifying origami structures are used for groups of these farm animals.

Swimming Duck

Ducks are curious and friendly. They live in groups called rafts, teams, or paddlings. Their waterproof feathers allow them to safely dive deep underwater. They see finer detail with more colors than humans and can move each eye independently. While the ducklings are still in their egg, they peep to try to hatch at the same time.

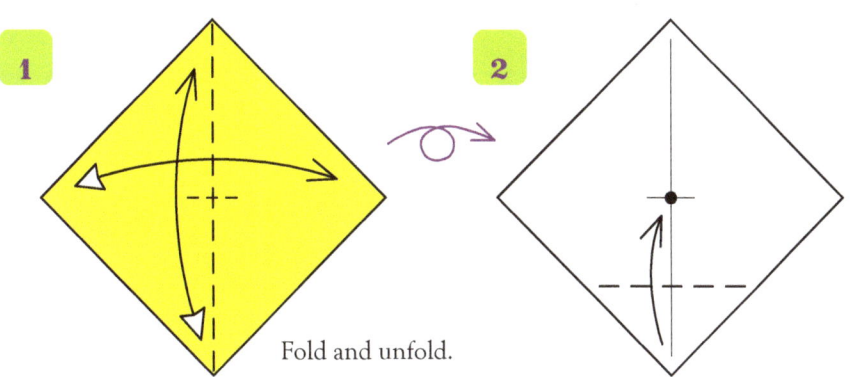

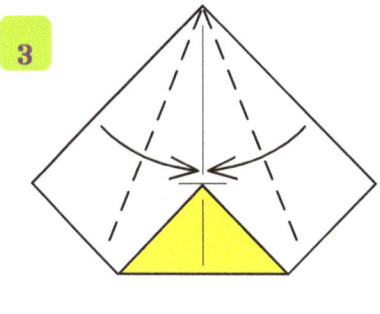

1. Fold and unfold.
2.
3.

Swimming Duck **45**

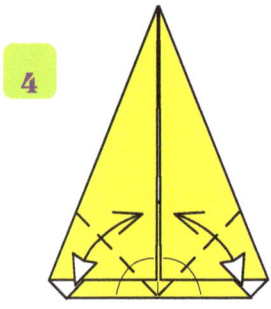

Fold and unfold.

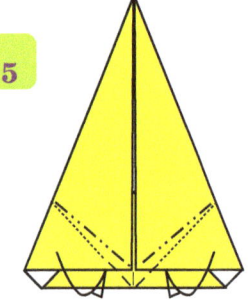

Valley-fold the lower layers along the creases for these reverse folds.

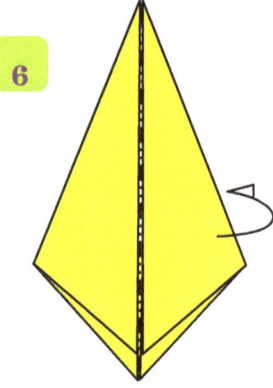

Fold in half and rotate.

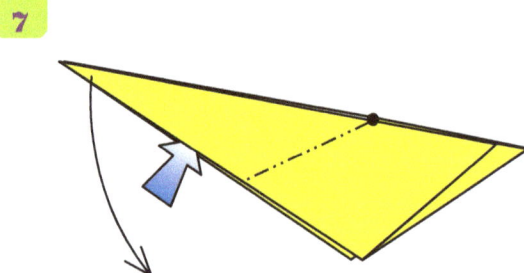

Reverse-fold.

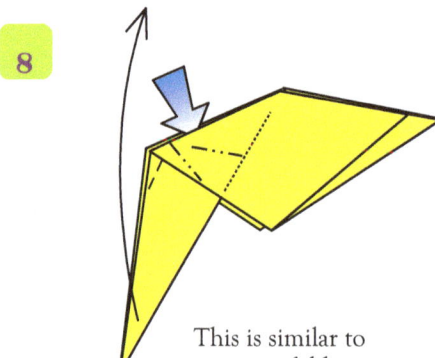

This is similar to a reverse fold.

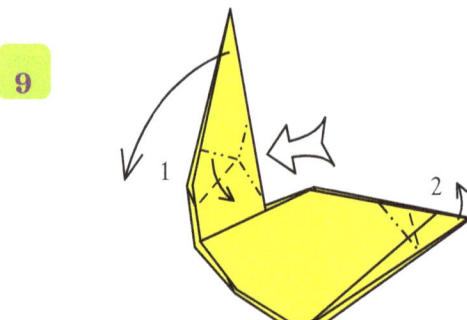

1. Push in on the right and make a crimp fold.
2. Crimp-fold.

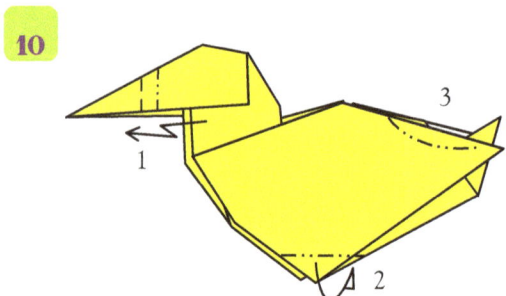

1. Crimp-fold.
2. Fold inside, repeat behind.
3. Curl the wing, repeat behind.

Swimming Duck

46   Origami Symphony No. 7

Standing Duck

How do you get down from an elephant? You don't, you get down from a duck. But the duck won't be happy. While some ducks are white, the colorful ones turn white with age. Ducks are fine walking in the snow or swimming in cold water because their webbed feet are adapted to keep warm, and the feet cannot feel the cold. Ducks feed on aquatic plants, small fish, insects, worms, and bread from us.

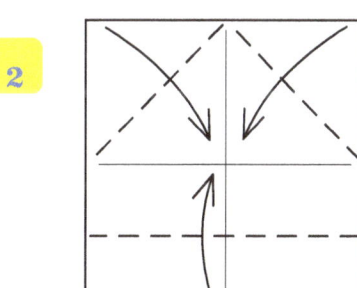

1

2

3

Fold and unfold.

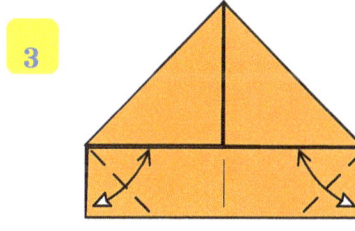

Fold and unfold.

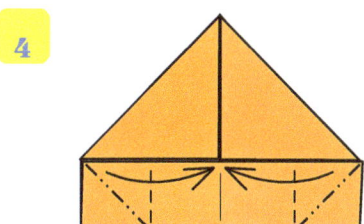

4

Make squash folds.

5

6

Fold to the center and swing out from behind.

Standing Duck **47**

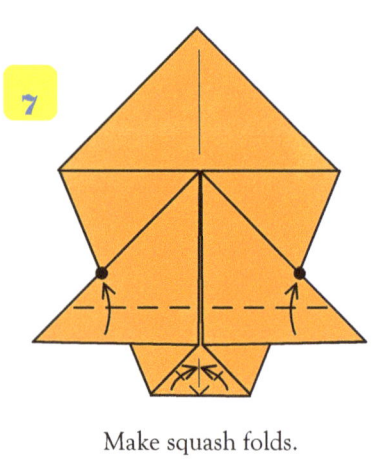

Make squash folds.

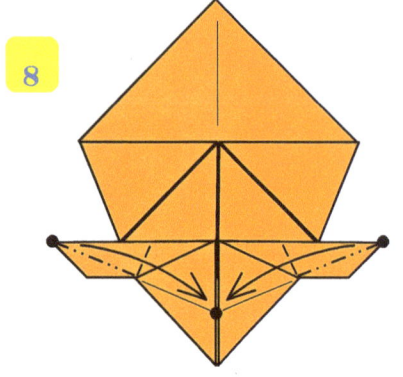

Make squash folds.

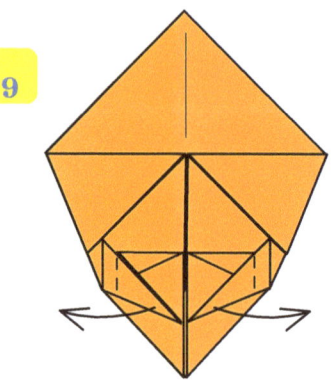

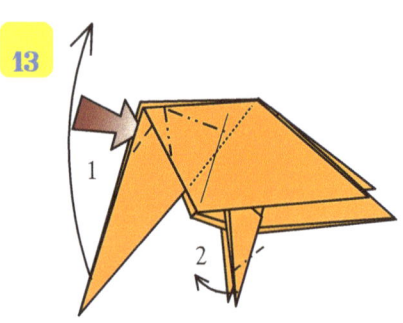

Make squash folds.

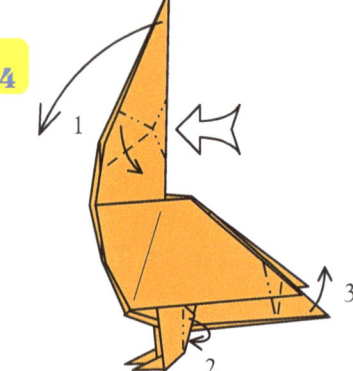

Fold in half and rotate.

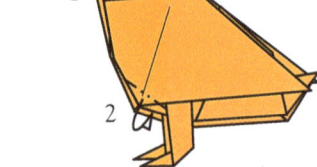

Reverse-fold.

1. This is similar to a reverse fold.
2. Reverse-fold, repeat behind.

1. Push in on the right and make a crimp fold.
2. Reverse-fold, repeat behind.
3. Crimp-fold.

1. Pull out and slide the paper down.
2. Fold inside. Repeat behind.

1. Crimp-fold.
2. Curl the wing, repeat behind.

Standing Duck

48 Origami Symphony No. 7

Goose

Geese are very social and get along with other animals, especially on a farm. Known as imprinting, a gosling will bond to anything that moves, including people. Among the largest of waterfowl, they feed on grasses, water plants, and insects. They swim and spend much time on land. In flight, geese form a V shape which makes it easier for the ones in the back. While flying, they take turns going to the front as they honk loudly for all to stay together.

1 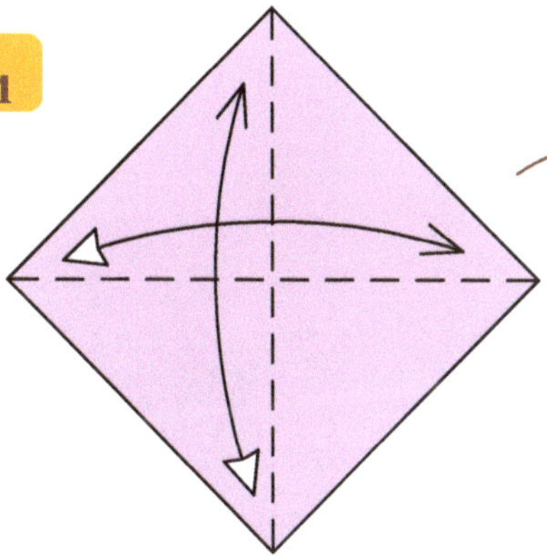 Fold and unfold.

2 Fold and unfold.

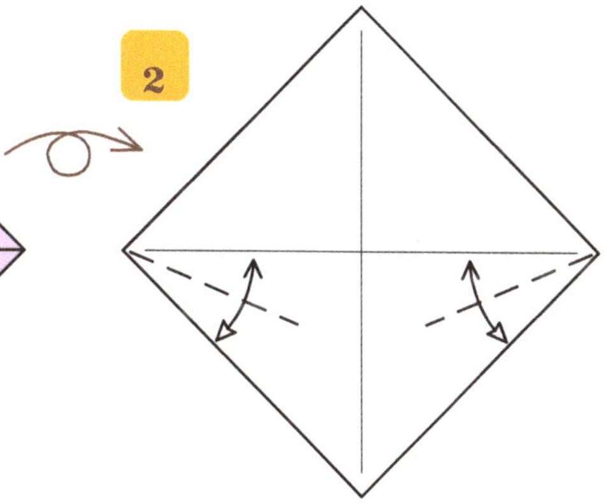

3 Fold and unfold.

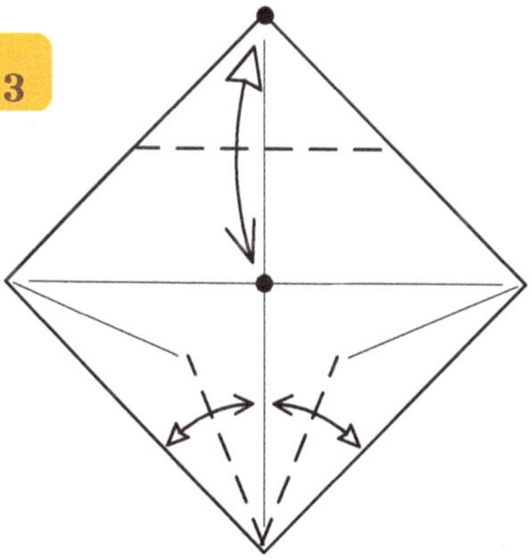

4 Fold along the creases.

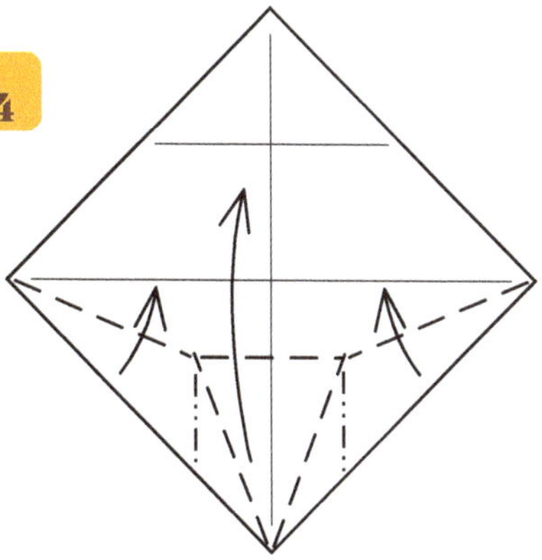

5

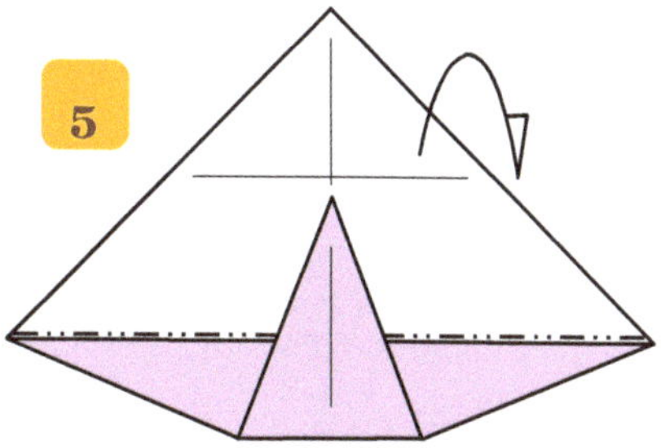

6

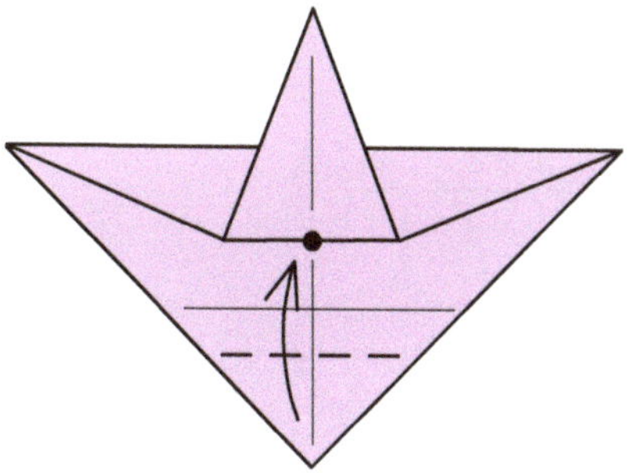

Goose **49**

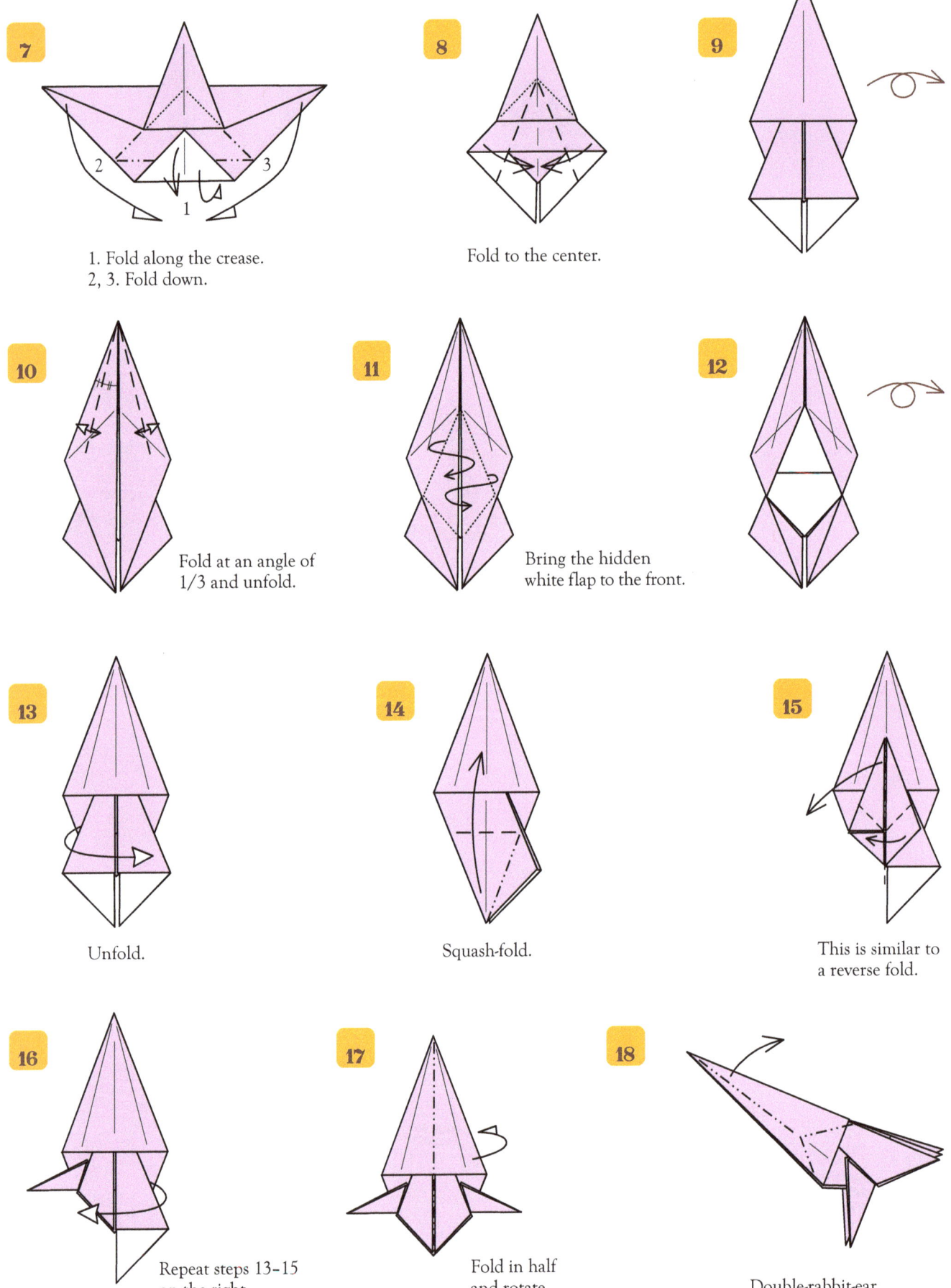

1. Reverse-fold.
2. Fold inside on each side. Repeat behind.

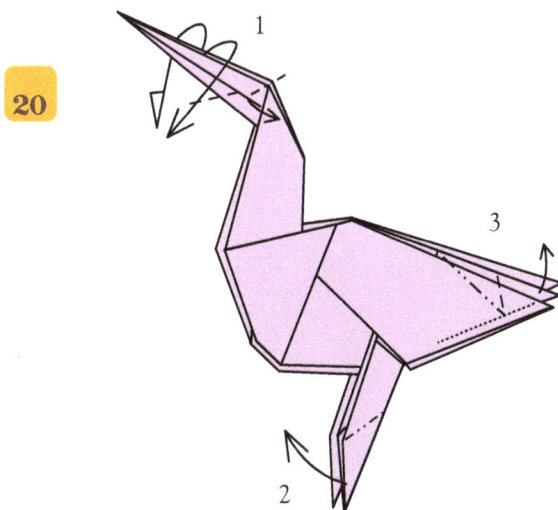

1. Outside-reverse-fold and spread.
2. Reverse-fold, repeat behind.
3. Crimp-fold the tail.

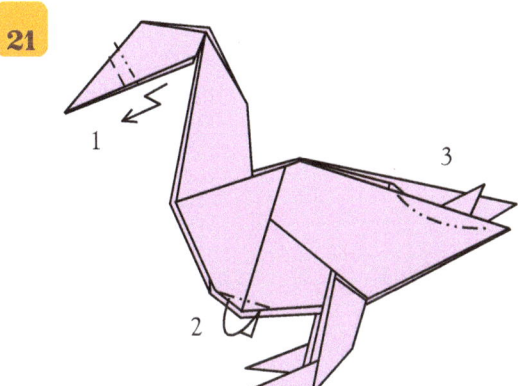

1. Crimp-fold.
2. Fold inside, repeat behind.
3. Curl the wing, repeat behind.

Goose

Goose **51**

Swimming Swan

Swans represent elegance. They are among the largest waterfowl and the heaviest flying birds in North America. They weigh between 15 to 30 pounds and have a wing span of 10 feet across. Swans feed on aquatic plants, insects, and small fish. Listen to them honk loudly.

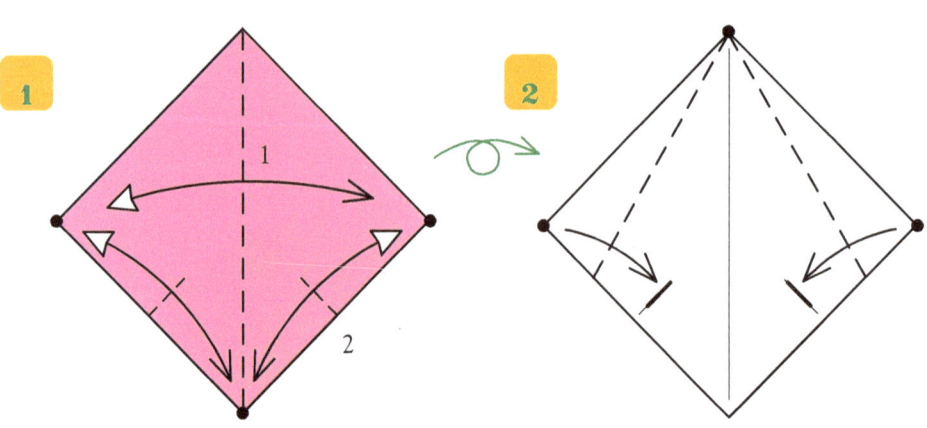

1. Fold and unfold.
2. Fold and unfold on the edge.

Bring the corners to the lines.

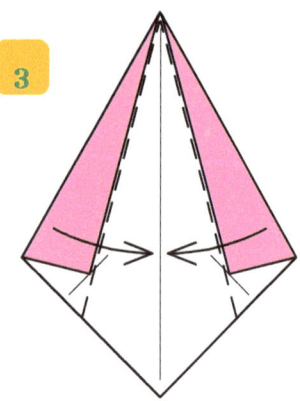

Fold to the center.

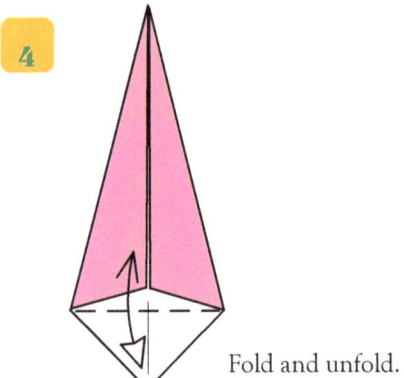

Fold and unfold.

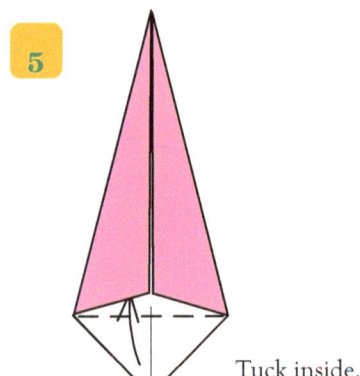

Tuck inside.

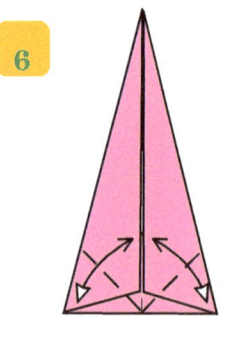

Fold and unfold.

52   Origami Symphony No. 7

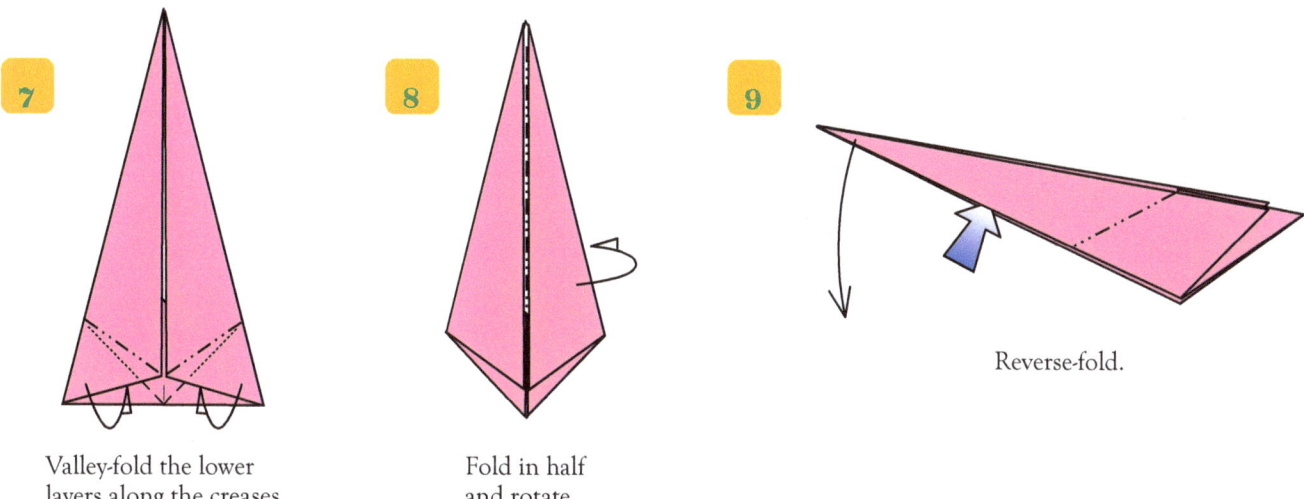

7

Valley-fold the lower layers along the creases for these reverse folds.

8

Fold in half and rotate.

9

Reverse-fold.

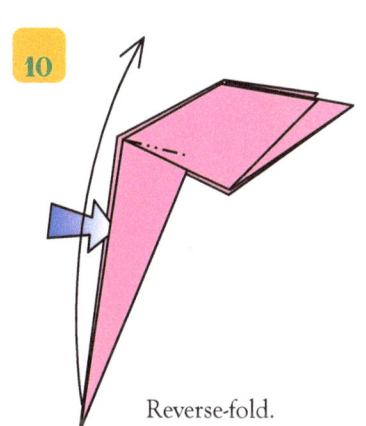

10

Reverse-fold.

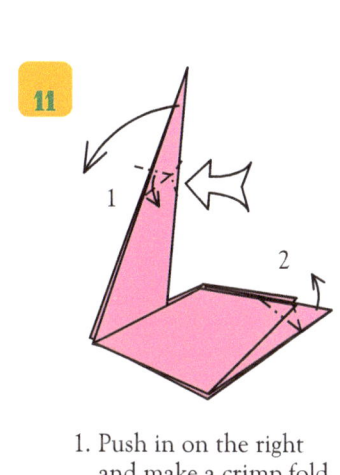
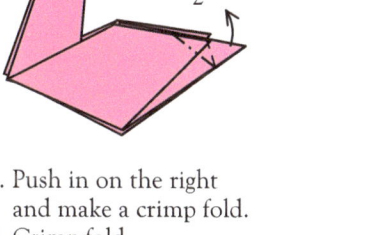

11

1. Push in on the right and make a crimp fold.
2. Crimp-fold.

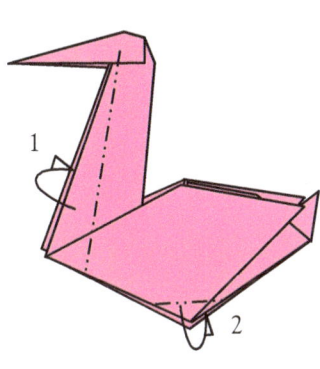

12

Fold inside at 1 and 2. Repeat behind.

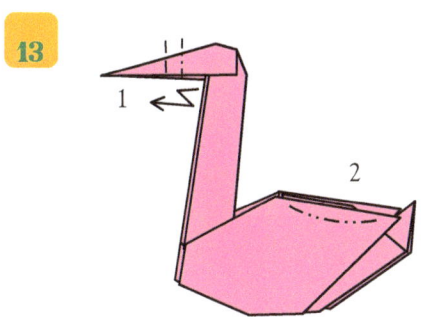

13

1. Crimp-fold.
2. Curl the wing, repeat behind.

14

Swimming Swan

Swimming Swan **53**

Standing Swan

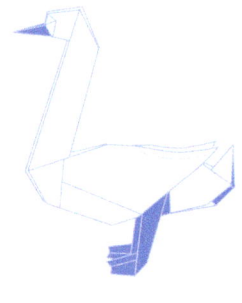

Swans are territorial and aggressive, especially guarding their young. They can live to 30 years. The trumpeter swan of North America is white with a black bill. A group of swans is a bevy or wedge.

1. Fold and unfold.
2. Fold and unfold.
3. Fold and unfold.
4. Fold along the creases.
5. 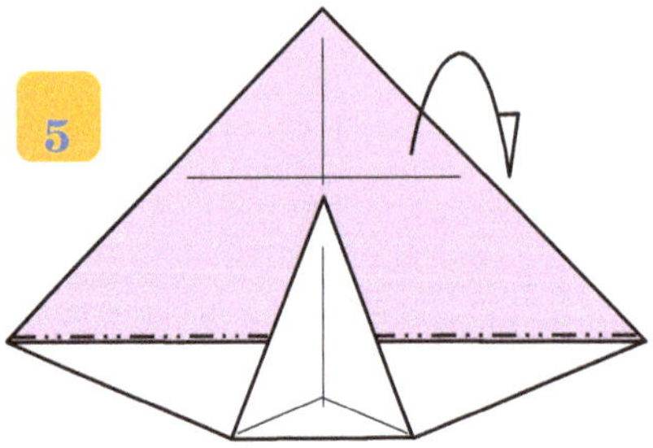
6.

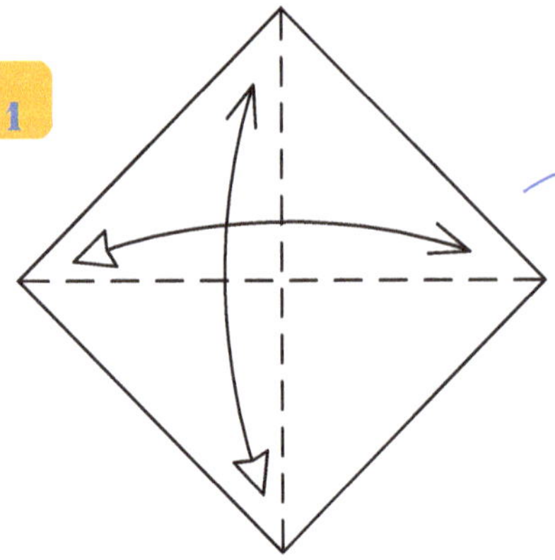

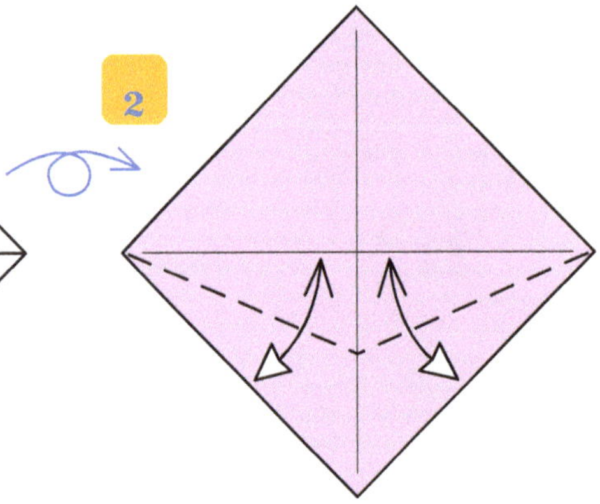

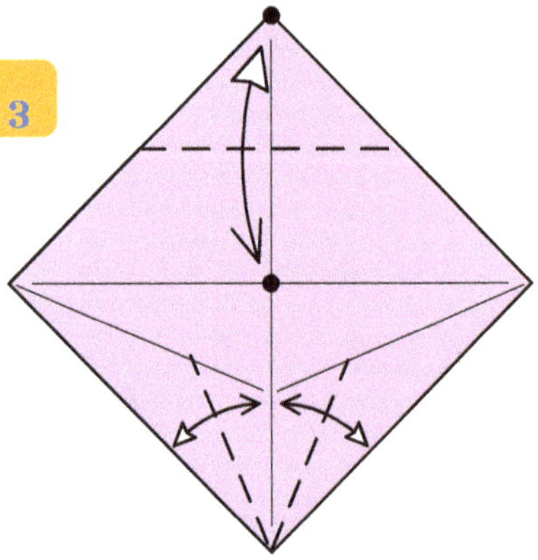

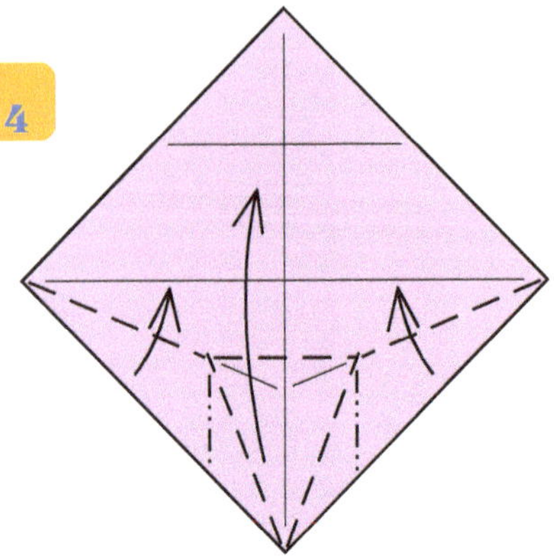

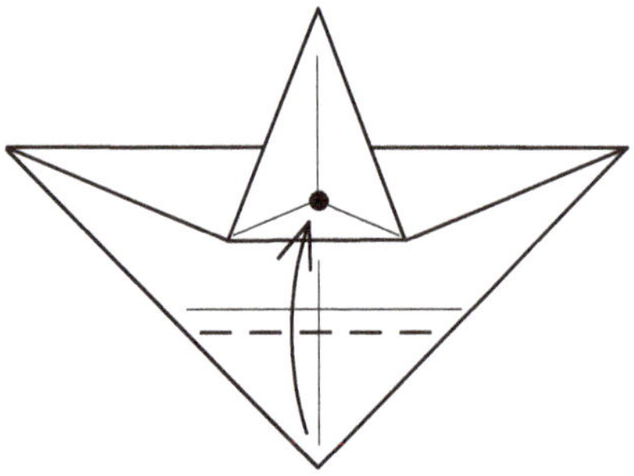

54   Origami Symphony No. 7

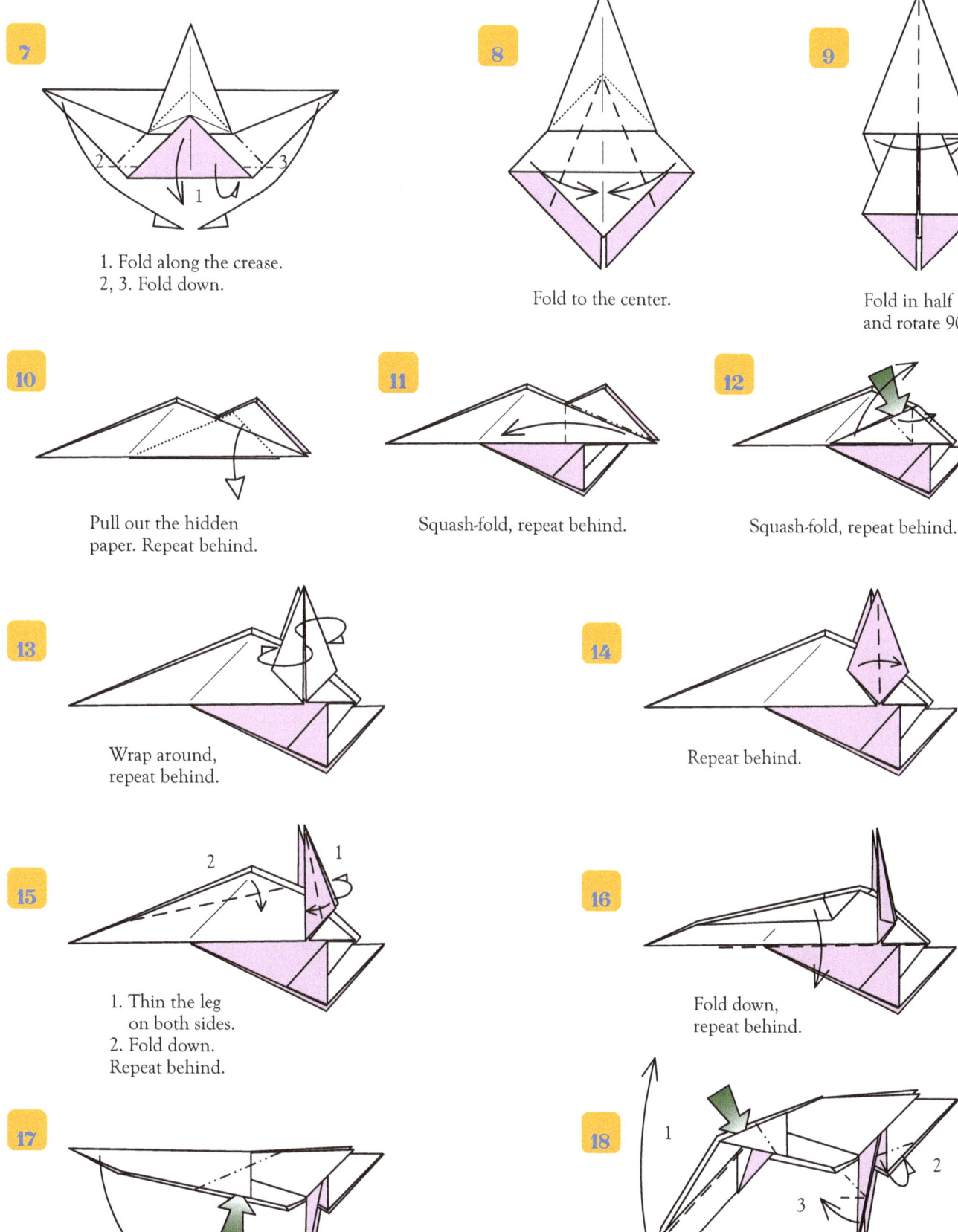

Standing Swan

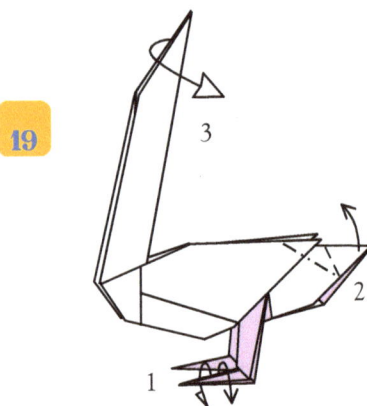

1. Unlock on both sides, repeat behind.
2. Crimp-fold.
3. Unfold.

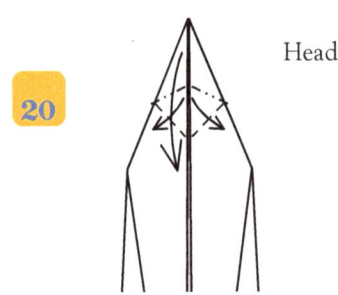

Head.

Fold down and spread.

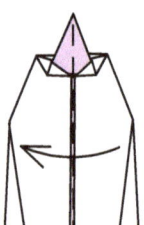

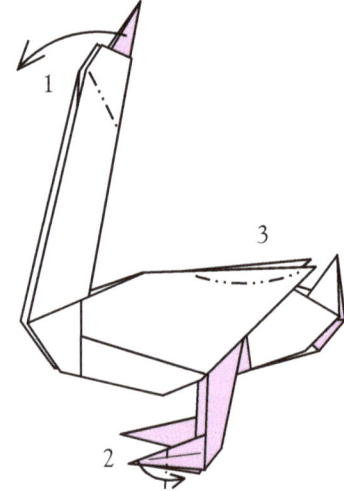

1. Reverse-fold.
2. Reverse-fold and flatten, repeat behind.
3. Curl the wing, repeat behind.

The Swan can stand.

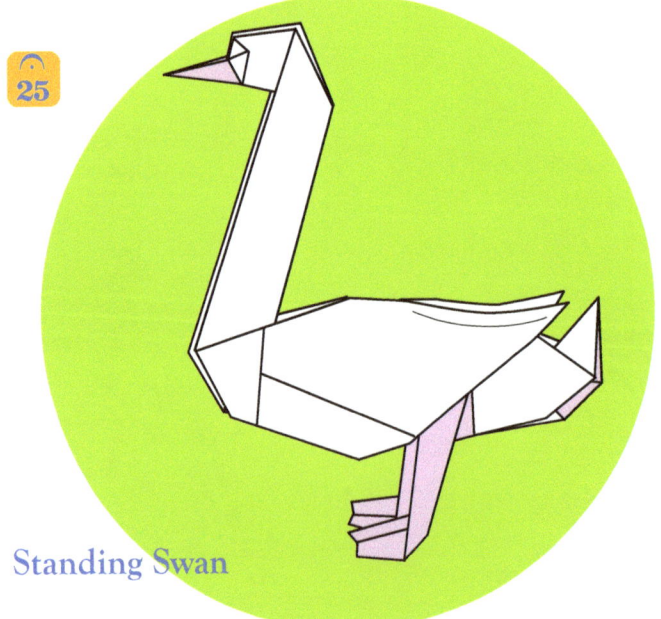

Standing Swan

Crow

Crows are some of the smartest animals in the world. They use tools for food, and especially like our leftovers. Though their caw calls are not so melodic, they are songbirds. Including the variety of "caws" they have 250 calls. The young crows help their parents raise chicks. These social, noisy birds can recognize human faces. Some have given gifts to people they like, such as shiny beads.

1. Fold and unfold.

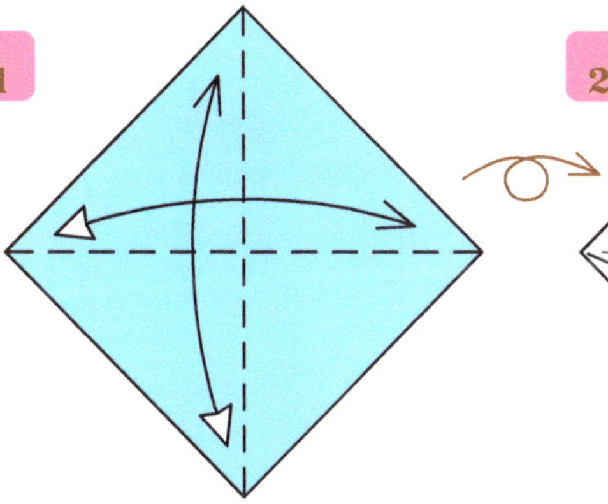

2. Fold and unfold.

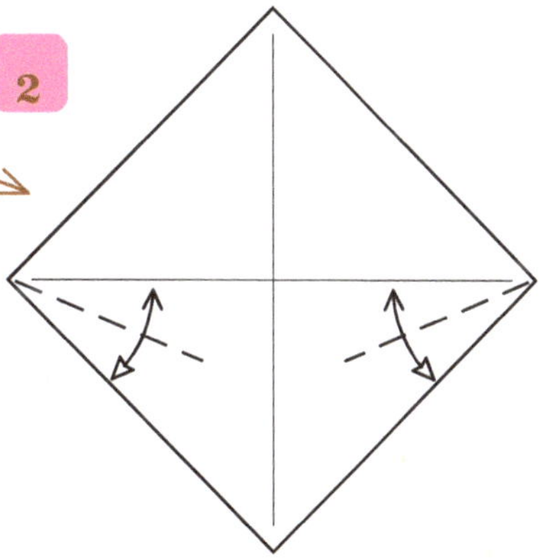

3. Fold and unfold.

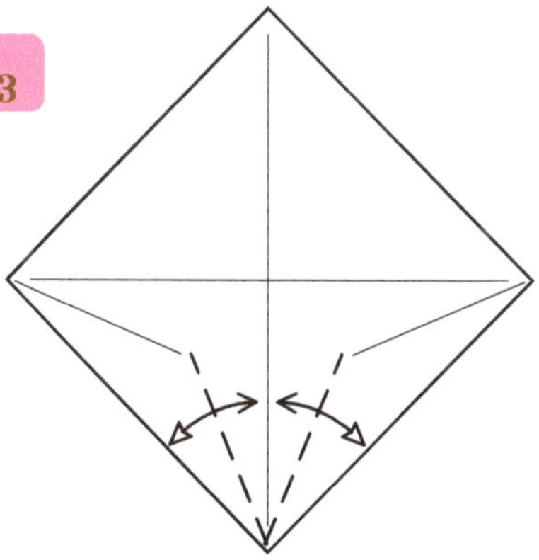

4. Fold along the creases.

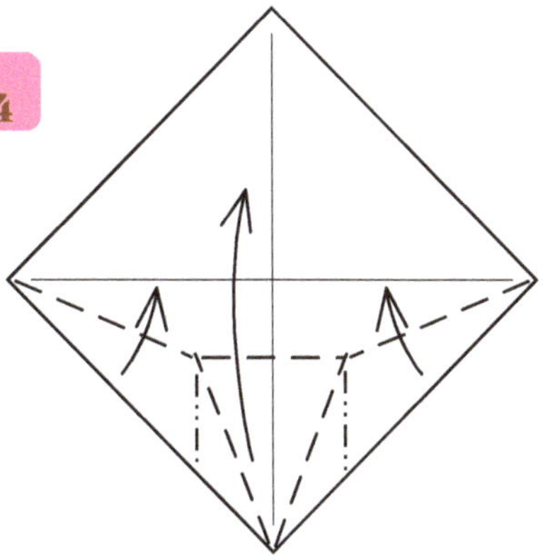

5.

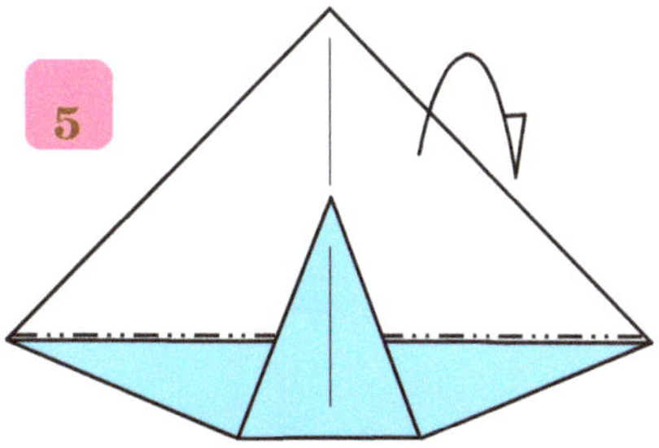

6.

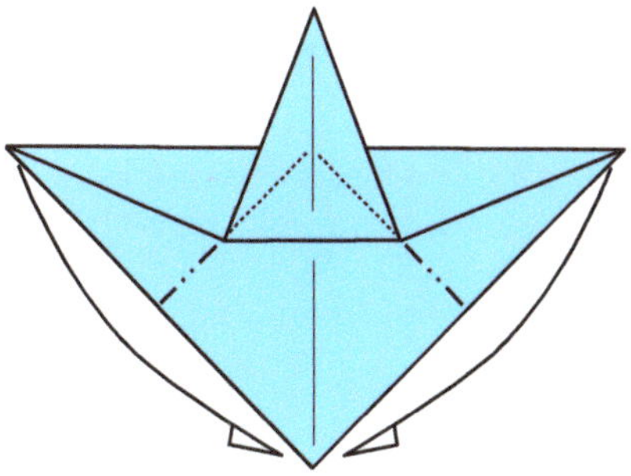

Crow 57

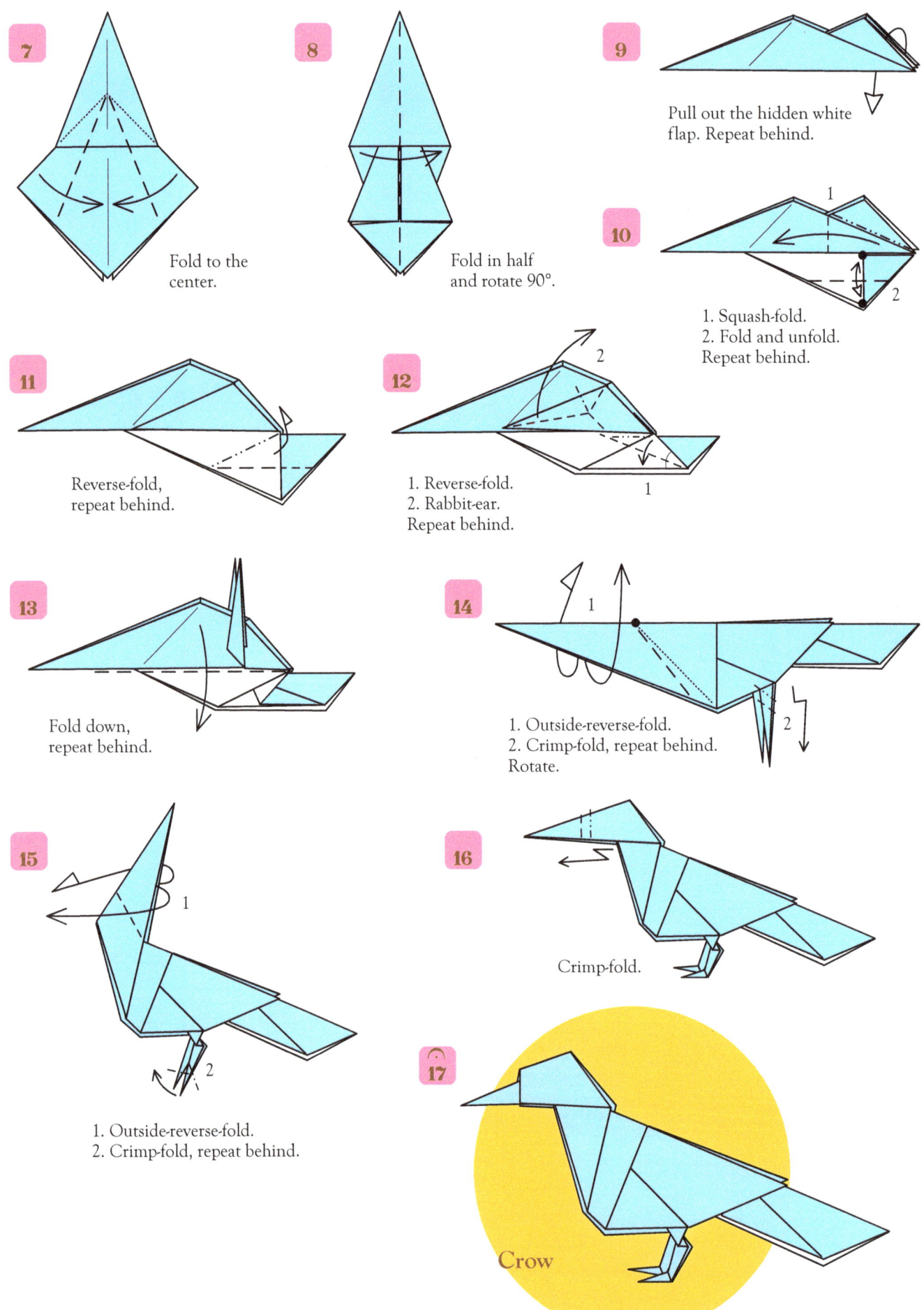

Chick

Chicks are so cure. While still in their eggs, they can hear the mother hen and peep back to her. Once hatched, they will follow the mother hen and can recognize her voice. From the hen, chicks learn which foods are good to eat and which to avoid. Chicks are playful, they run around and jump.

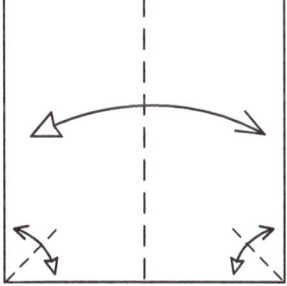

Fold and unfold.

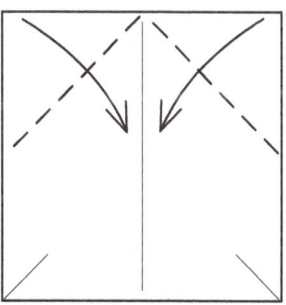

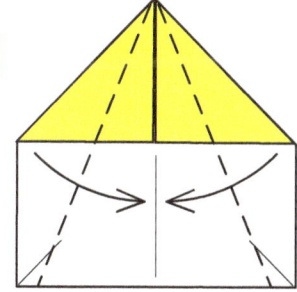

Fold to the center.

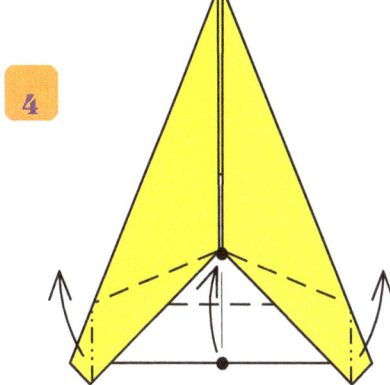

Make squash folds.

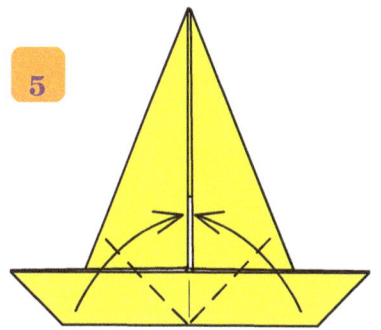

Fold to the center.

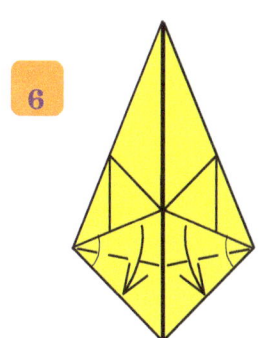

Chick 59

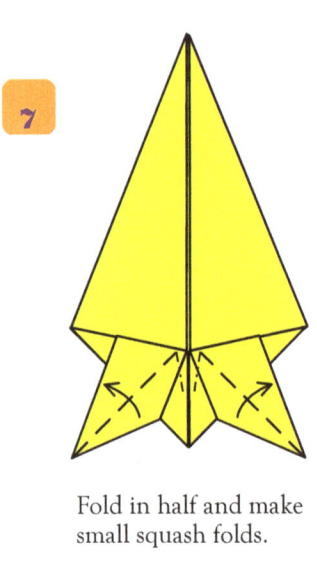

Fold in half and make small squash folds.

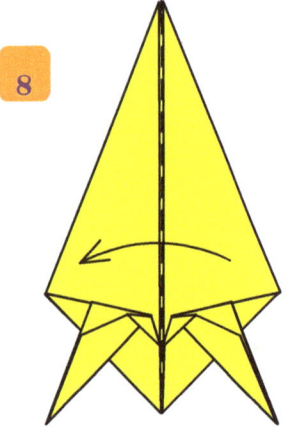

Fold in half and rotate.

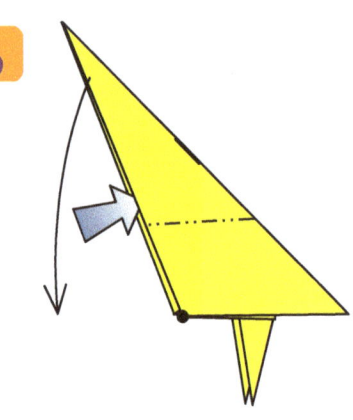

Reverse-fold so the edge goes to the dot.

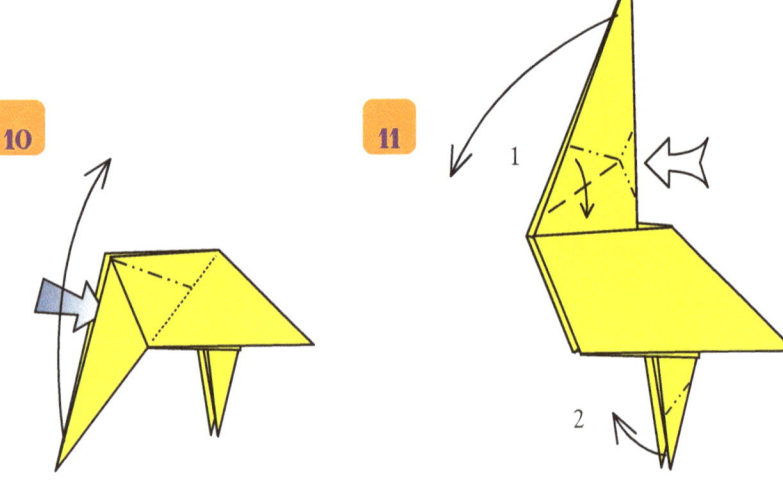

Reverse-fold.

1. Push in on the right and make a crimp fold.
2. Reverse-fold, repeat behind.

Crimp-fold.

Chick

60 *Origami Symphony No. 7*

Hen

The mother hen takes good care of her chicks. Of all the birds, the chicken is the most primitive and dinosaur-like. They are the closest living relative to the tyrannosaurus rex. They can only fly short distances. Domesticated in Southern China 8,000 years ago, there are 25 billion chickens in the world, surpassing all other bird species.

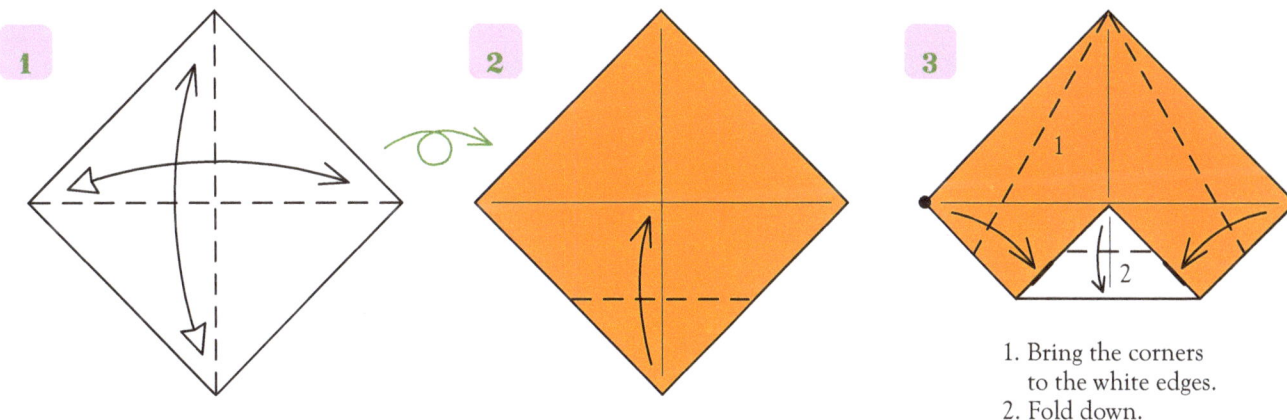

1. Fold and unfold.

2. (turn over)

3.
   1. Bring the corners to the white edges.
   2. Fold down.

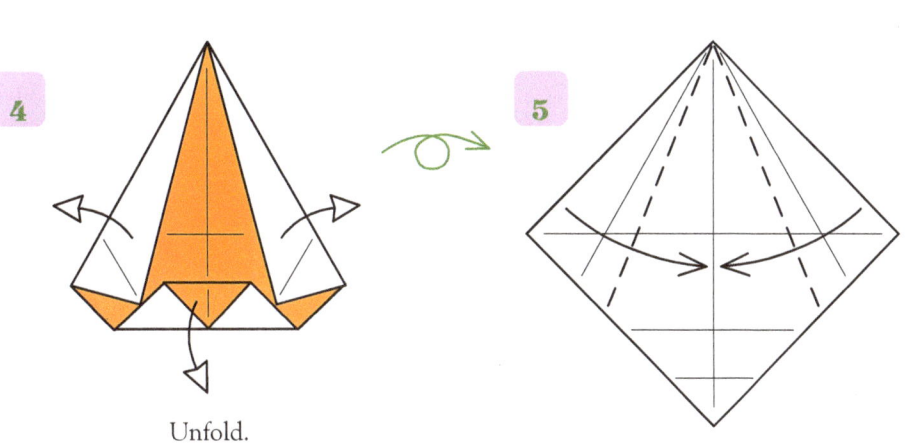

4. Unfold.

5. Fold to the center.

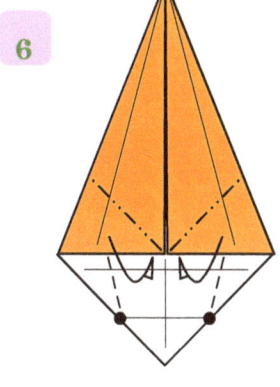

6. Make reverse folds.

Hen 61

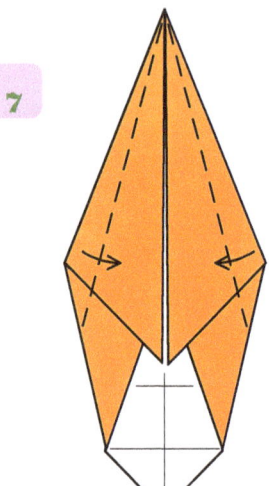

7 Fold along the creases.

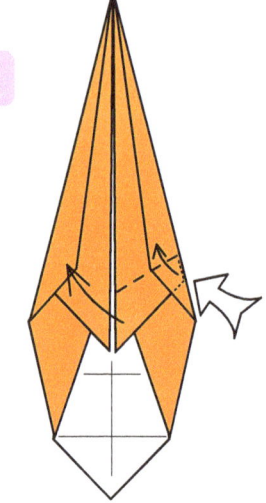

8 Reverse-fold.

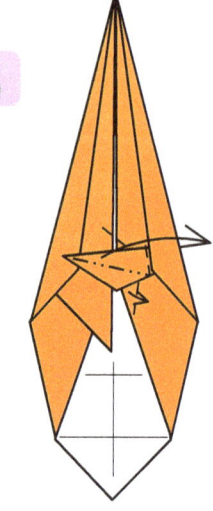

9 Squash-fold with a smaller squash fold.

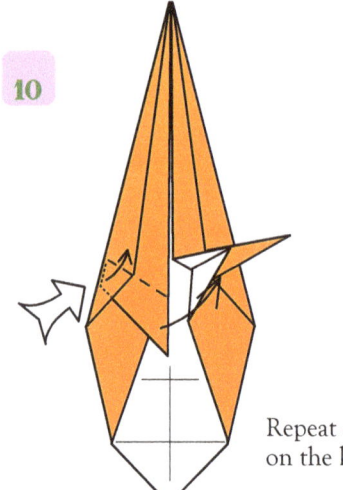

10 Repeat steps 8–9 on the left.

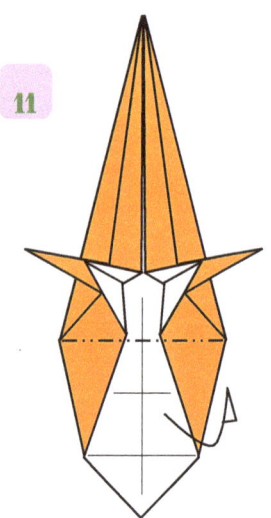

11

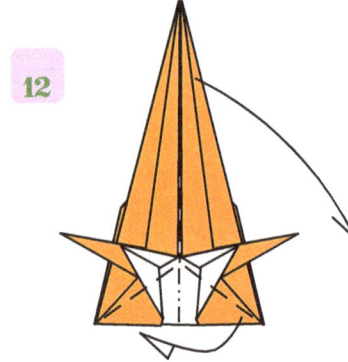

12 This is similar to a rabbit ear.

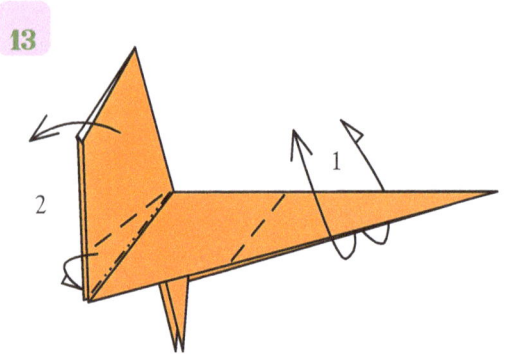

13
1. Outside-reverse-fold.
2. Crimp-fold.

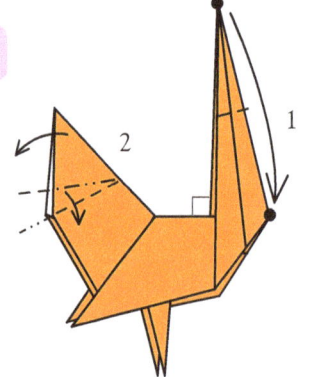

14 Note the right angle.
1. Outside-reverse-fold.
2. Crimp-fold.

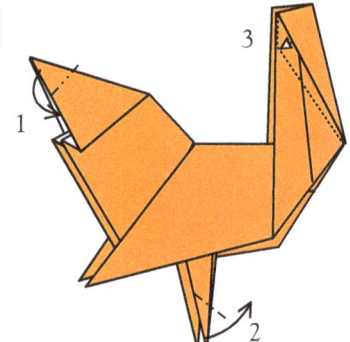

15
1. Reverse-fold.
2. Reverse-fold, repeat behind.
3. Pull out, repeat behind.

16 Head and Neck.

Outside-reverse-fold so the dot goes near the top.

17 Outside-reverse-fold.

18 Pivot at the top to slide the paper a little bit.

19 Crimp-fold.

20
1. Fold inside.
2. Fold inside.
Repeat behind.

21

Hen

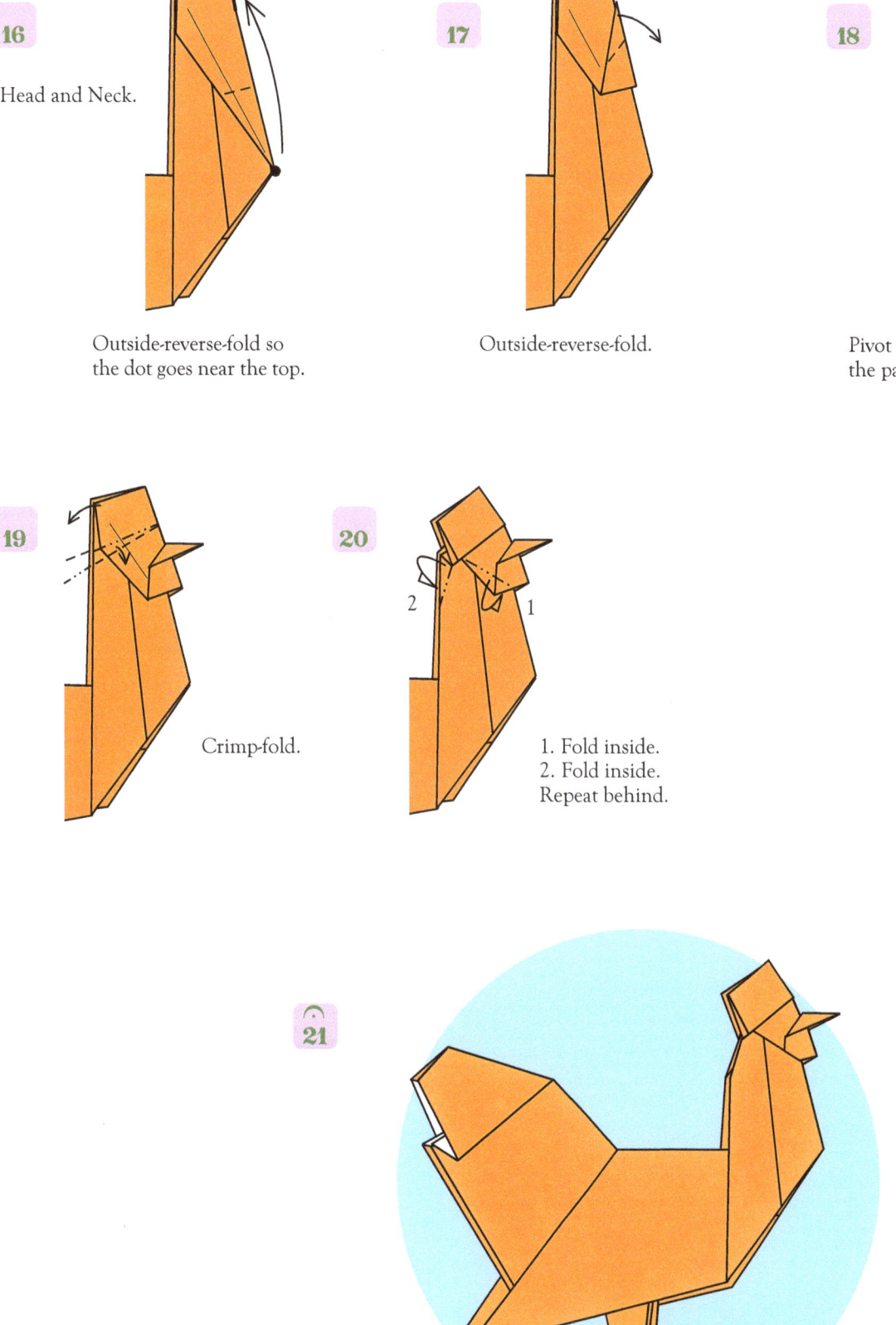

Hen 63

Rooster

Chickens are one of the few birds to have a comb and two wattles. The larger and brighter, the more attractive the rooster is to the hen. Roosters do a dance called "tidbitting" where they move their head and make funny calls, to attract hens. Several roosters can live together and protect the flock. Chickens can recognize human faces and farm animals. Being very social and intelligent, they have a vocabulary of 30 distinct sounds.

1. 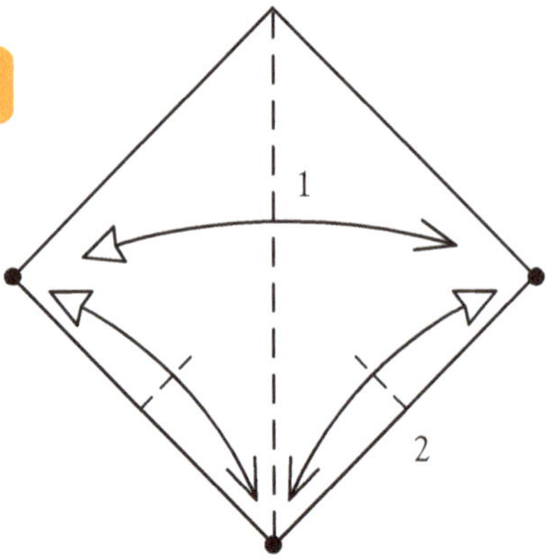
1. Fold and unfold.
2. Fold and unfold on the edge.

2. 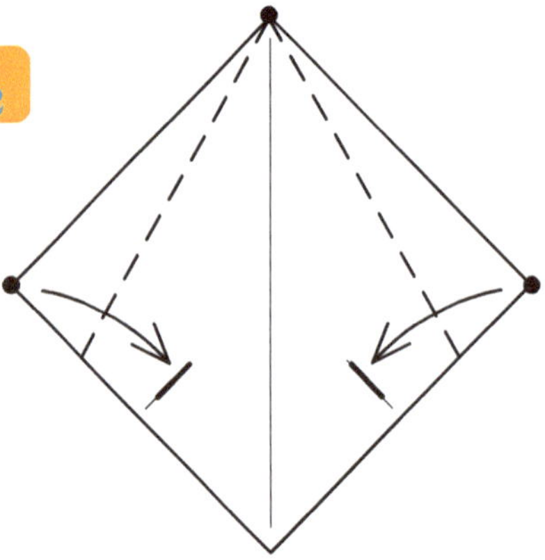
Bring the corners to the lines.

3. 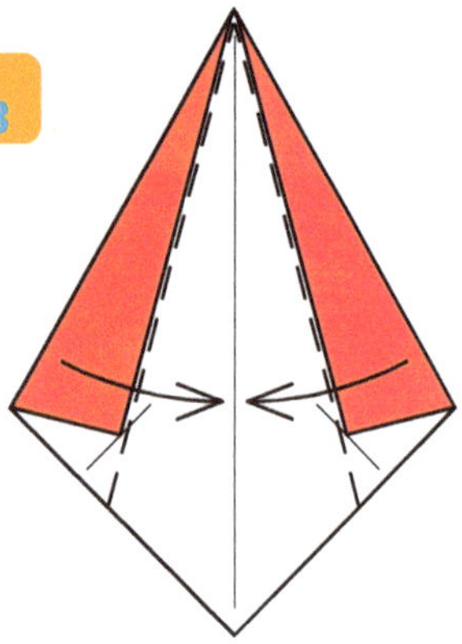
Fold to the center.

4. 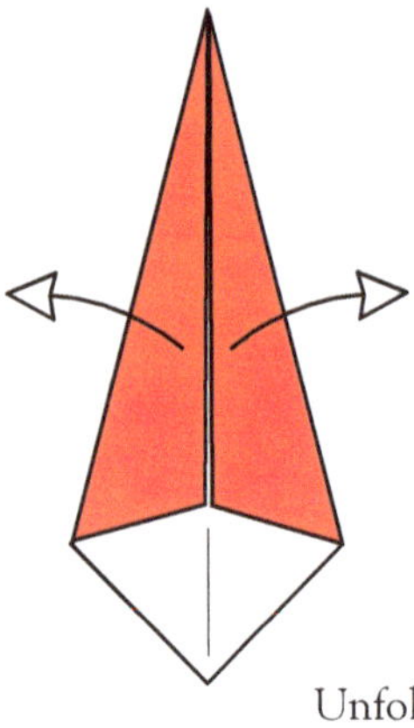
Unfold.

5.

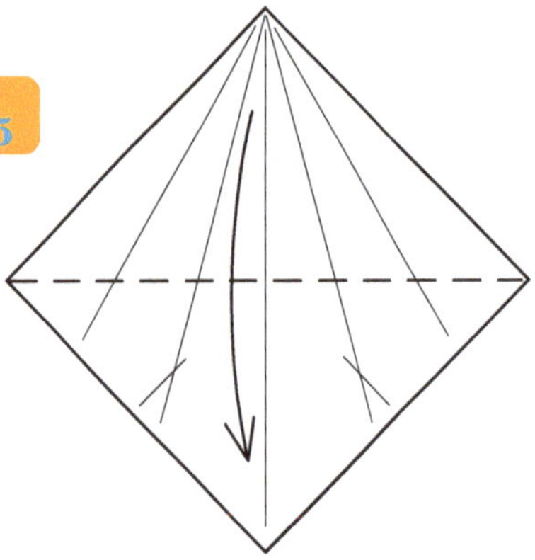

6.
Fold to the center. 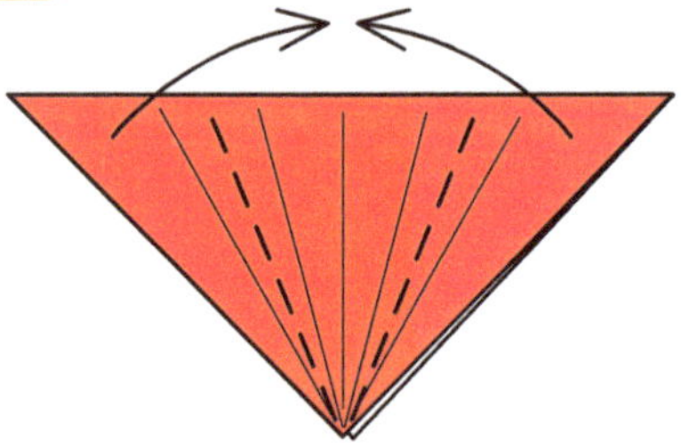

64   Origami Symphony No. 7

7

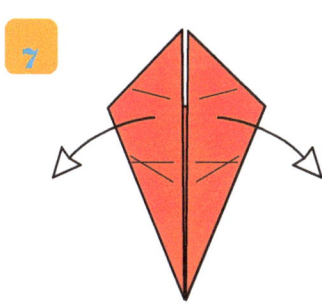

Unfold everything.

8

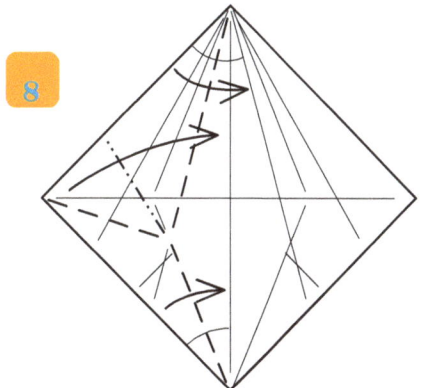

Fold along some of the creases for this rabbit ear.

9

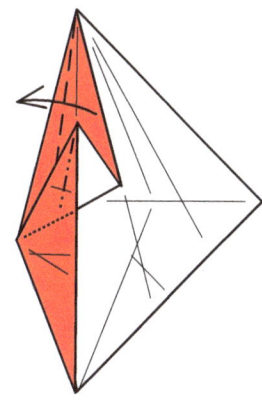

Valley-fold along the crease for this reverse fold.

10

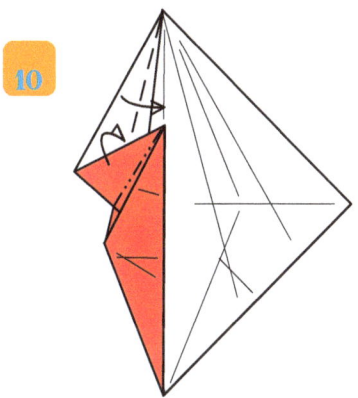

Valley-fold along the crease for this reverse fold.

11

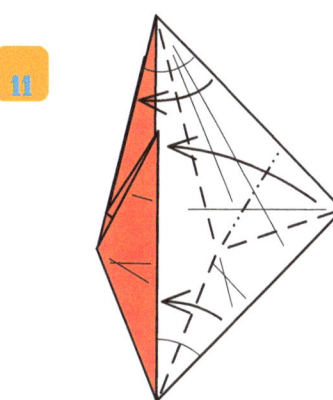

Repeat steps 8–10 on the right.

12

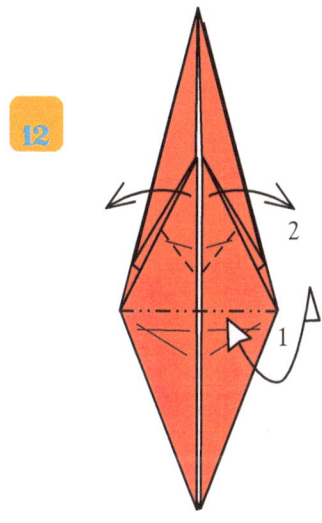

1. Fold and unfold.
2. Make squash folds.

13

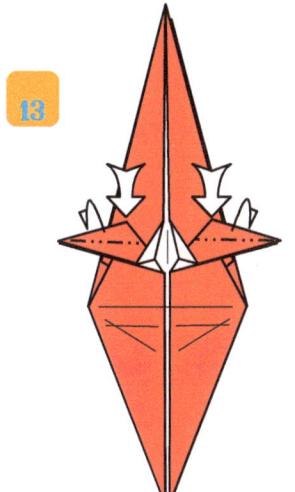

Make reverse folds.

14

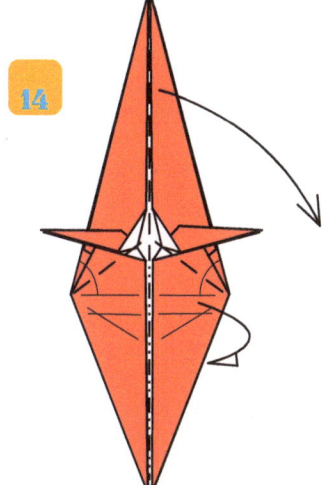

This is similar to a rabbit ear.

15

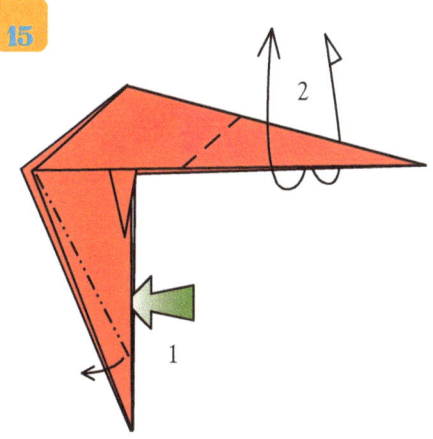

1. Slide the top layer, repeat behind.
2. Outside-reverse-fold.

Rooster **65**

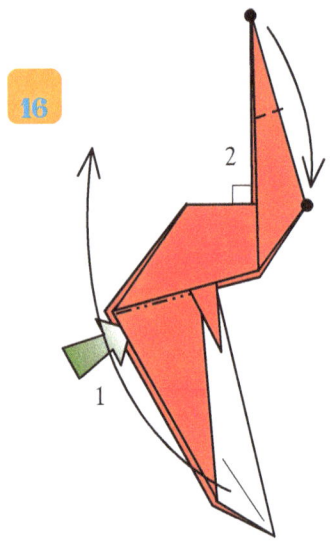

Note the right angle.
1. Outside-reverse-fold.
2. Reverse-fold.

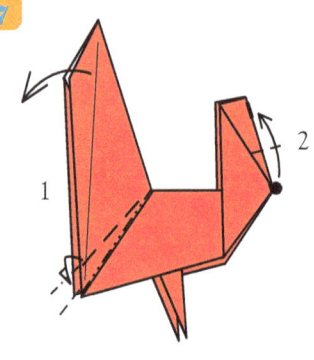

1. Outside-reverse-fold so the dot goes near the top.
2. Crimp-fold.

1. Make crimp folds.
2. Crimp-fold, repeat behind.
3. Outside-reverse-fold.

Head.

Pivot at the top to slide the paper a little bit.

Crimp-fold.

Fold inside, repeat behind.

Rooster

Pig

Pigs are incredibly smart, ranked within the top ten of the most intelligent animals. They are smarter and more trainable than dogs. Mother pigs sing to their piglets. They can learn their names and have 20 distinct grunts. Pigs are very social, bond with humans, and enjoy listening to music. It is believed they dream. Their sense of smell is 2000 times more sensitive than ours.

1.

Fold and unfold.

2.

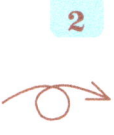

Fold to the center and unfold.

3.

Fold to the lines.

4.

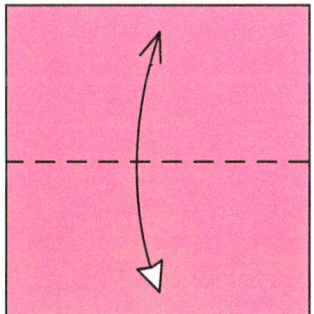

5.

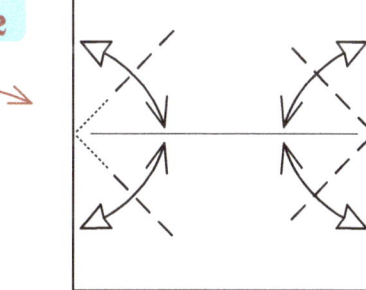

1. Make squash folds.
2. Make reverse folds.

6.

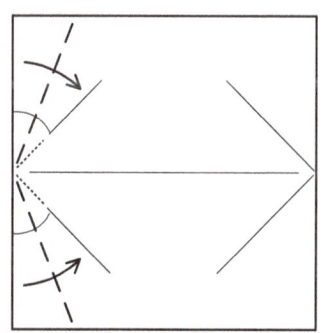

1. Fold the legs.
2. Pleat-fold.

Pig **67**

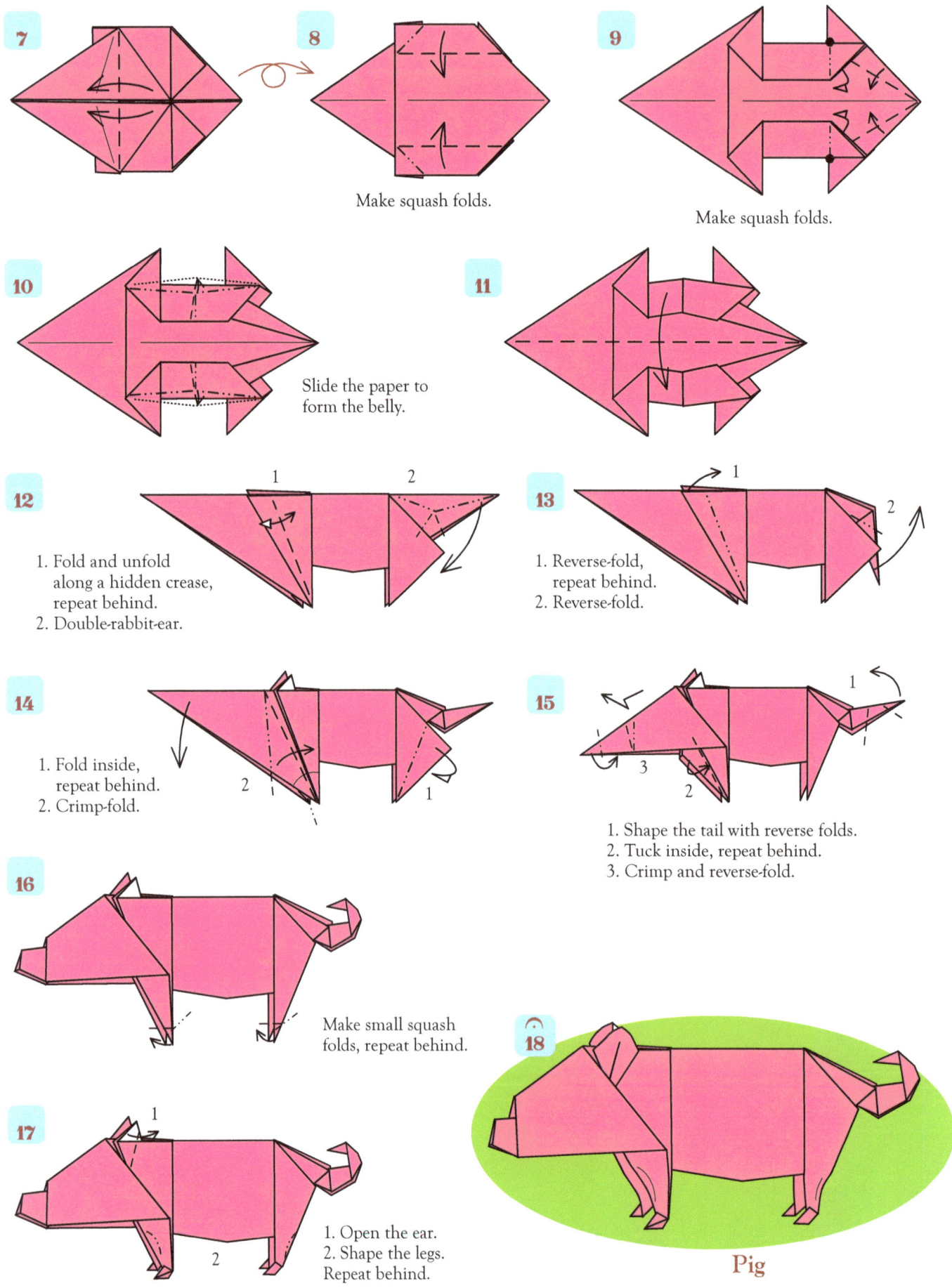

Pig

Sheep

There are over 1 billion sheep around the world. These animals are very social and can recognize each other, and humans, too. They can see almost all around themselves, protecting them from predators. Sheep uses vocal sounds to express fear, excitement, and boredom. Their wool grows forever.

1.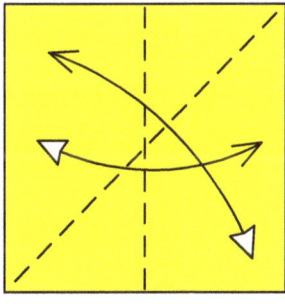

   Fold and unfold.

2.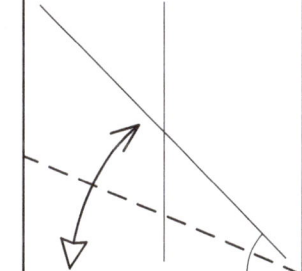

   Fold and unfold.

3.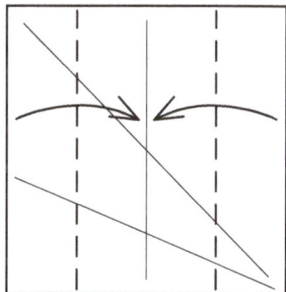

   Fold to the center.

4.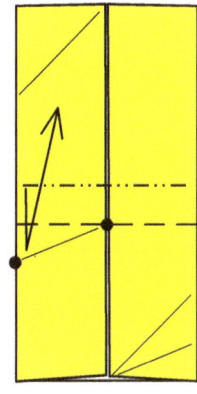

   Pleat-fold.

5.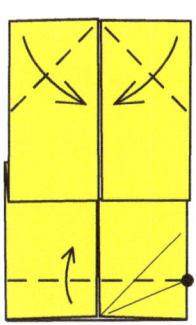

6.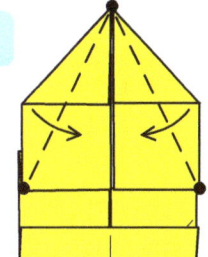

7.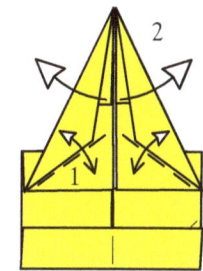

   1. Fold and unfold along the edges.
   2. Unfold.

Sheep **69**

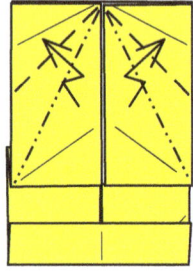

8

Make crimp folds along the creases.

9

Make reverse folds. Rotate 90°.

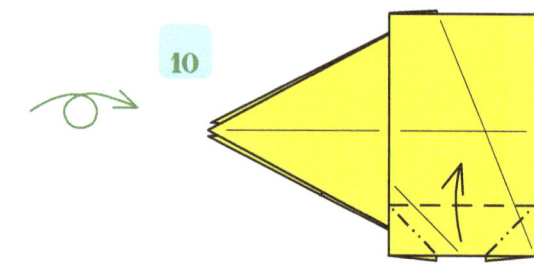

10

Petal-fold.

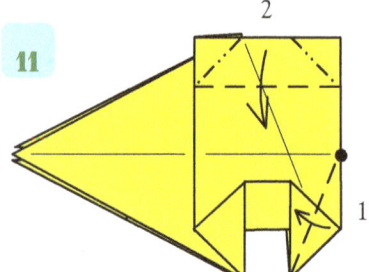

11

1. Thin the leg.
2. Repeat steps 10–11 on the top.

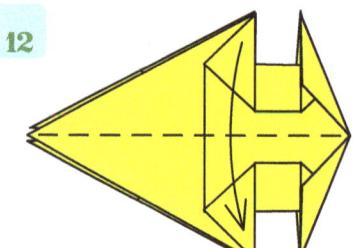

12

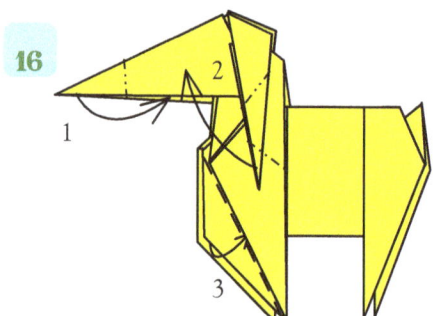

13

Mountain-fold along the crease for this crimp fold.

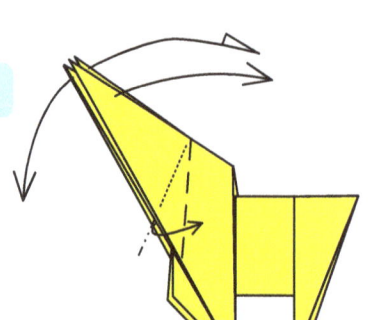

14

Crimp-fold.

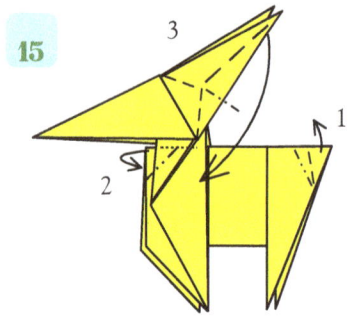

15

1. Crimp-fold.
2. Reverse-fold.
3. Rabbit-ear, repeat behind.

16

1. Reverse-fold.
2. Shape the horns with reverse folds, repeat behind.
3. Tuck inside, repeat behind.

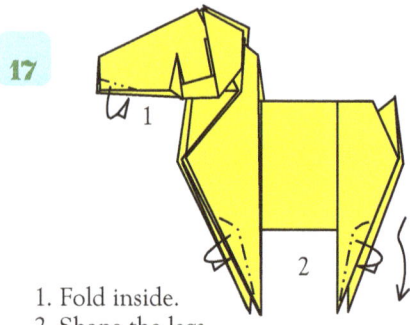

17

1. Fold inside.
2. Shape the legs. Repeat behind.

18

Sheep

70 Origami Symphony No. 7

Cow

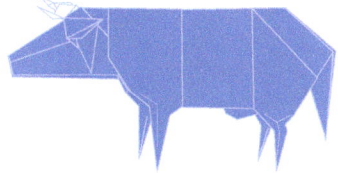

The cow is the female and the bull is the male. Each day these social animals spend 8 hours eating 40 pounds of grass and plants. With eyes on the side of their heads, they can see almost all the way around themselves. They are colorblind. In a bull fight, the bright red cape looks yellow-gray to them.

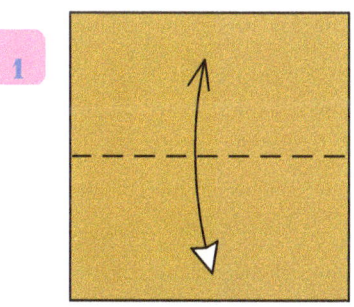

Fold and unfold.

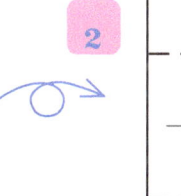

Fold and unfold.

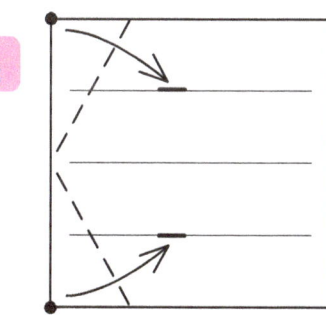

Unfold.

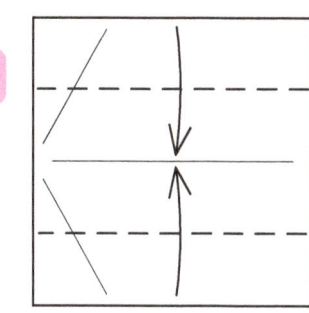

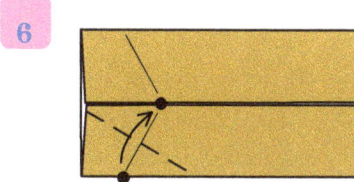

Cow **71**

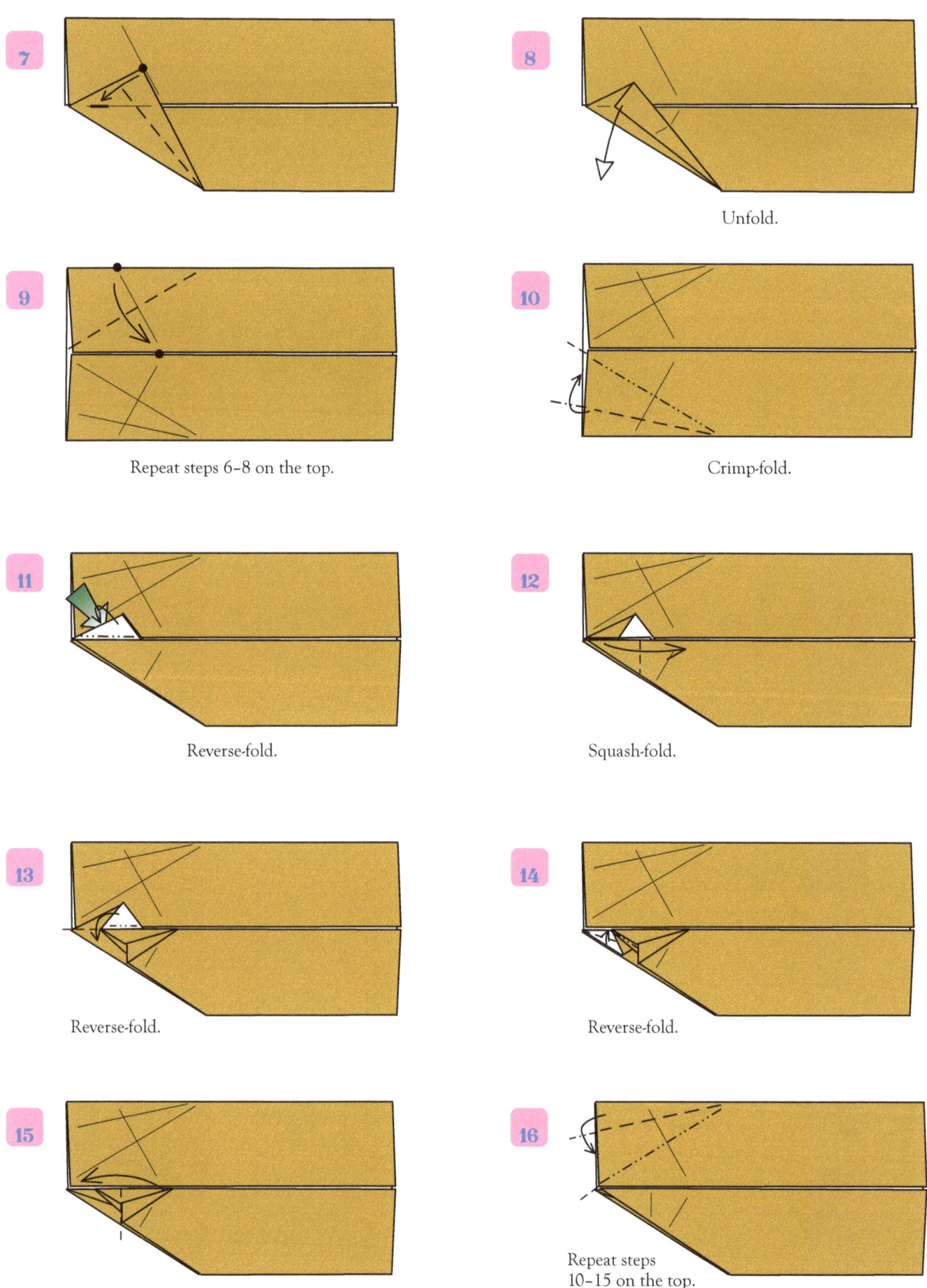

72 *Origami Symphony No. 7*

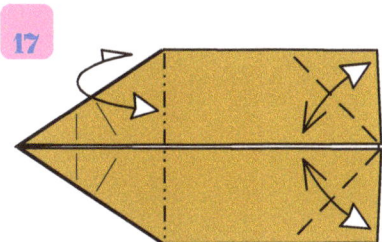
Fold and unfold.

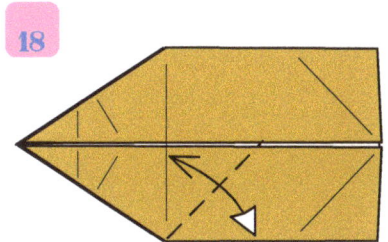
Fold and unfold the lower half.

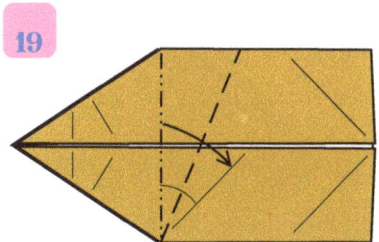

Unfold.

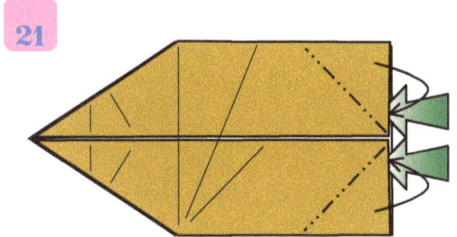
Make reverse folds.

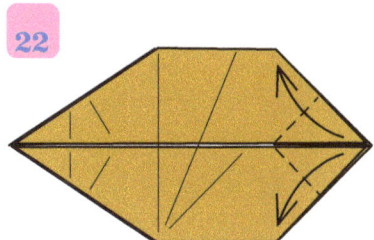

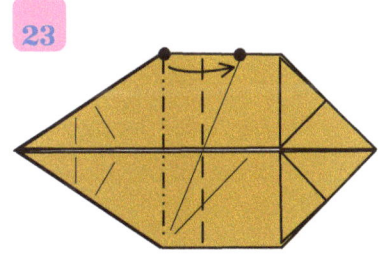

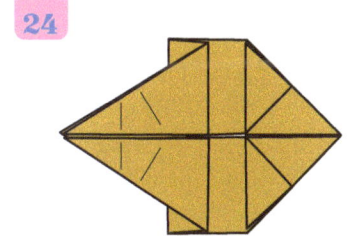

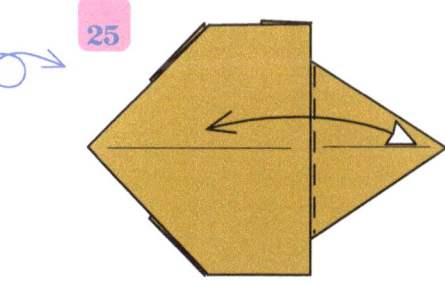
Fold and unfold.

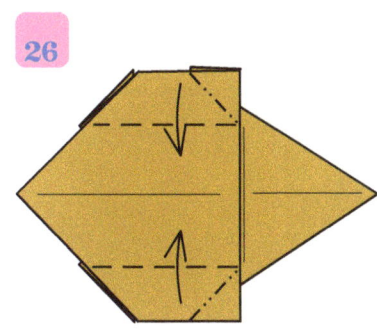
Make squash folds.

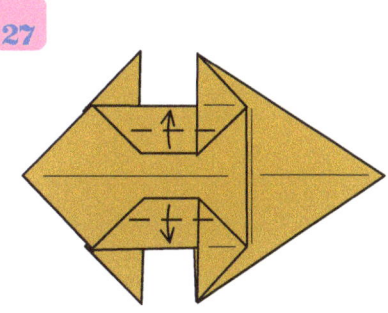

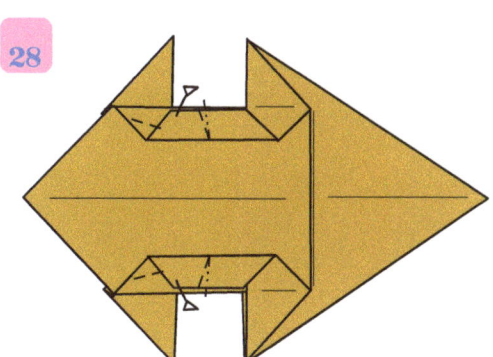

Cow 73

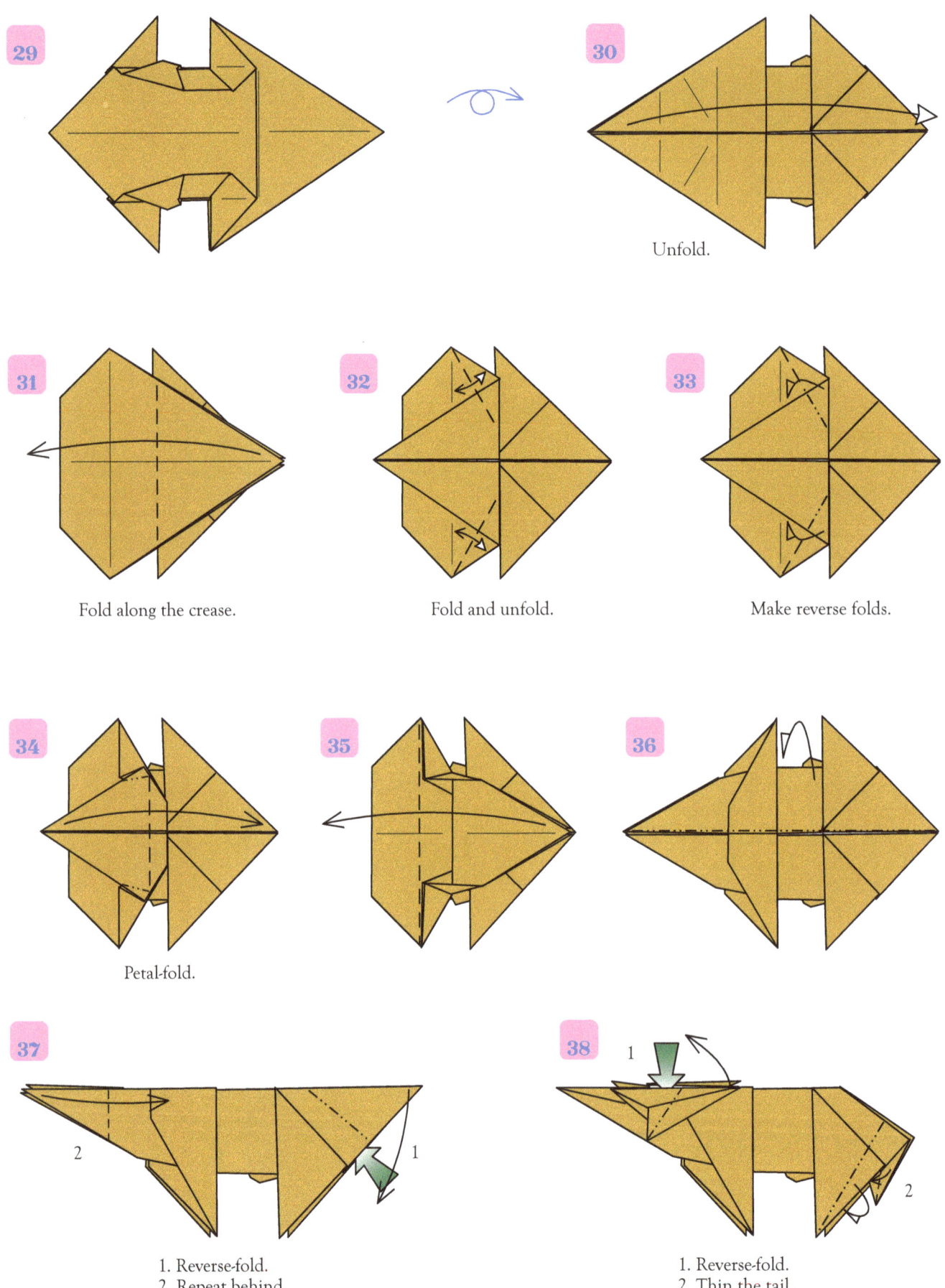

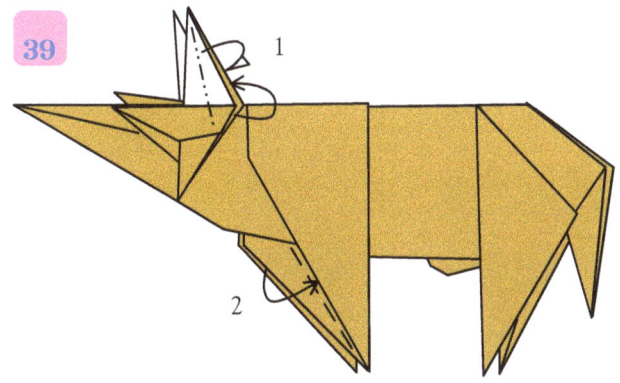

1. Fold inside on both sides.
2. Tuck inside.
Repeat behind.

Crimp-fold.

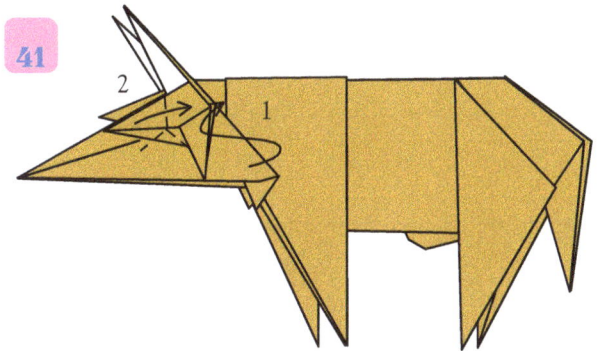

1. Tuck inside.
2. Fold the ear.
Repeat behind.

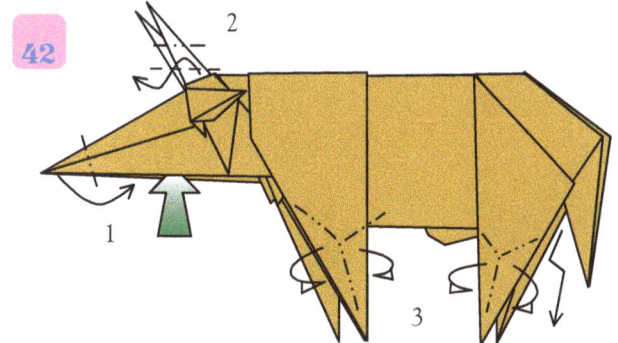

1. Reverse-fold.
2. Shape the horn.
3. Shape the legs.
Repeat behind.

Cow

Cow **75**

Third Movement

Minuet of Antiprisms with a Trio of Stars

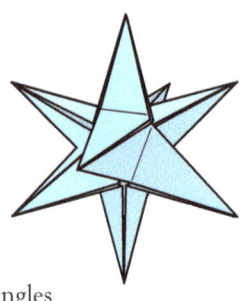

Antiprisms have identical polygon bases on the top and bottom but are staggered with a band of triangles along the sides. Here is a collection of antiprisms with triangular, square, pentagonal, hexagonal, and octagonal bases. These form elegant stands to exhibit the reptiles, monkeys, and more. The trio of stars shines through the night on the farm and elsewhere. The stars will guide you from the farm to the monkeys.

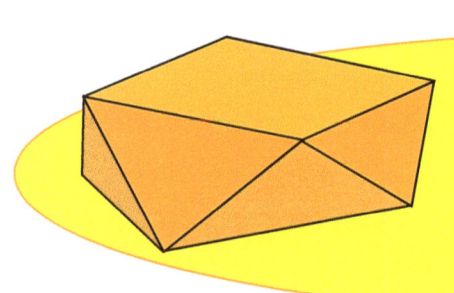
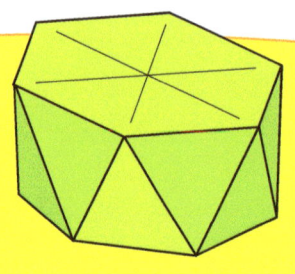
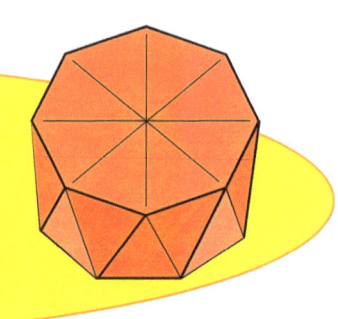

Octahedron

The octahedron is composed of eight equilateral triangles. According to Plato, the octahedron represented air because it appears to be suspended. As an antiprism, the top and bottom are triangles with six triangles connecting them.

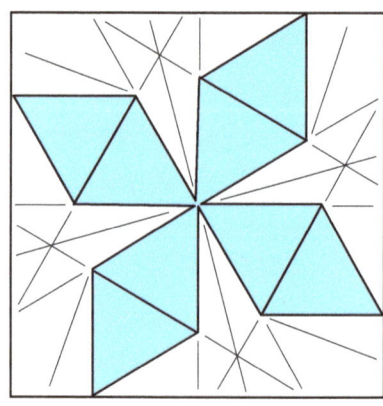

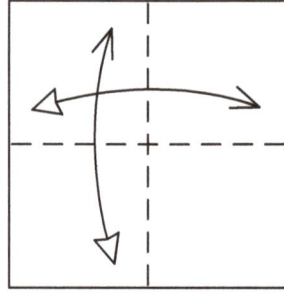
Fold and unfold.

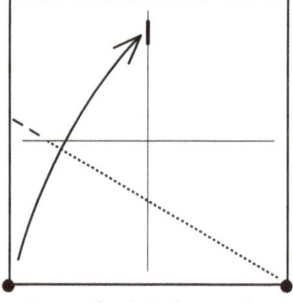
Bring the left dot to the line. Crease on the left.

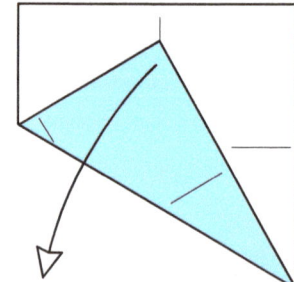
Unfold and rotate 90°.

76 *Origami Symphony No. 7*

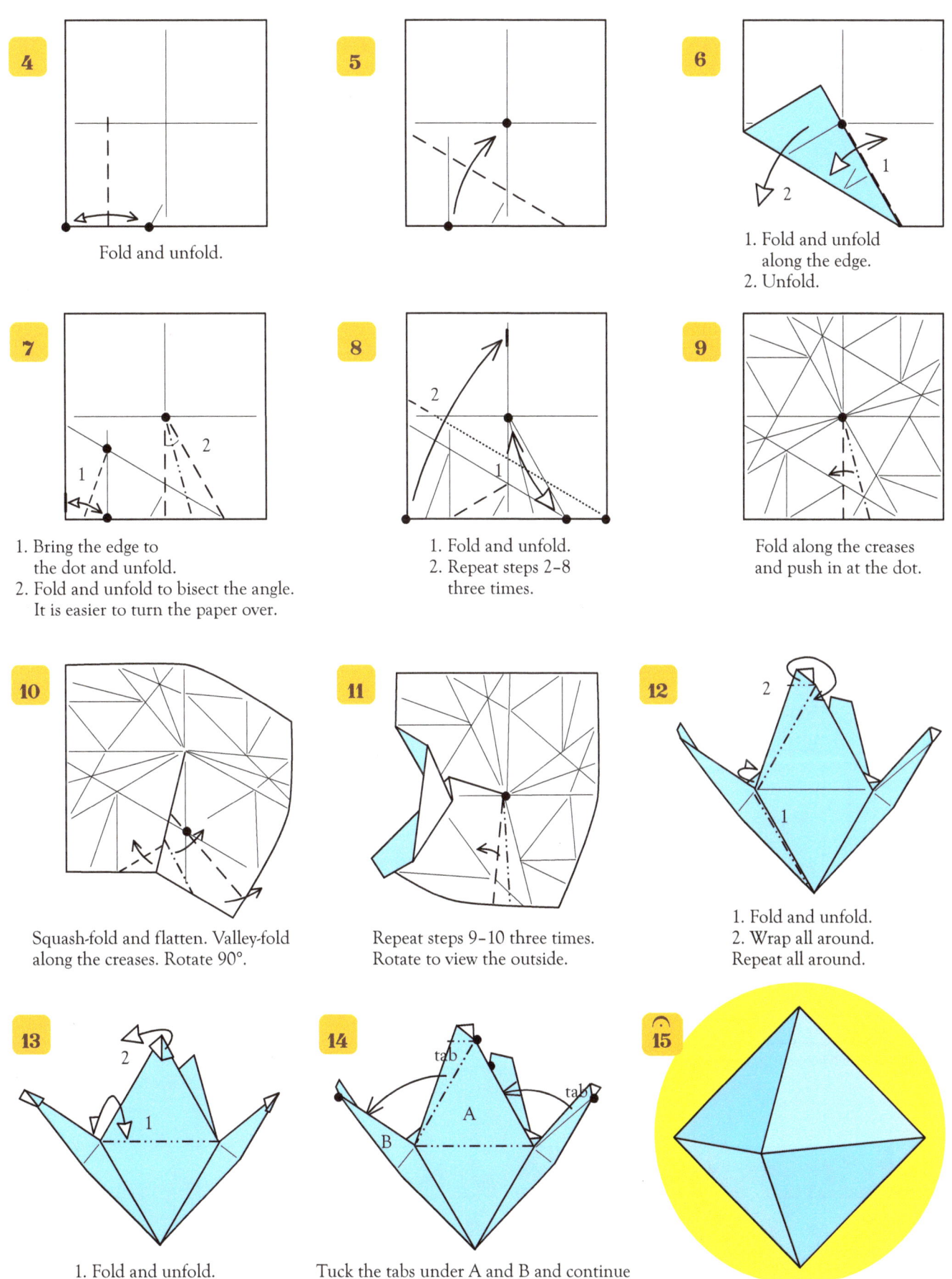

Square Antiprism

This antiprism is composed of two squares and eight isosceles triangles. Each triangle has angles 90°, 45°, and 45°. The layout shows square symmetry.

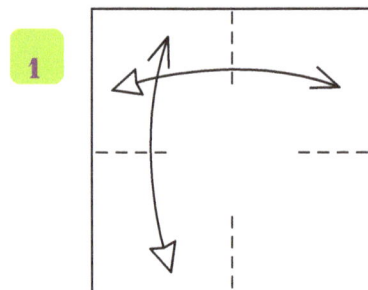

1. Fold and unfold.

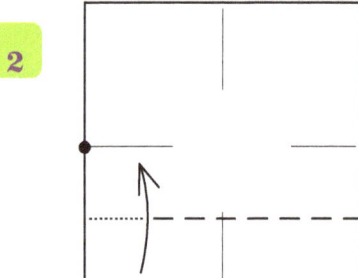

2.

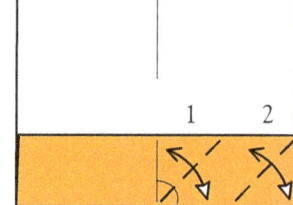

3. Fold and unfold.

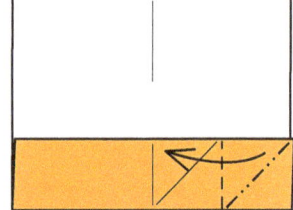

4. Squash-fold.

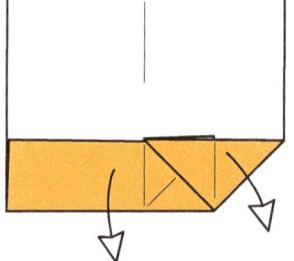

5. Unfold and rotate 90°.

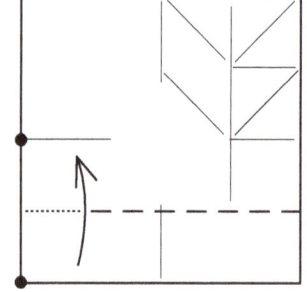

6. Repeat steps 2–5 three times. Rotate 45°.

78   *Origami Symphony No. 7*

7

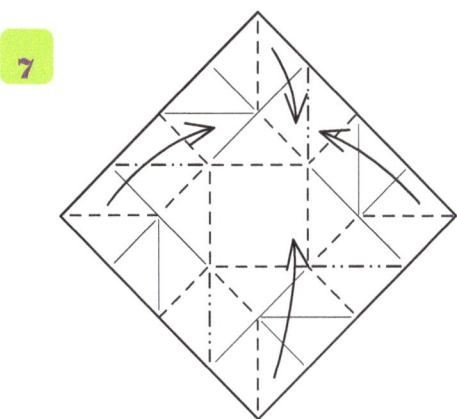

Fold along the creases. The model will become 3D and the corners will be pointing up.

8

Fold each flap down to flatten the top. Repeat all around.

9

Tuck inside.

10

Repeat step 9 three times.

11

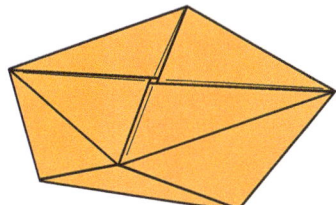

Rotate the top to the bottom.

12

Square Antiprism

Pentagonal Antiprism

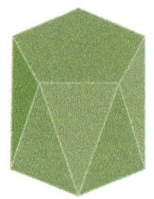
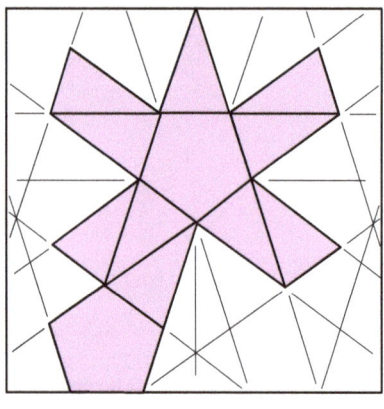

A pentagonal antiprism is composed of 10 triangles and two pentagons. In this one, the angles of each triangle are 36°, 72°, and 72°.

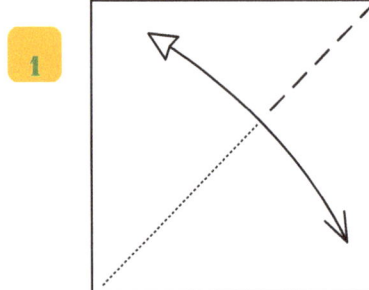

1. Fold and unfold by the top.

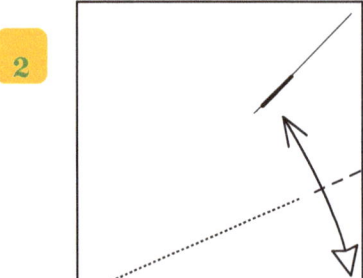

2. Fold and unfold on the right.

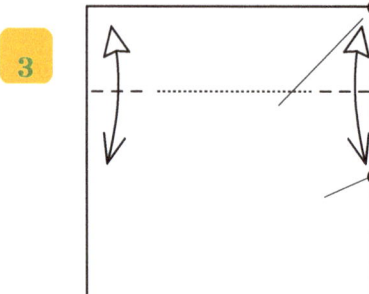

3. Fold and unfold on the edges.

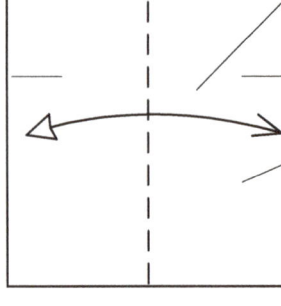

4. Fold and unfold, creasing lightly.

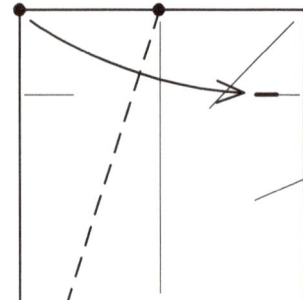

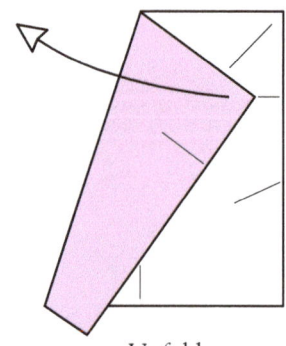

6. Unfold.

Origami Symphony No. 7

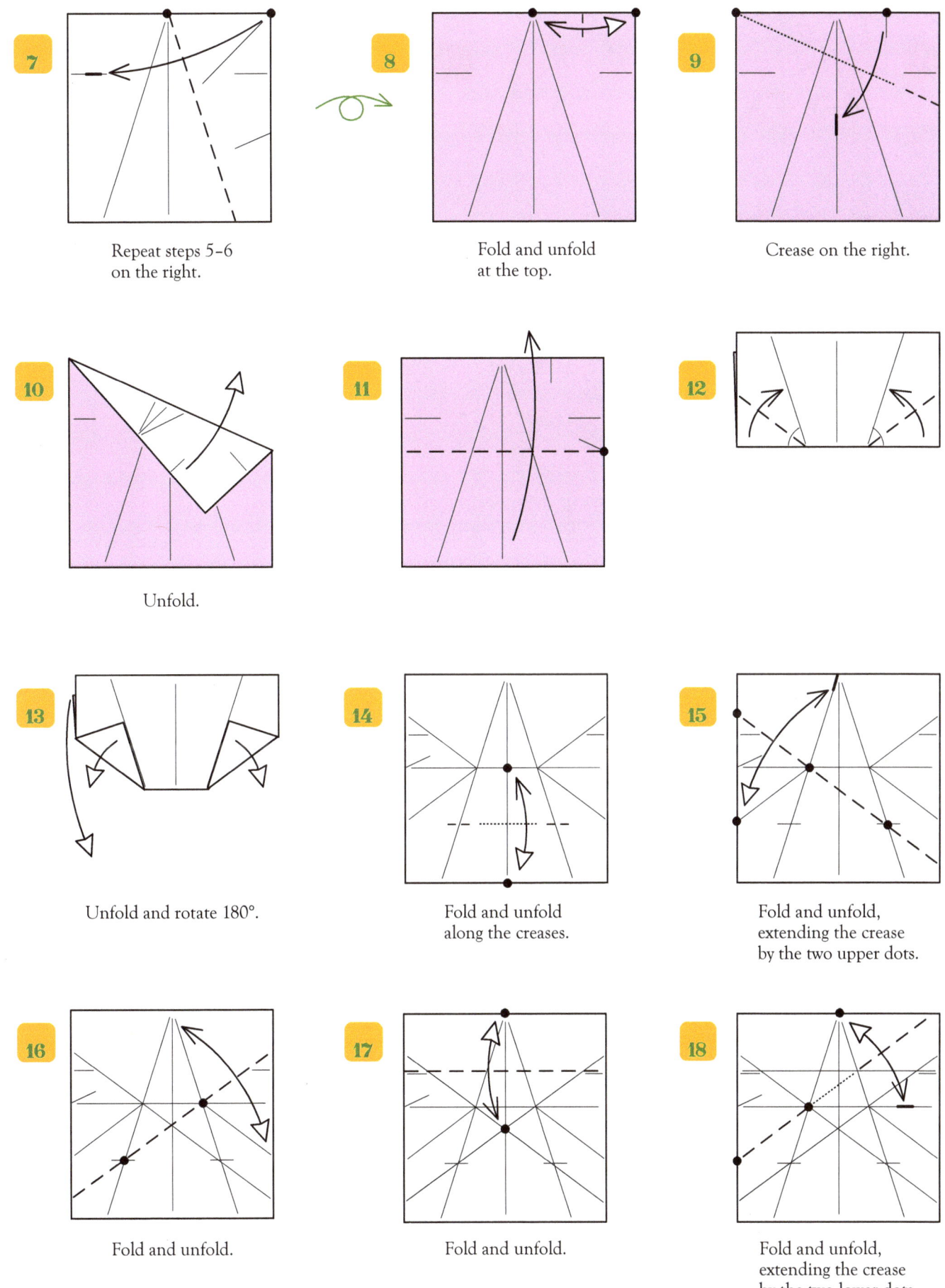

Golden Pentagonal Antiprism

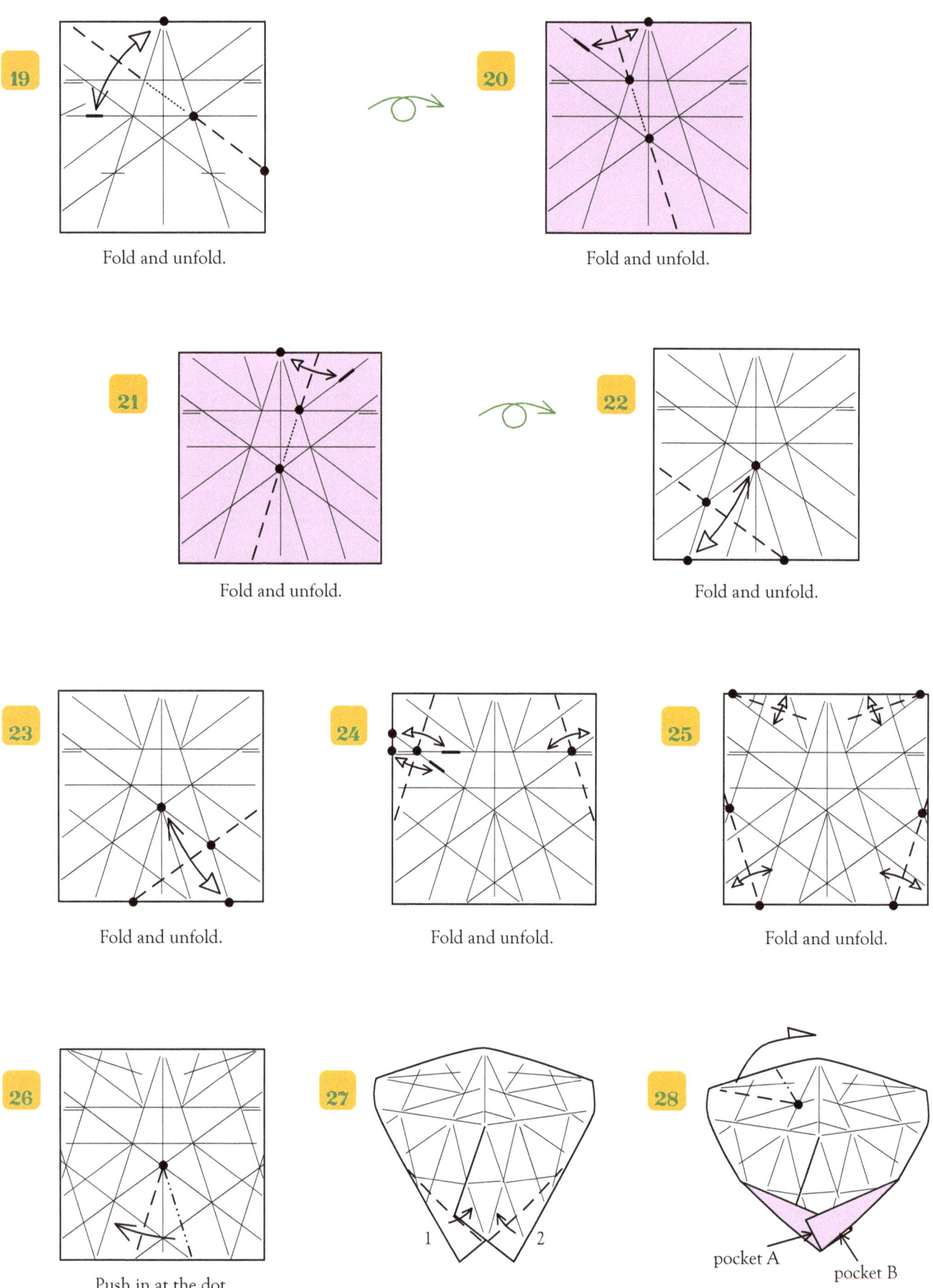

82 *Origami Symphony No. 7*

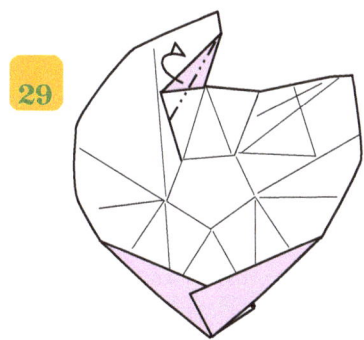

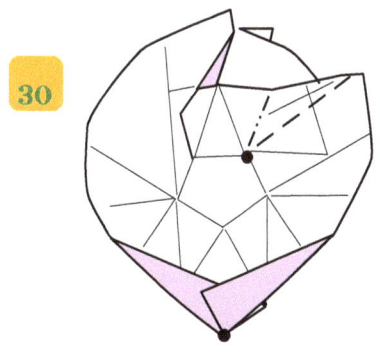

Repeat steps 28–29 on the right. Rotate to view the outside so the dot at the bottom goes to the top.

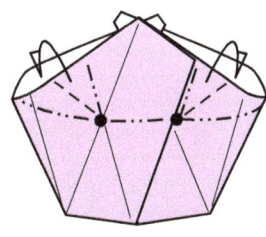

Puff out at the dots and flatten inside. Rotate slightly to view the left.

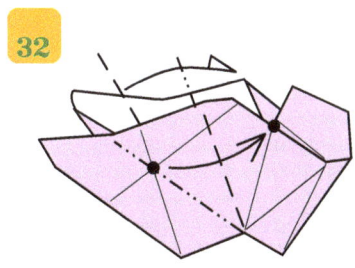

Repeat behind.

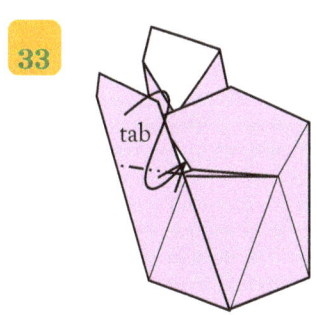

Tuck the tab into pocket A.

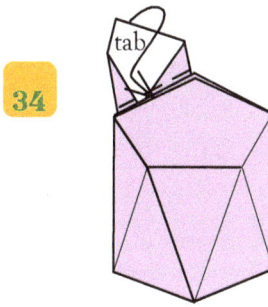

Tuck the tab into pocket B.

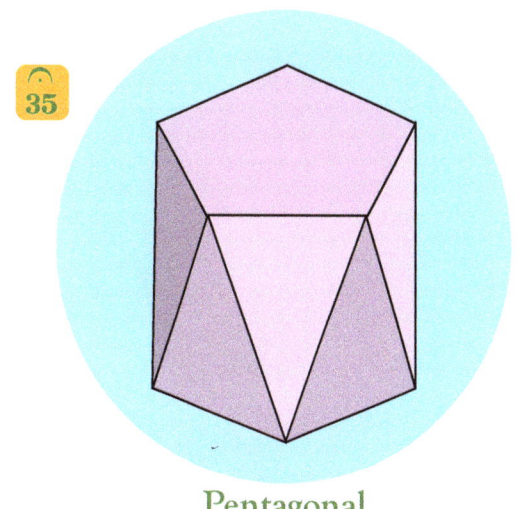

Pentagonal Antiprism

Golden Pentagonal Antiprism **83**

Hexagonal Antiprism

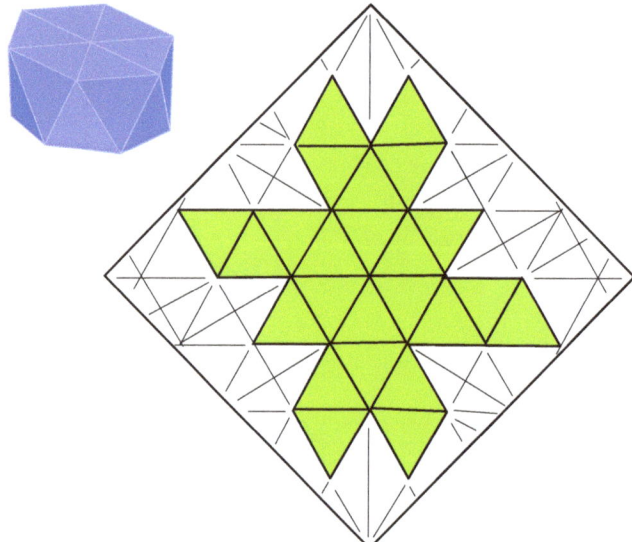

This antiprism is composed of two hexagons and twelve equilateral triangles. This is the uniform hexagonal antiprism.

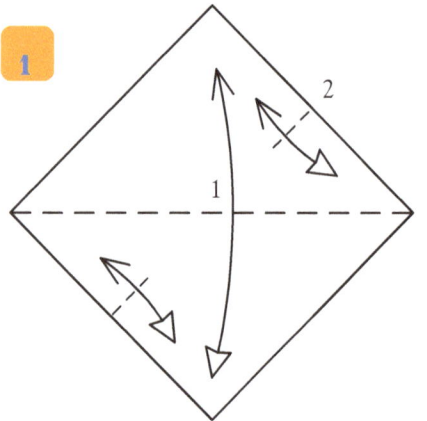

1. Fold and unfold.
2. Fold and unfold on the edges.

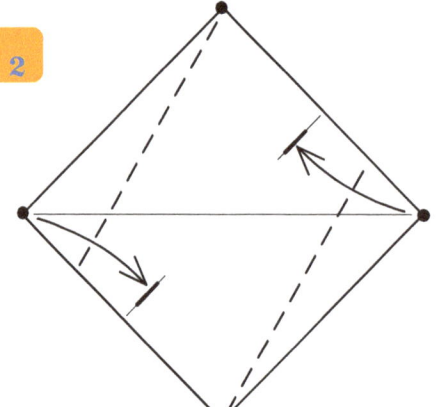

Bring the corners to the lines.

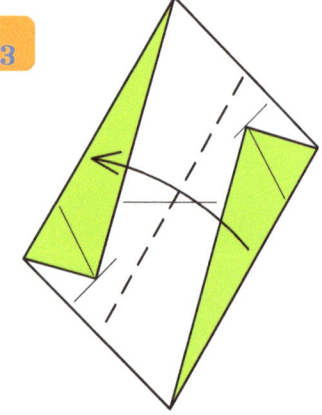

Fold in half.

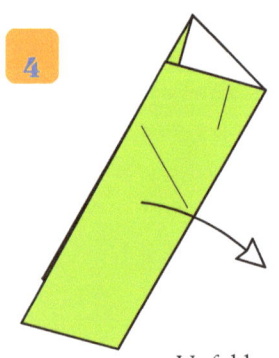

Unfold.

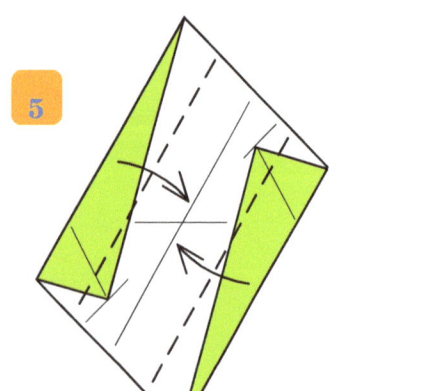

Fold to the center.

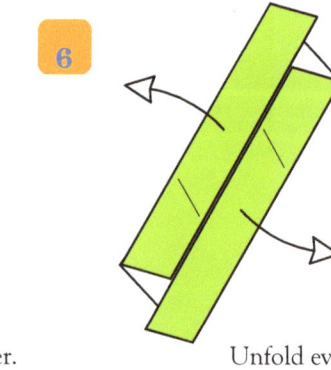

Unfold everything.

84 Origami Symphony No. 7

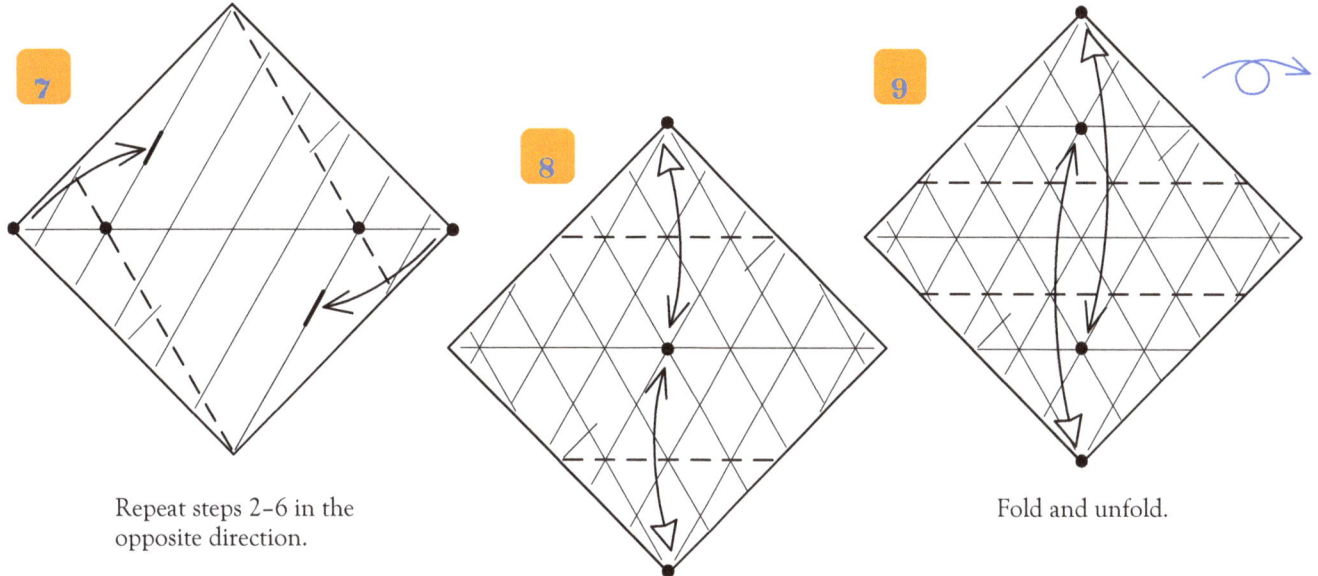

7. Repeat steps 2–6 in the opposite direction.

8. Fold to the center and unfold.

9. Fold and unfold.

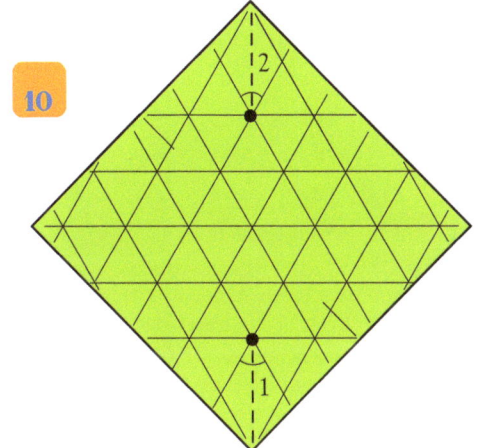

10. Fold and unfold at 1 and 2.

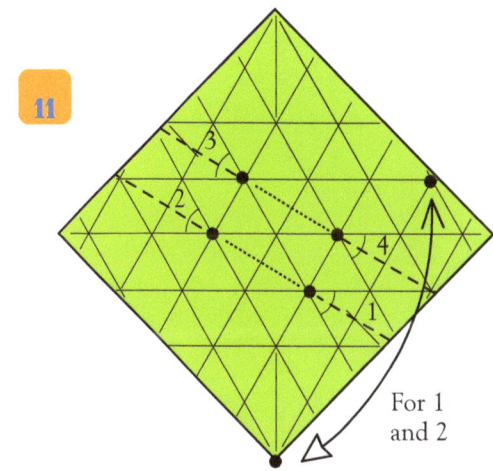

11. Fold and unfold at 1 and 2. Rotate 180° for 3 and 4 (same as 1 and 2).

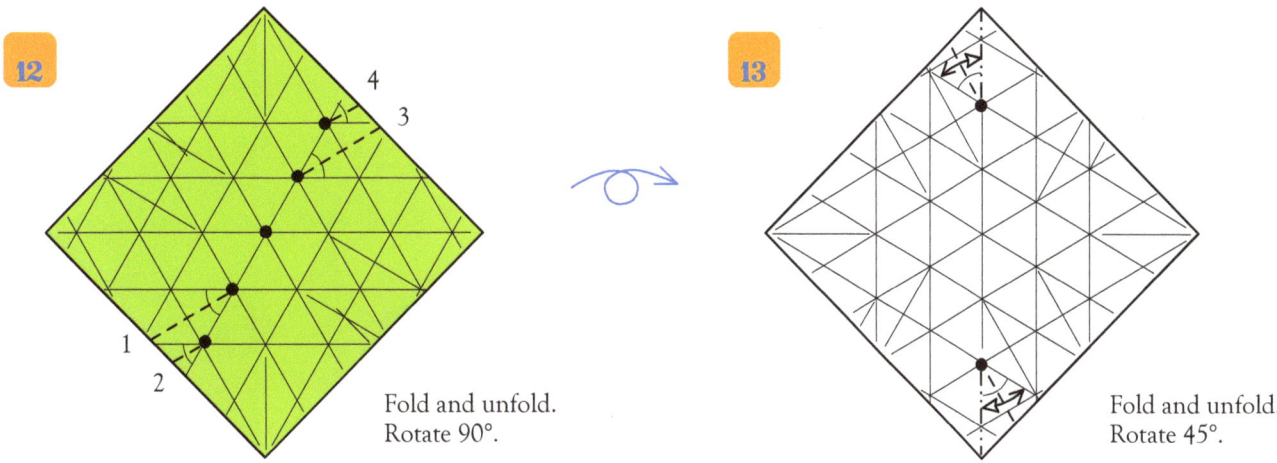

12. Fold and unfold. Rotate 90°.

13. Fold and unfold. Rotate 45°.

Hexagonal Antiprism **85**

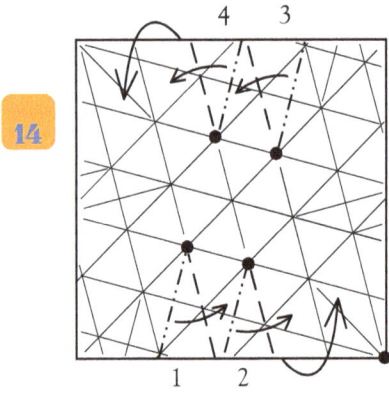

Fold along the creases and push in at the center dots. Rotate so the corner dot goes to the top and center.

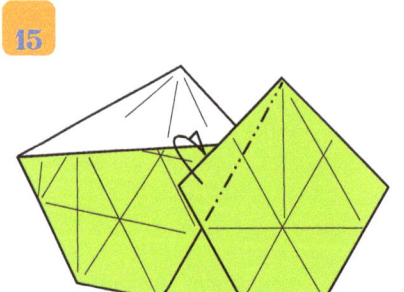

Wrap around. Turn over and repeat.

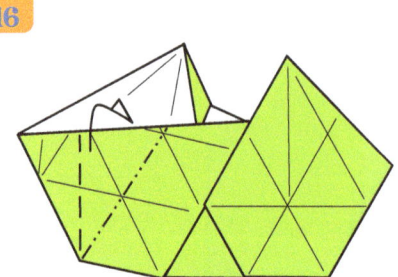

Fold along the creases. Turn over and repeat.

 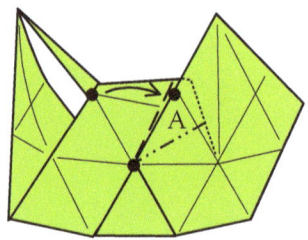

Fold along the creases which are hidden under triangle A. Puff out at the lower dot, the other dots will meet. Turn over and repeat.

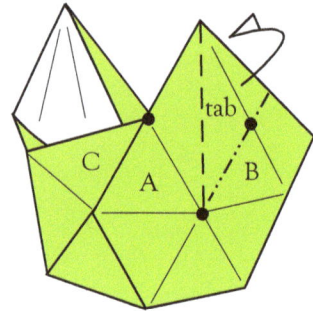

Tuck the tab into layers which are hidden from view. Puff out at the lower dot, the other dots will meet. C, A, and B are three of the six triangles that form the top hexagon.

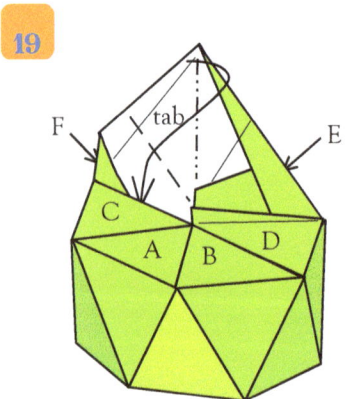

Four of the six triangles on top are shown. E and F are the remaining triangles to finish the model. Tuck the tab inside, same as step 18.

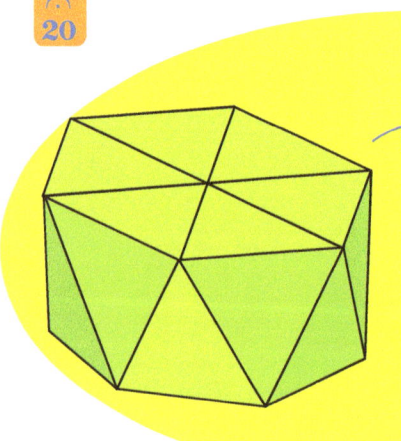

Hexagonal Antiprism

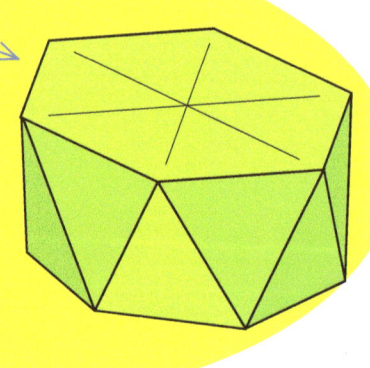

86 *Origami Symphony No. 7*

Octagonl Antiprism

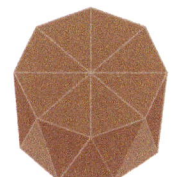

This antiprism is composed of two octagons and sixteen isosceles triangles. Each triangle has angles 45°, 67.5°, and 67.5°. The layout shows square symmetry.

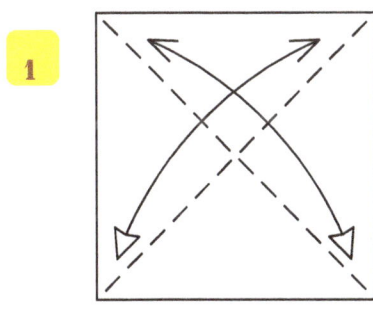

1. Fold and unfold.

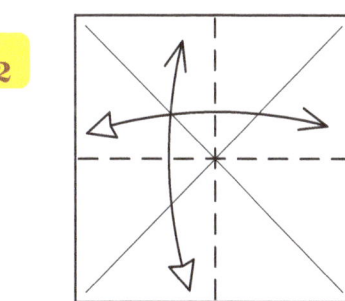

2. Fold and unfold.

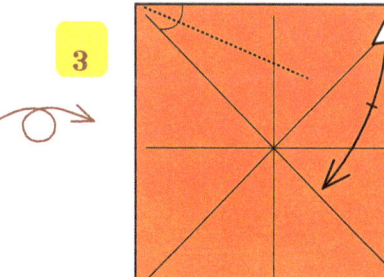

3. Fold and unfold.

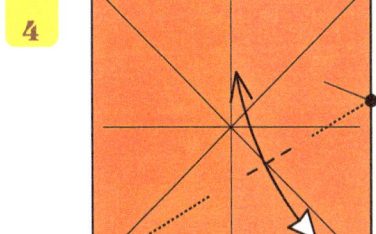

4. Fold and unfold along the diagonal.

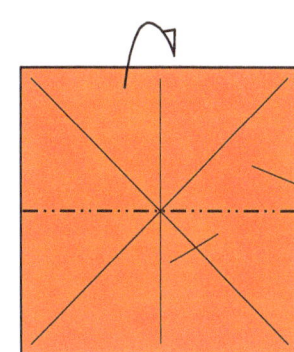

5.

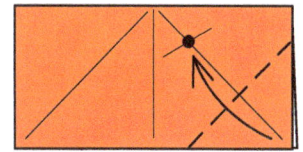

6. Repeat behind.

Octagonal Antiprism **87**

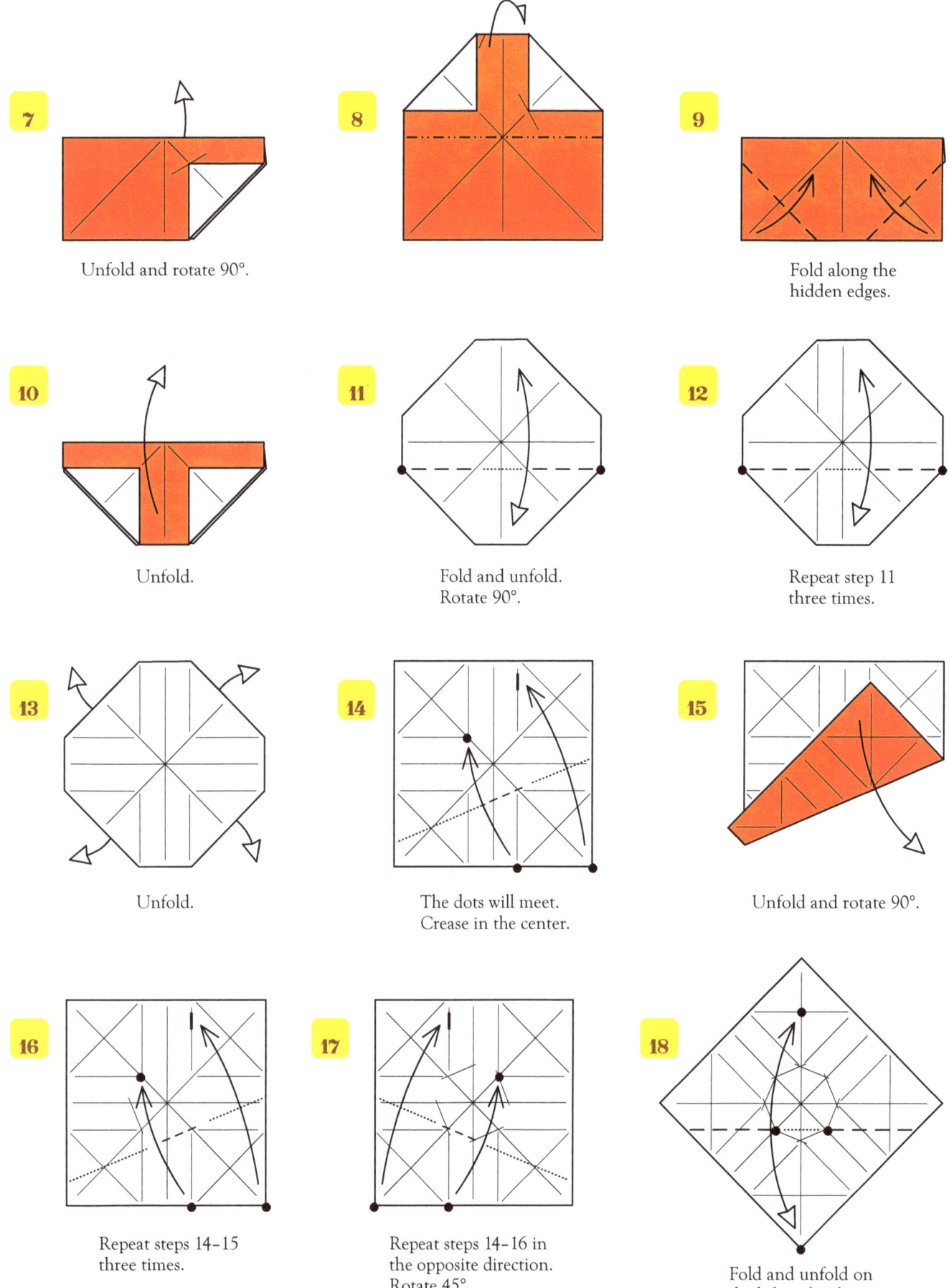

88 Origami Symphony No. 7

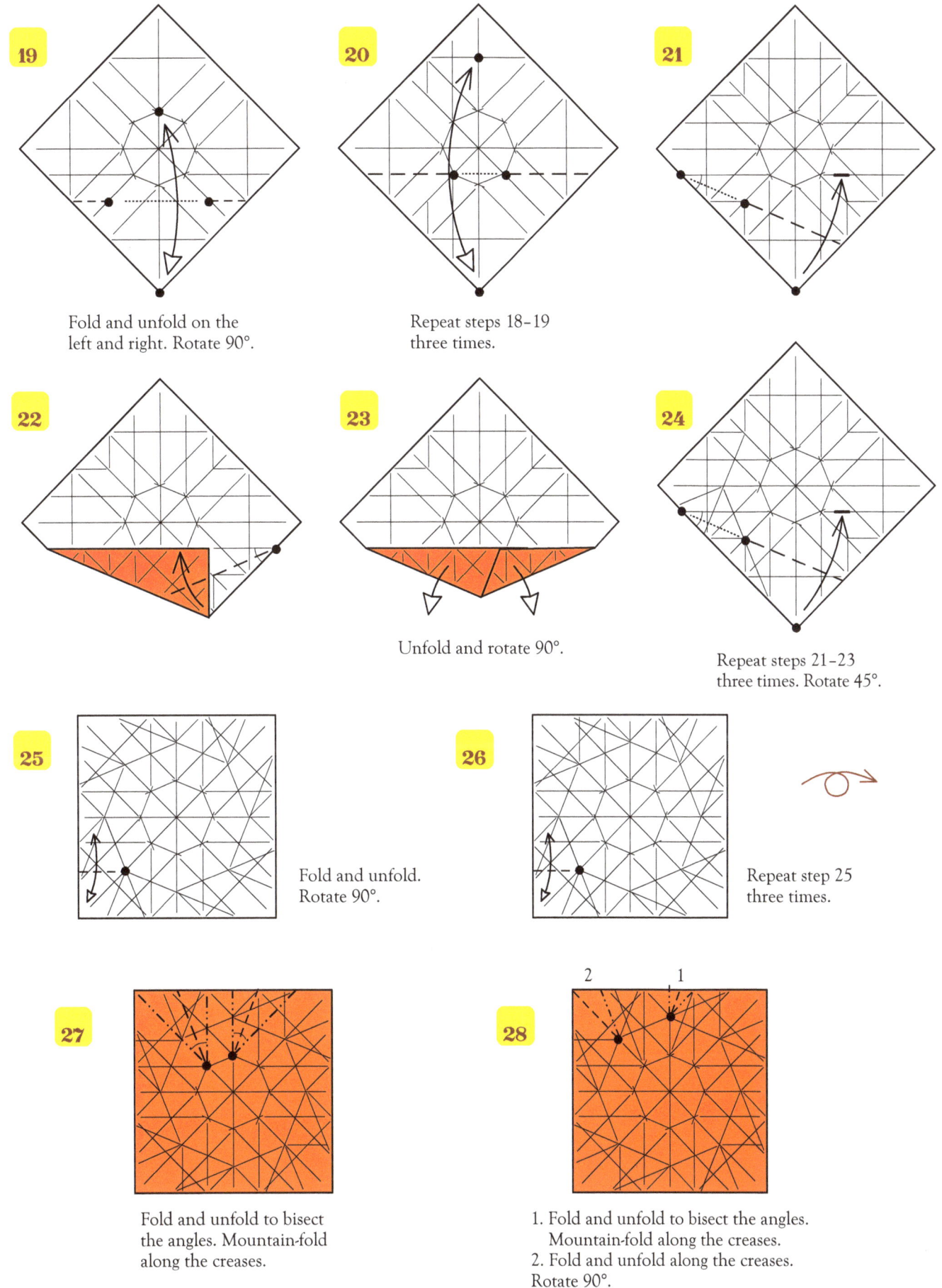

19. Fold and unfold on the left and right. Rotate 90°.

20. Repeat steps 18–19 three times.

21.

22.

23. Unfold and rotate 90°.

24. Repeat steps 21–23 three times. Rotate 45°.

25. Fold and unfold. Rotate 90°.

26. Repeat step 25 three times.

27. Fold and unfold to bisect the angles. Mountain-fold along the creases.

28.
1. Fold and unfold to bisect the angles. Mountain-fold along the creases.
2. Fold and unfold along the creases. Rotate 90°.

Octagonal Antiprism **89**

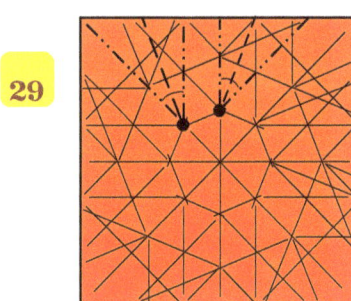

Repeat steps 27–28 three times.

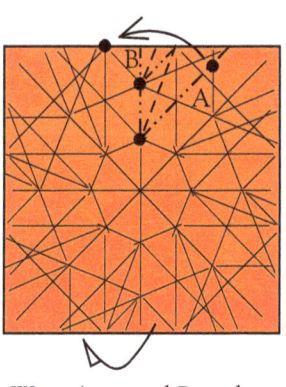

Wrap A around B so the upper dots meet. Puff out at the two center dots.

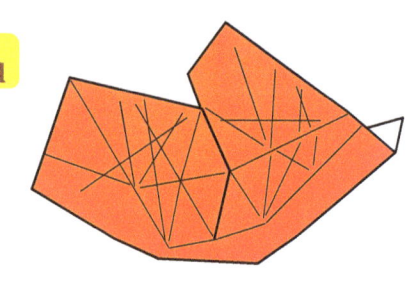

Repeat step 30 three times on the other edges.

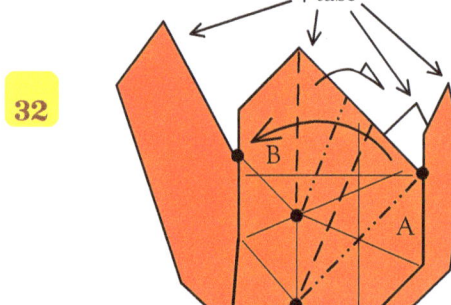

The four corners at the top are the four tabs that will lock the model. Begin with the first tab. Wrap A around B so the upper dots meet. Puff out at the two lower dots.

Repeat step 32 three times. The model closes with a four-way twist lock.

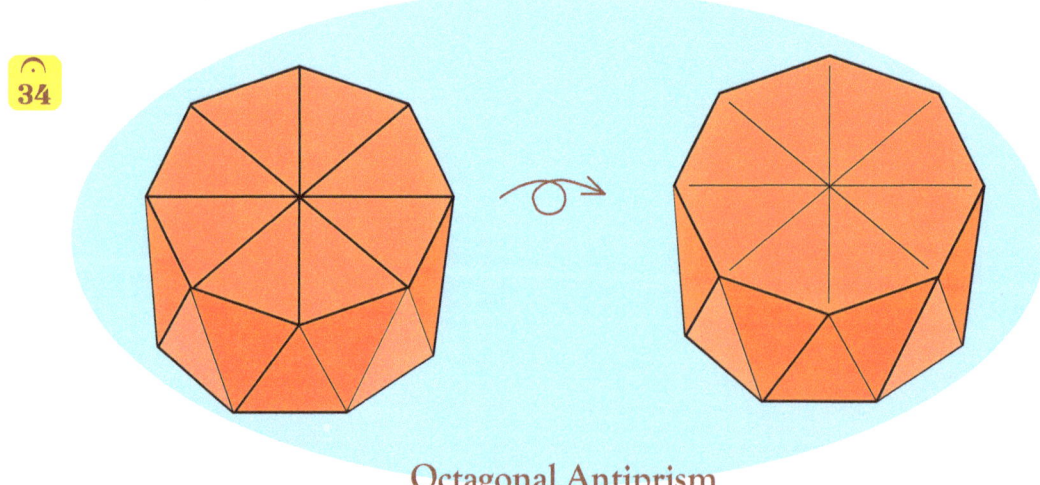

Octagonal Antiprism

90 *Origami Symphony No. 7*

Trio of Stars

Night has arrived and the stars are shining. This trio of stars can be seen by the animals in the other movements. Stars can be formed from collapsed polyhedra. The eight corners of a cube become the eight points of the Eight-Pointed Star by collapsing the cube.

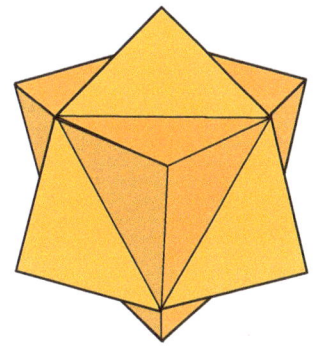

Stellated Octahedron

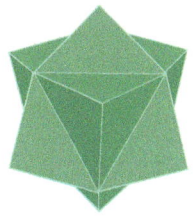

The stellated octahedron has eight points. The apex angle on each face is 90°. The paper is divided into sixths. It closes with a four-way lock.

Stellated Cube **91**

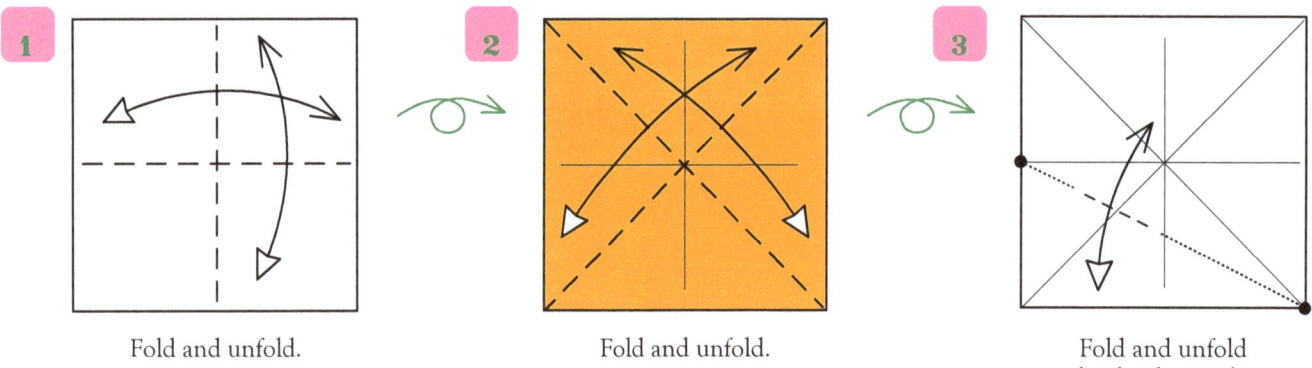
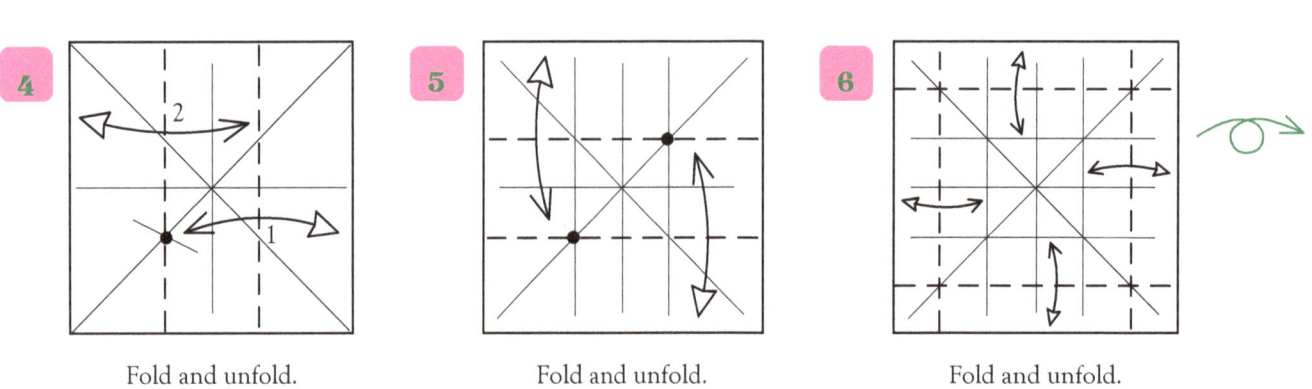
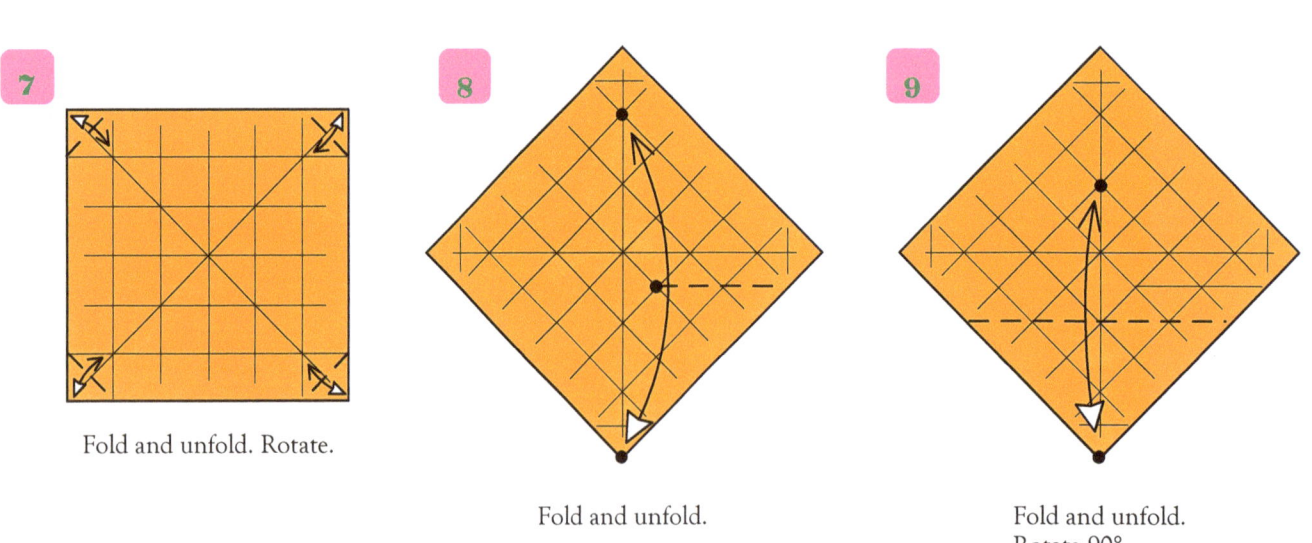

92 Origami Symphony No. 7

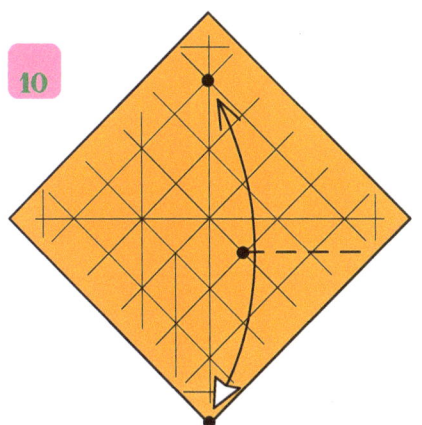

Repeat steps 8–9 three times.

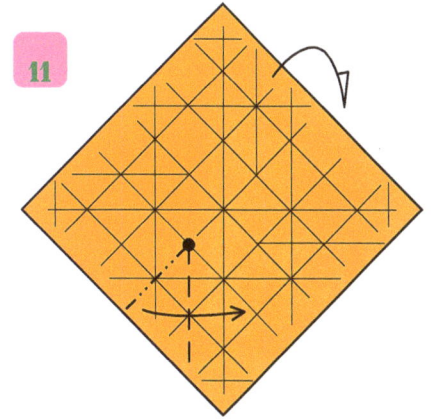

Puff out at the dot.

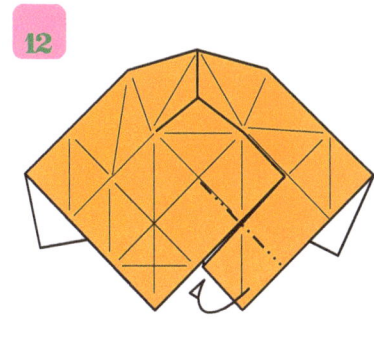

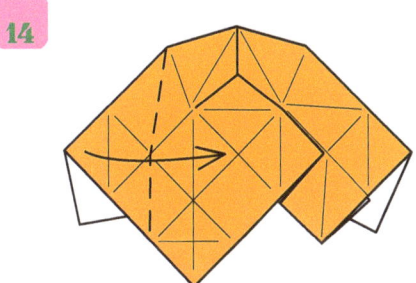

Fold and unfold.

Repeat steps 11–13 three times.

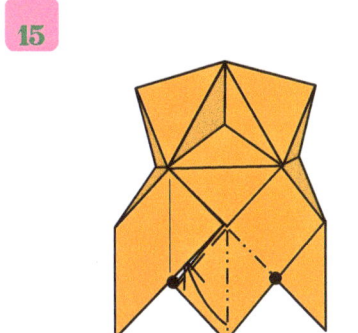

Tuck inside. The dots will meet. Repeat three times going around.

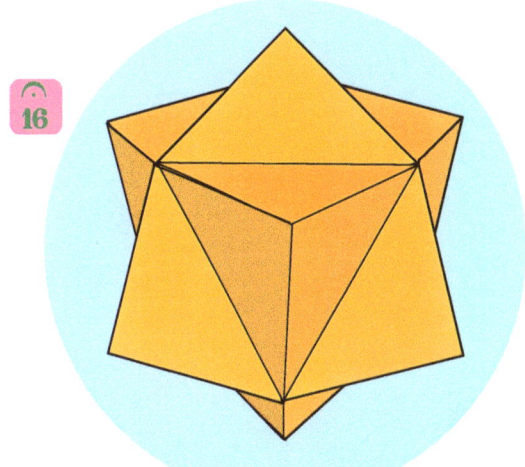

Stellated Octahedron

Stellated Cube **93**

Eight-Pointed Star

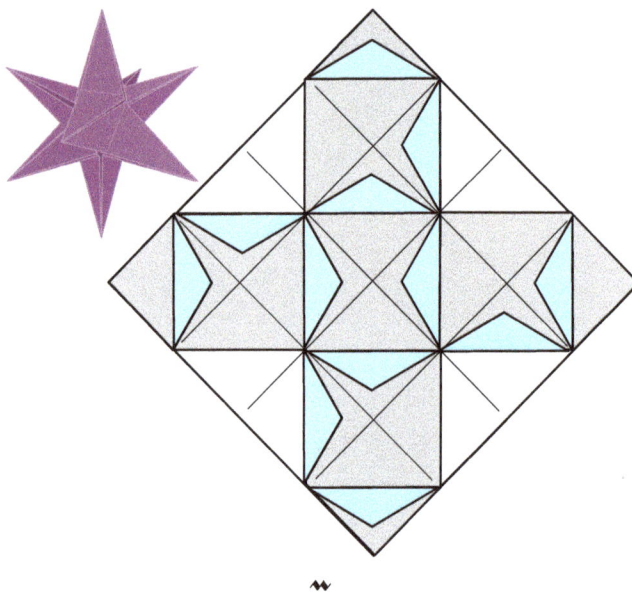

The eight-pointed star comes from a collapsed cube. The shaded regions in the layout shows the sides of the cube, and the colored parts show the arms of the star. Each of the eight arms has three sides, with angles of 30° at the vertices.

1 Fold and unfold. Rotate 45°.

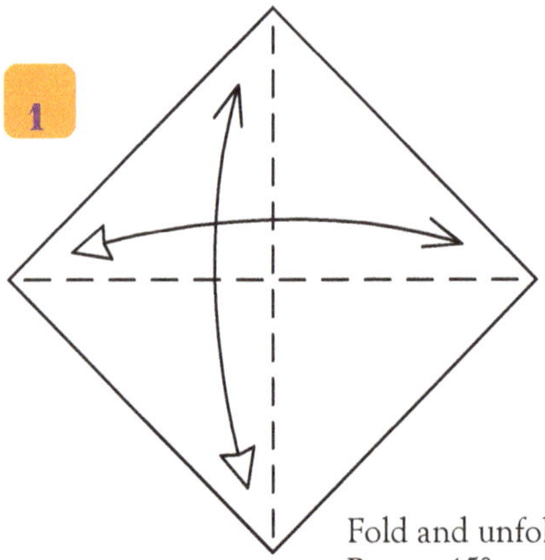

2 Fold and unfold.

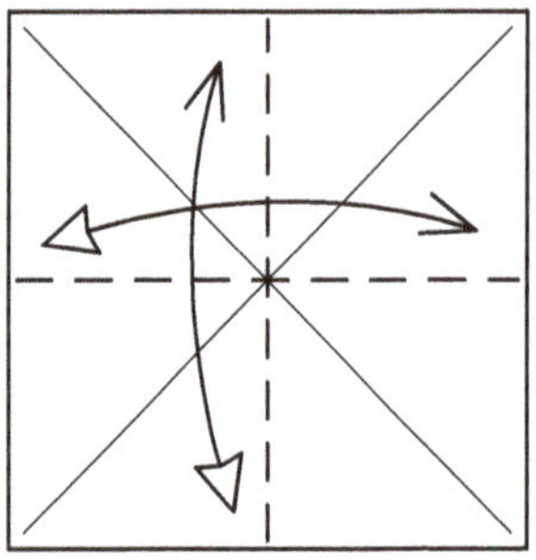

3 Fold to the center and unfold.

4 Fold and unfold. Rotate 90°.

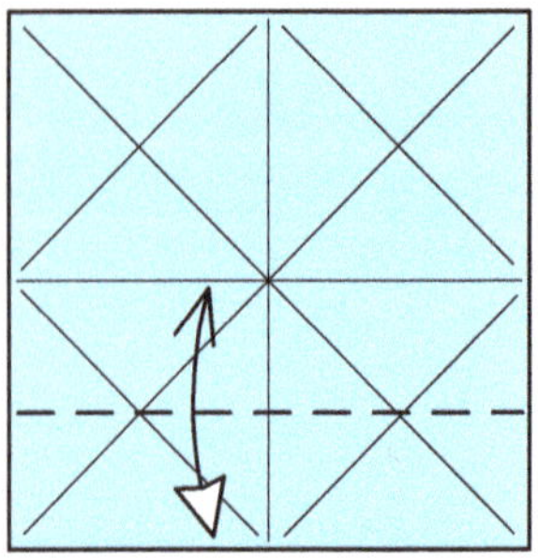

5 Rpeat step 4 three times. Rotate 45°.

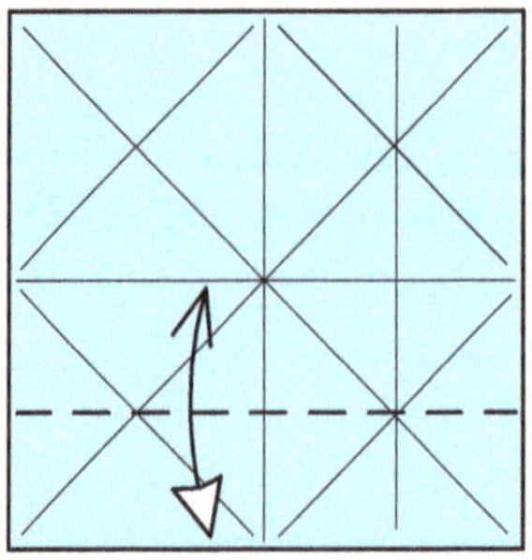

6 Fold and unfold. Rotate 90°.

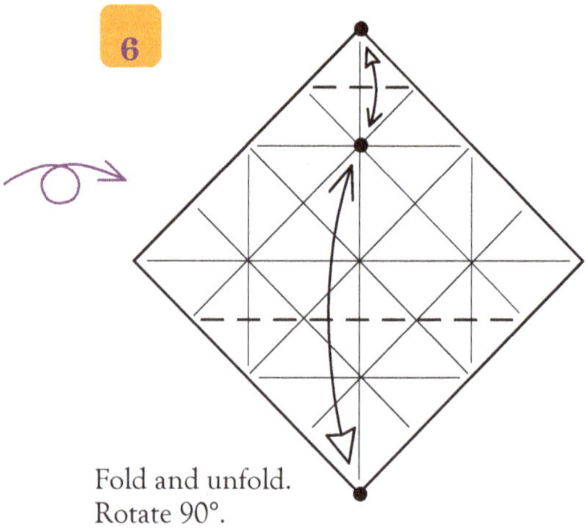

94 Origami Symphony No. 7

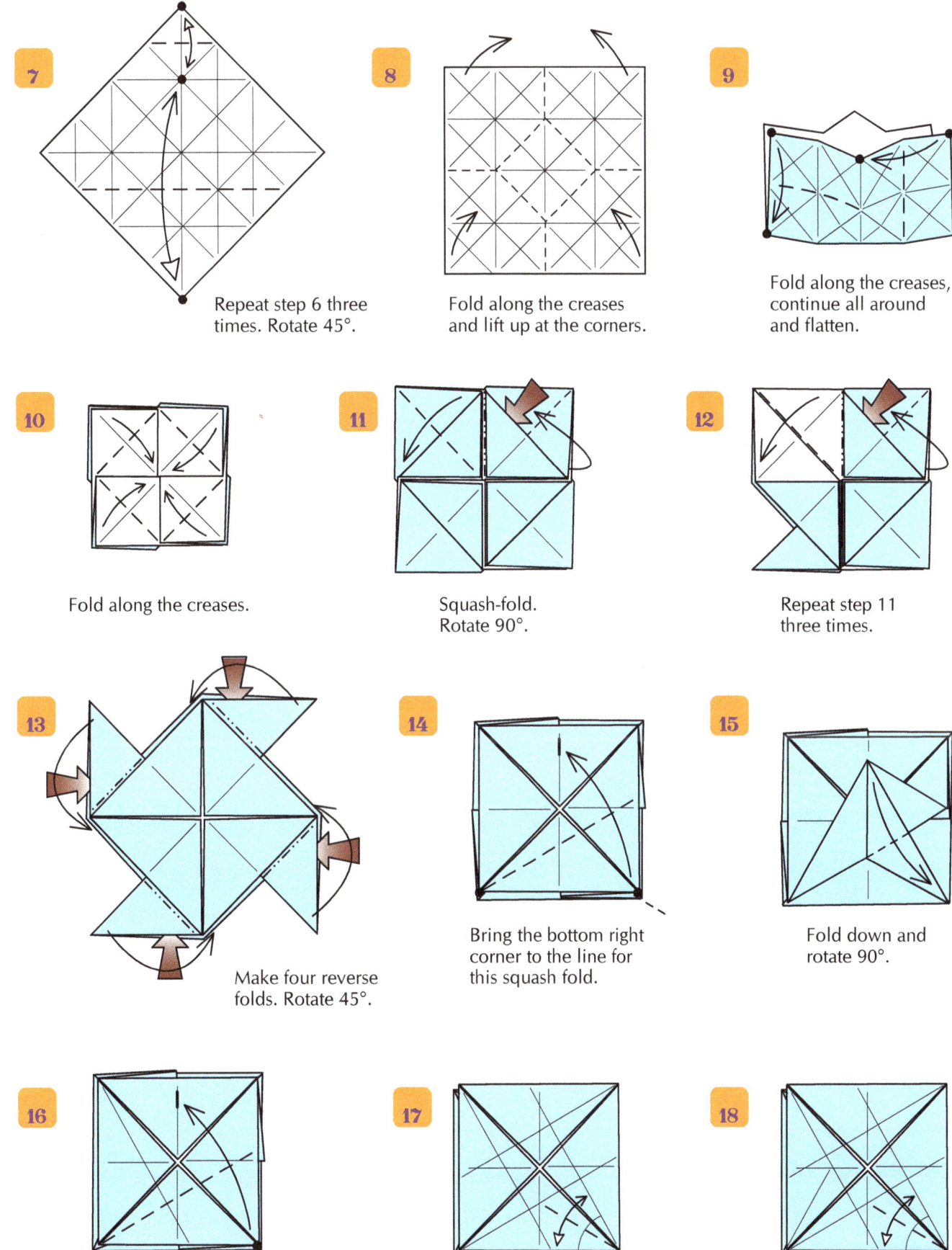

Eight-Pointed Star

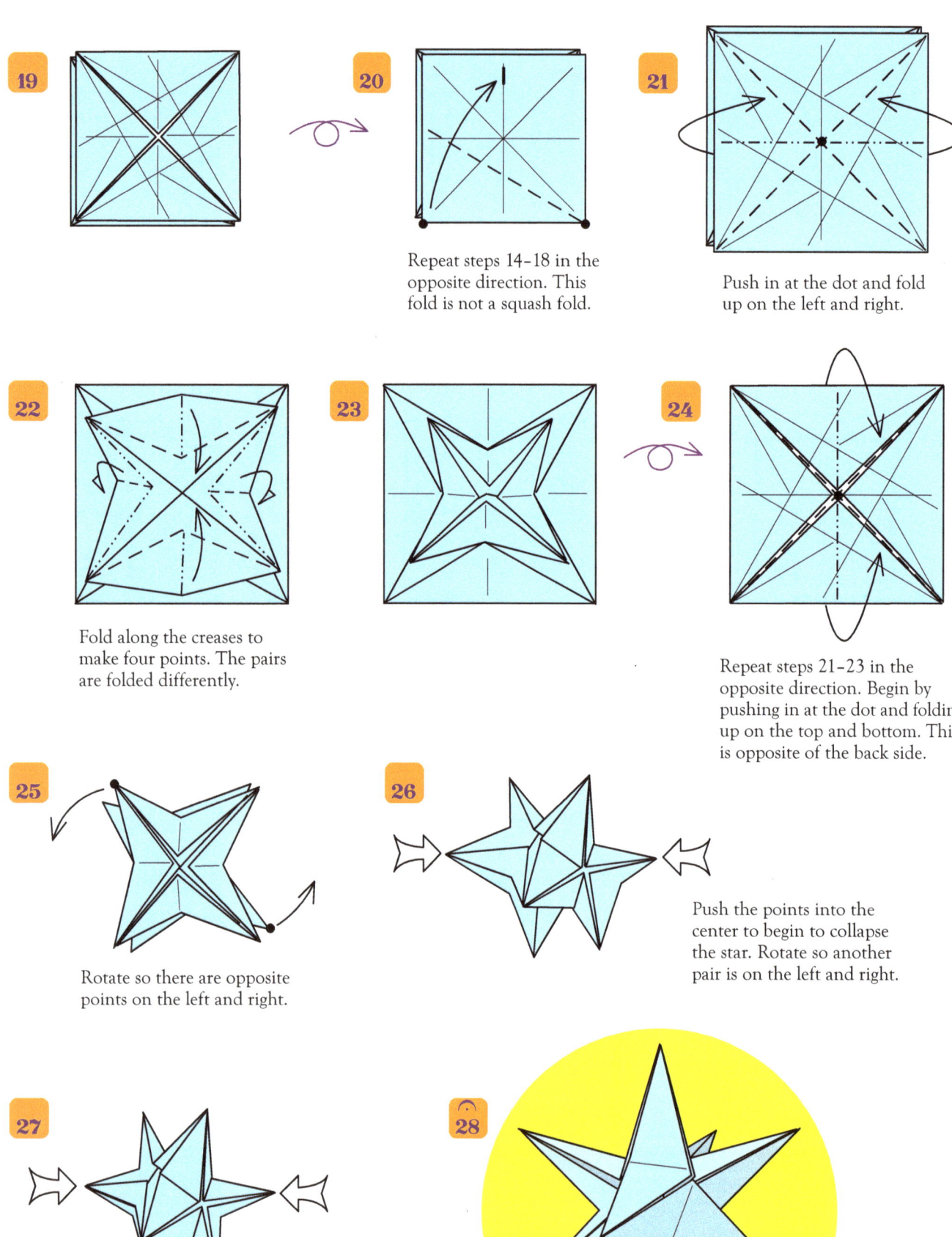

Eight-Pointed Star

96 *Origami Symphony No. 7*

Omega Star

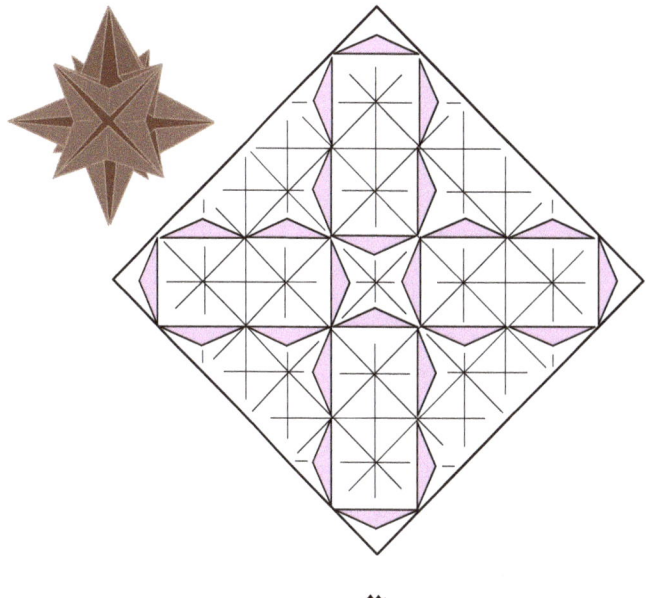

The omega star has twelve points. The geometry of the finished model is based on the 3D shape shown in step 15.

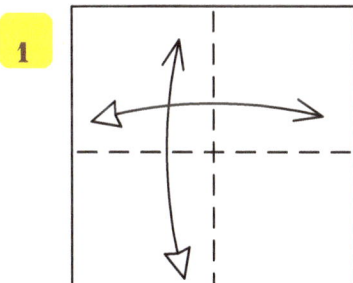

1

Fold and unfold.

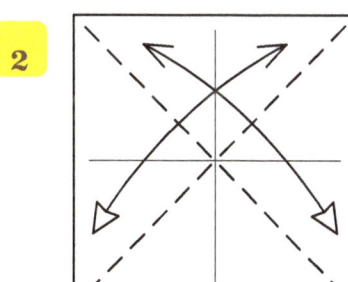

2

Fold and unfold.

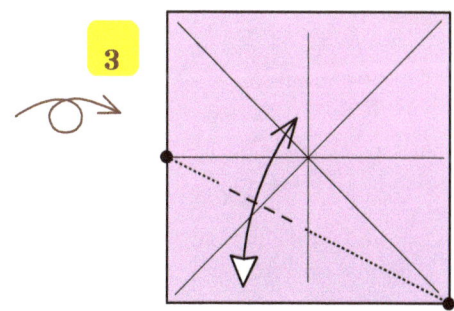

3

Fold and unfold by the diagonal.

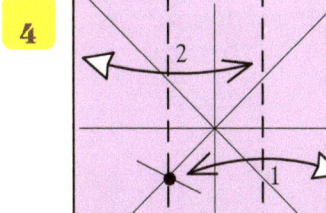

4

Fold and unfold.

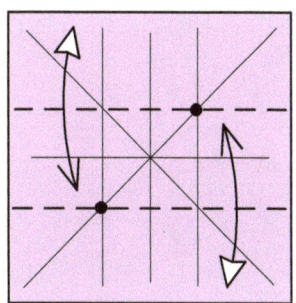

5

Fold and unfold.

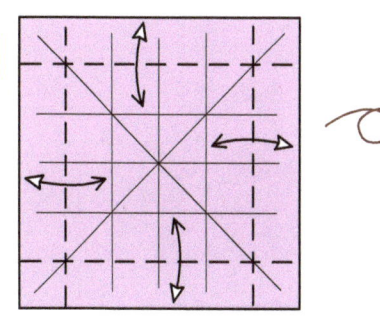

6

Fold and unfold. Rotate 45°.

Omega Star **97**

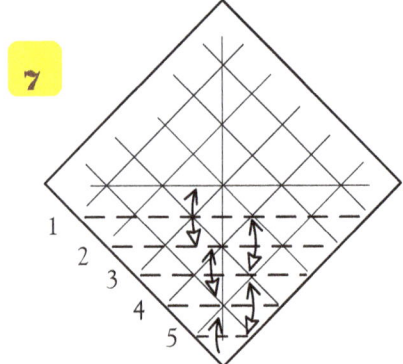
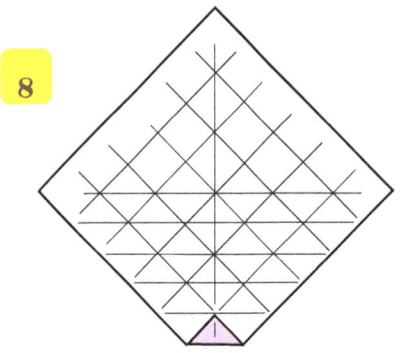
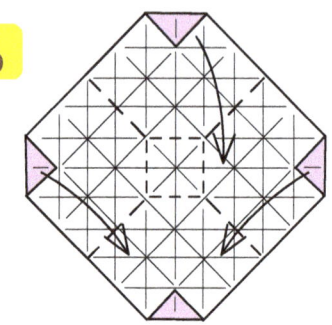

7 Fold and unfold starting with the highest one. Do not unfold the last one.

8 Repeat step 7 on the three other corners.

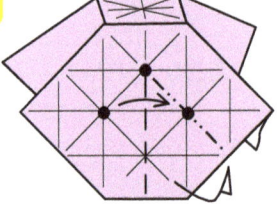
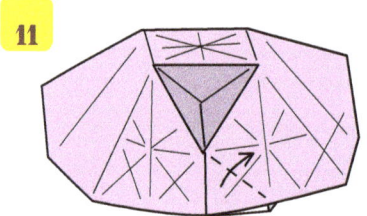

10 Push in at the upper dot to form a sunken triangle.

12 Repeat steps 10–11 three times.

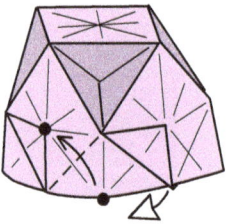

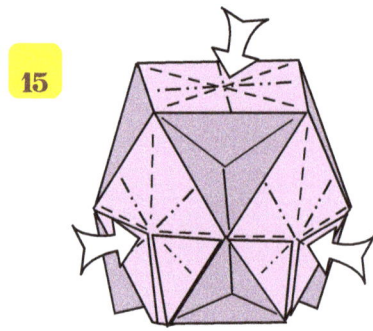

13 Spread at the bottom to form a sunken triangle.

14 Repeat step 13 three times.

15 Sink the sides first, then the top. Repeat all around.

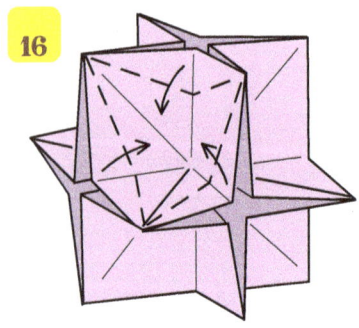
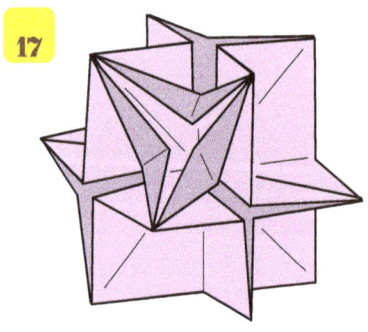

16 Fold inward.

17 Repeat step 16 all around.

Omega Star

98 *Origami Symphony No. 7*

Fourth Movement

March of the Boisterous and Frolicsome Monkeys

𝄢 It's Monkey time! The apes have no tail and walk on two legs. The Old World monkeys live in Africa and Asia while the New World Monkeys live in the jungles of Central and South America. The Old World monkeys are larger, spend time on the ground and in trees, and feed on leaves and grasses. The New World monkeys live mainly in trees, feed on fruit, and have prehensile tails that can grab onto branches. They all have a hoot to hoot and a song to sing.

Gorilla

The gorilla is the largest and most powerful primate. At 4 to 6 feet tall, they can weigh over 400 pounds and are many times stronger than humans. They live in large social groups, exhibit personalities, can laugh, show compassion and grief. Eating all day long, they can eat over 40 pounds every day, feeding on leaves, shoots, bark, fruit, snails, ants, and caterpillars. They communicate with 16 types of calls, including roaring, hooting, and short barks. Koko, the gorilla, knew over 1000 signs. They have opposable thumbs like us, but also have opposable big toes.

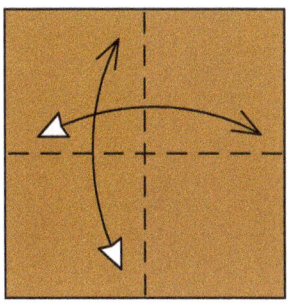

1. Fold and unfold.

2. Fold and unfold.

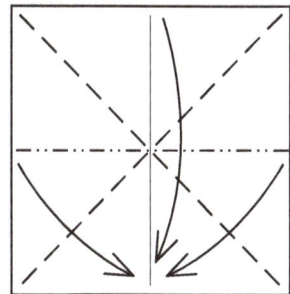

3. Fold along the creases to make a Waterbomb Base.

Gorilla 99

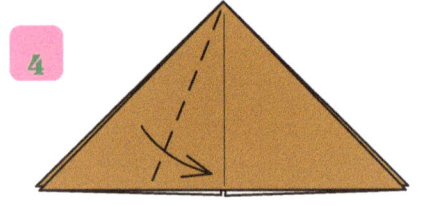
4
Repeat behind.

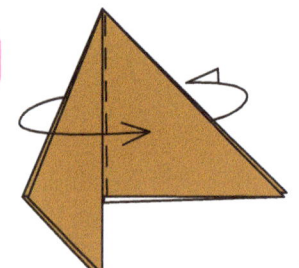
5

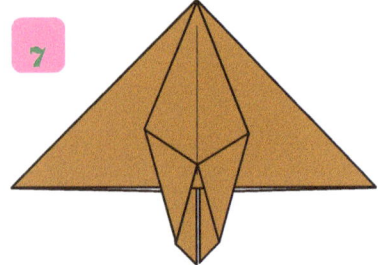
6
Bring the dots to the center.

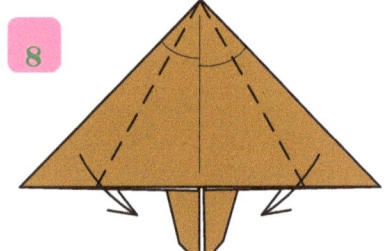
7

8

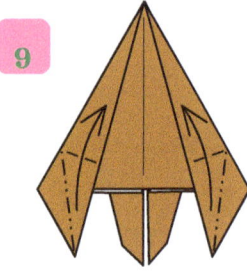
Fold at an angle of 1/3.

9
Make squash folds.

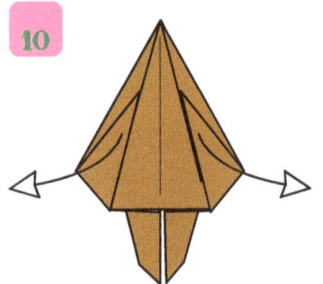
10
Unfold.

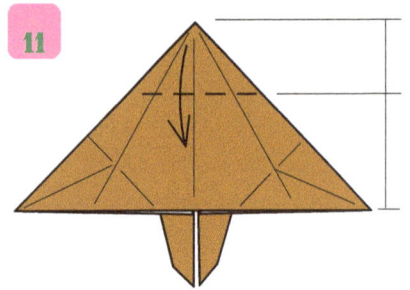
11
Fold down a little more than 1/3 of the height.

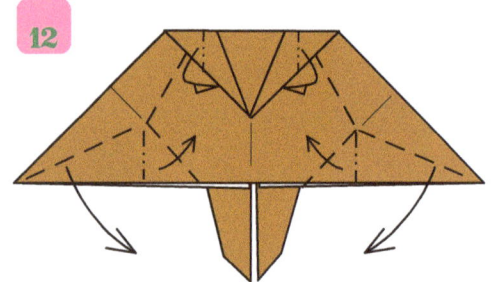
12
Fold along the creases and make small reverse folds at the head.

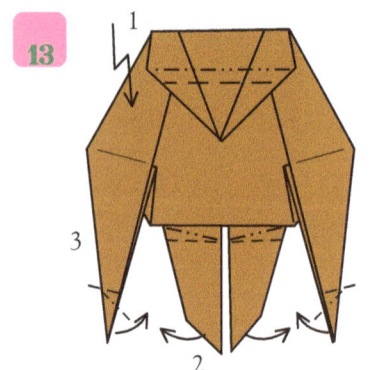
13
1. Pleat-fold.
2. Pleat-fold.
3. Squash-fold.

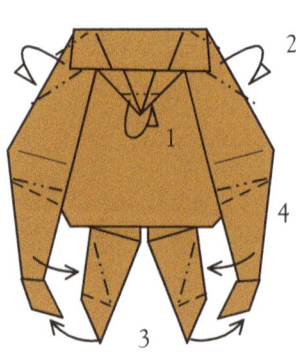
14
1. Fold behind.
2. Fold behind.
3. Pleat-fold.
4. Crimp-fold.

15

Gorilla

100 Origami Symphony No. 7

Gibbon

Gibbons are smaller apes that weigh between 10 to 30 pounds. As the fastest moving ape, they swing gracefully through trees with their longs arms, traveling at up to 35 miles per hour. They spend most of their time in treetops of the rainforest and sleep on branches. Though an omnivore, their favorite diet is fruit, especially figs. They walk on two legs with arms raised for balance. These social and intelligent apes live in family units. At sunrise they begin singing, creating all kinds of calls. It begins as a solo and others join in, see if you can find a YouTube of gibbons singing.

1. 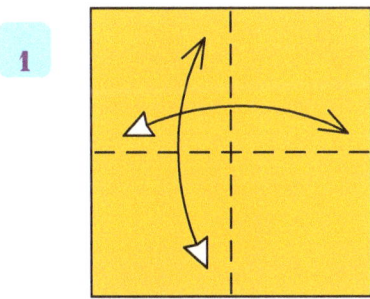 Fold and unfold.

2. 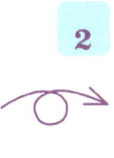 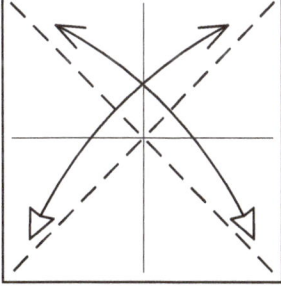 Fold and unfold.

3. 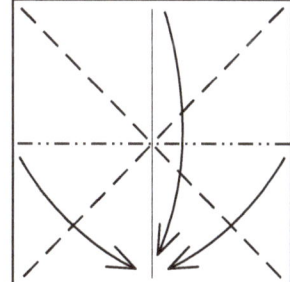 Fold along the creases to make a Waterbomb Base.

4.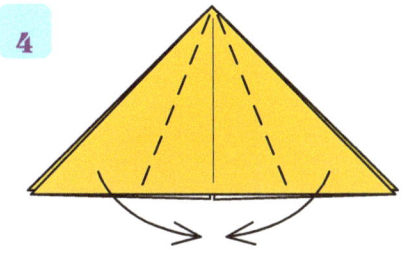

5. 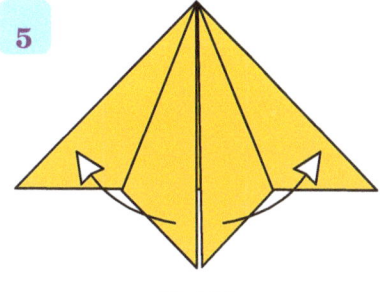 Unfold.

6. 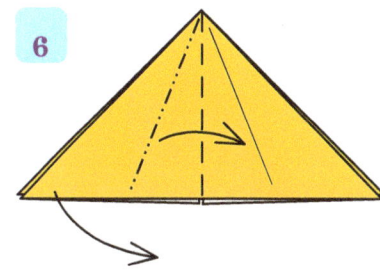 Squash-fold.

Gibbon **101**

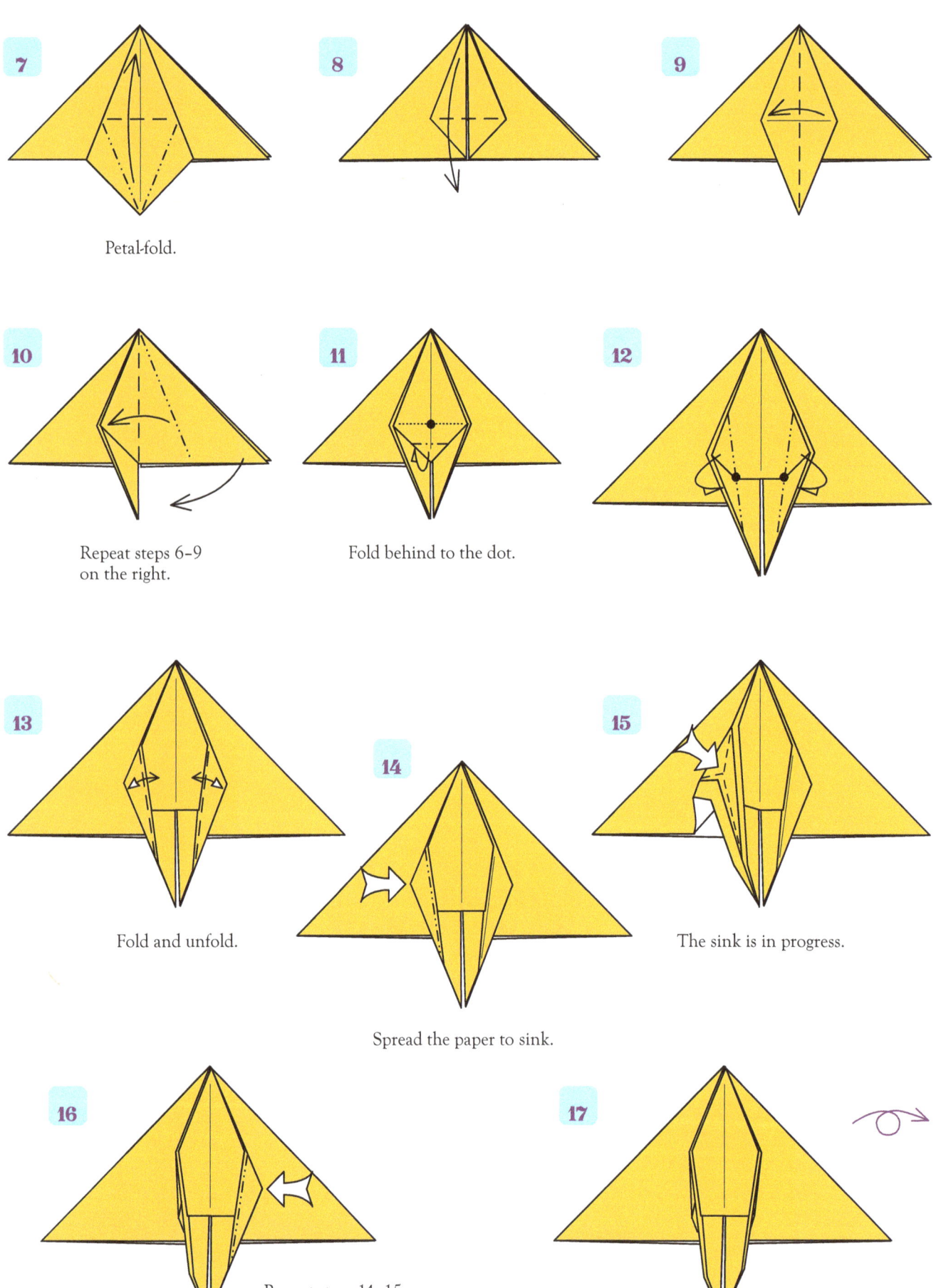

18

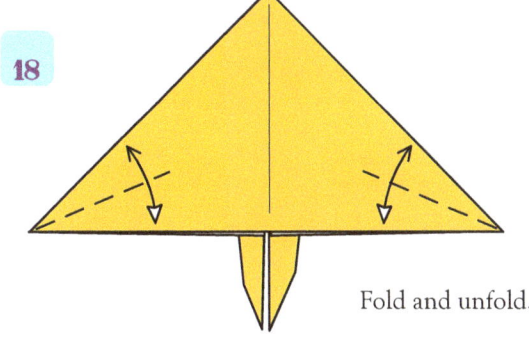

Fold and unfold.

19

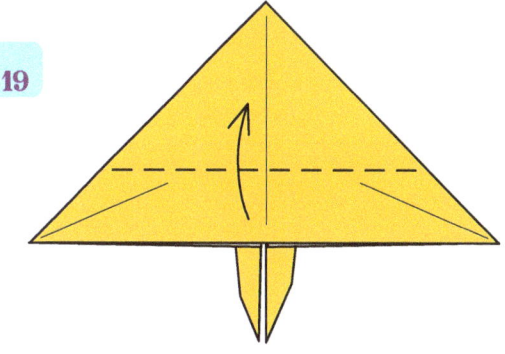

20

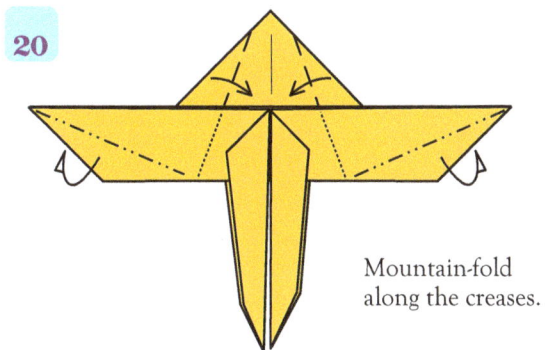

Mountain-fold along the creases.

21

22

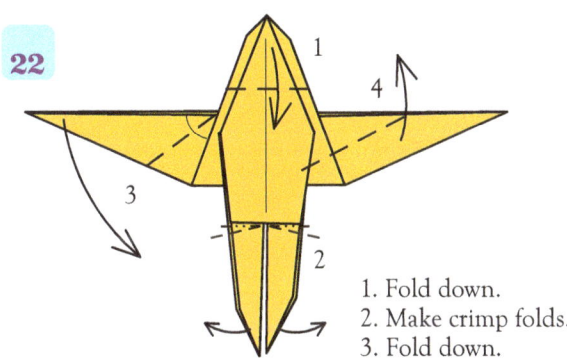

1. Fold down.
2. Make crimp folds.
3. Fold down.
4. Fold up.

23

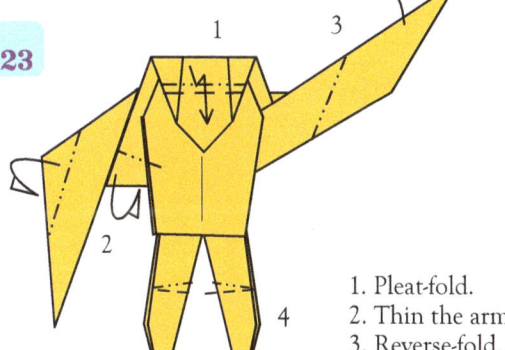

1. Pleat-fold.
2. Thin the arm.
3. Reverse-fold.
4. Make crimp folds.

24

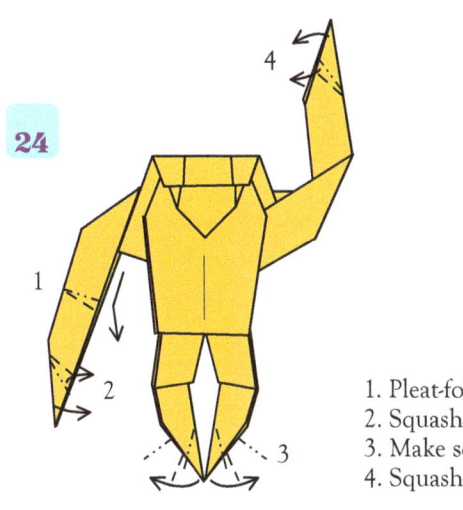

1. Pleat-fold.
2. Squash-fold.
3. Make squash folds.
4. Squash-fold.

25

Gibbon

Gibbon 103

Spider Monkey

The spider monkey is the most intelligent of the New World monkeys, residing in rainforest canopies of Central and South America. With long thin limbs, they have exceptionally long tails. They swing from limb to limb and can easily hang from their long, strong tail as they search for food. They eat mainly fruits and nuts but their diet includes eggs and insects. Weighing up to 25 pounds, these social primates live in large groups, each called a troop. When troops meet, they greet each other with hugs.

1. Fold and unfold.

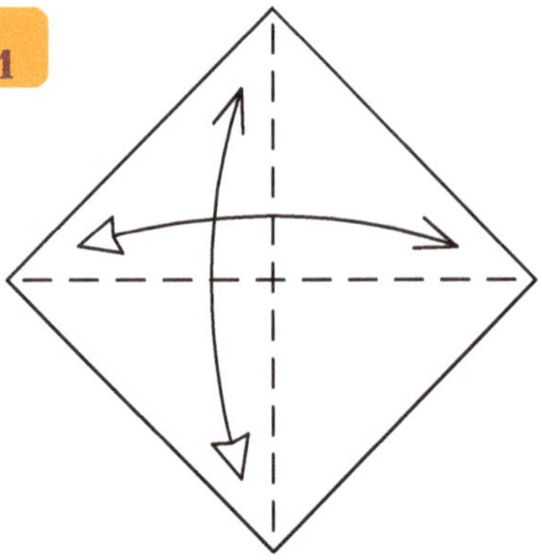

2. Fold to the center and unfold.

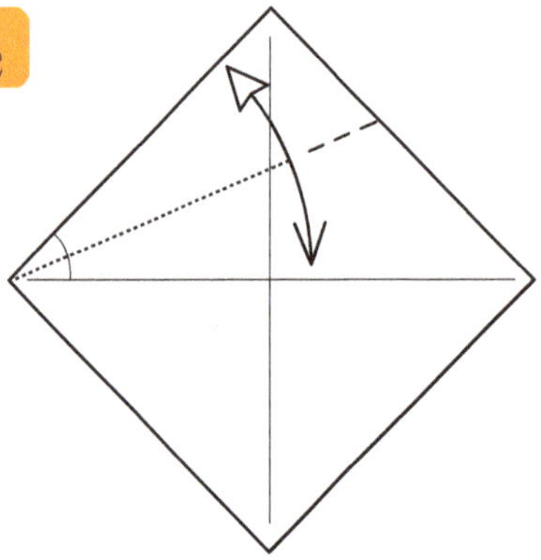

3. Fold and unfold on the diagonal.

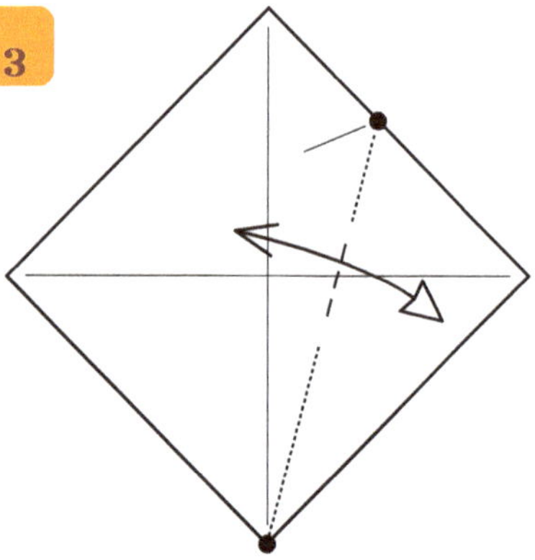

4. Bring the edge to the dot.

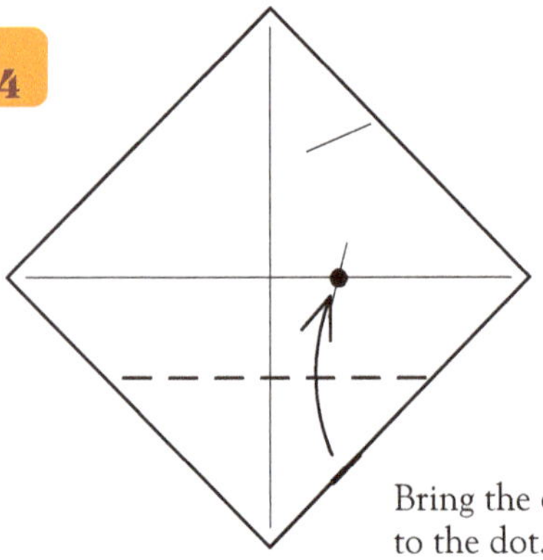

5.

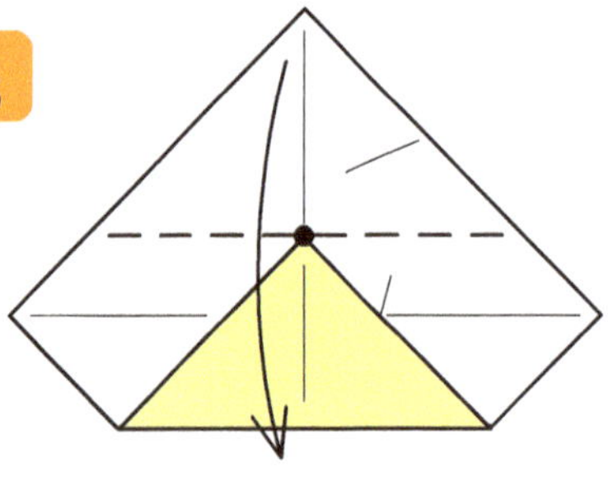

6.

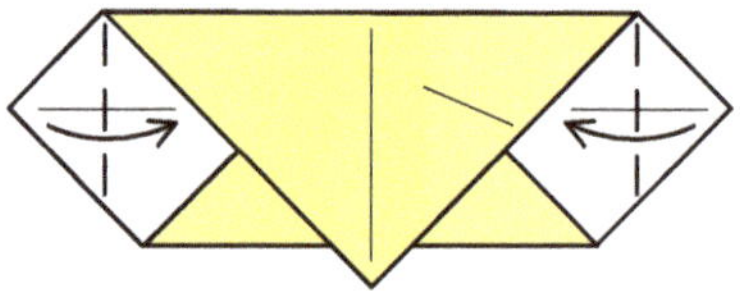

104 *Origami Symphony No. 7*

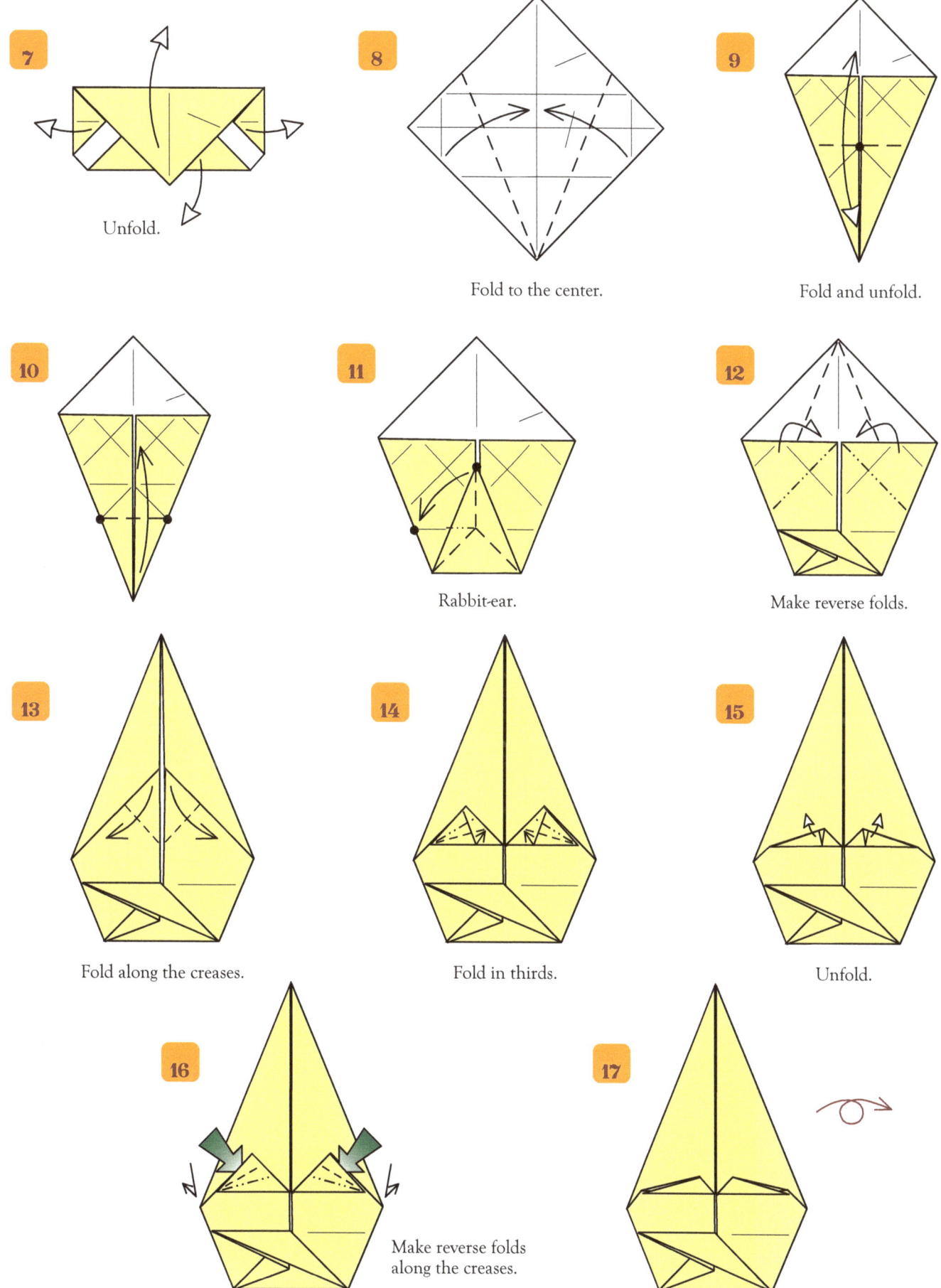

Spider Monkey

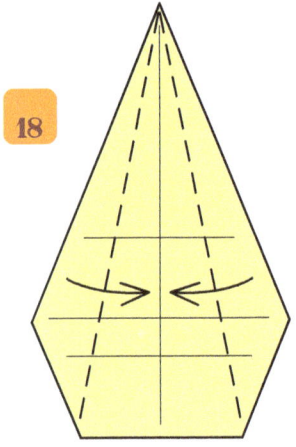

Fold to the center.

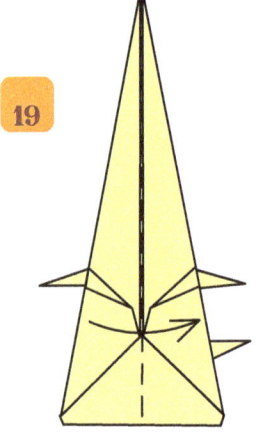

Fold in half and rotate 90°.

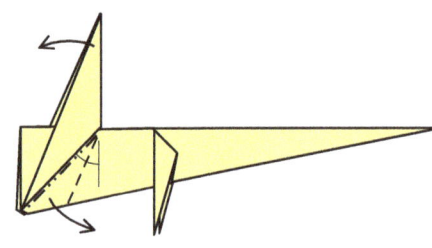

Crimp-fold.

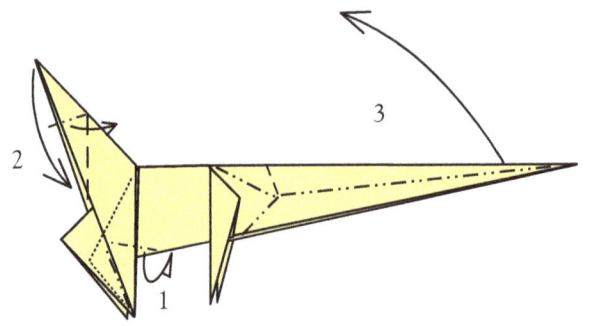

1. Squash-fold, repeat behind.
2. Squash-fold.
3. Double-rabbit-ear.

1. Shape the tail with reverse folds.
2. Crimp-fold, repeat behind.
3. Reverse-fold.
4. Pleat-fold.

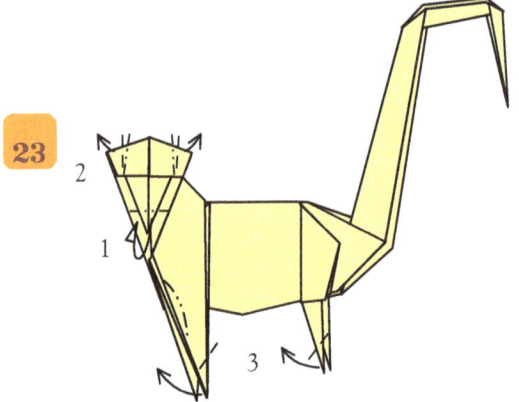

1. Fold inside.
2. Make pleat folds.
3. Outside-reverse-fold the feet and shape the legs. Repeat behind.

Spider Monkey

Vervet Monkey

The vervet monkey is a medium to large size monkey with a black face and lighter brown fur. They are found in abundance in East Africa, living a variety of habitats, including the savanna, open woodland, and forests. They like to be near water and trees. Climbing high in trees protects them from the large cats and other predators. They live in complex social groups, known as troops. The infants are especially well taken care of as others in the group like to play and spend time with them. They feed on leaves, shoots, fruit, insects, and rodents. In urban areas, they will find food in farms. During the day, they travel in groups searching for food, and at night sleep in trees.

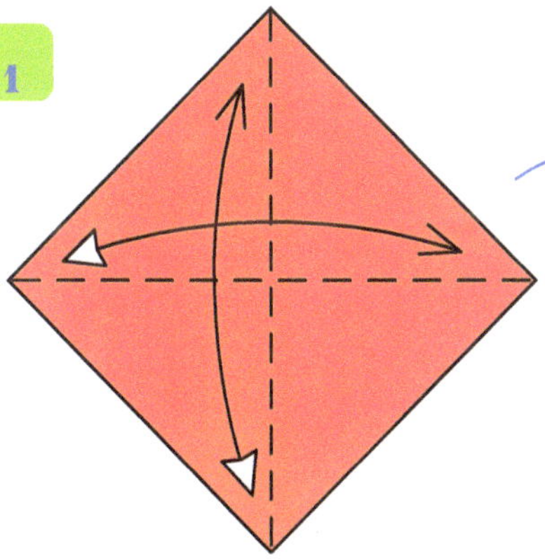

1. Fold and unfold.

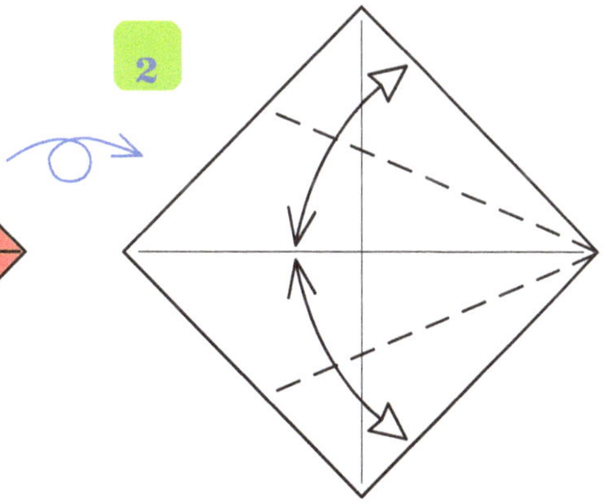

2. Fold to the center and unfold.

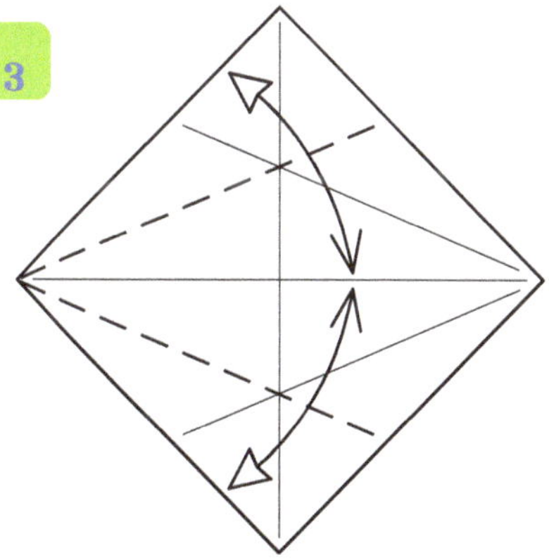

3. Fold to the center and unfold.

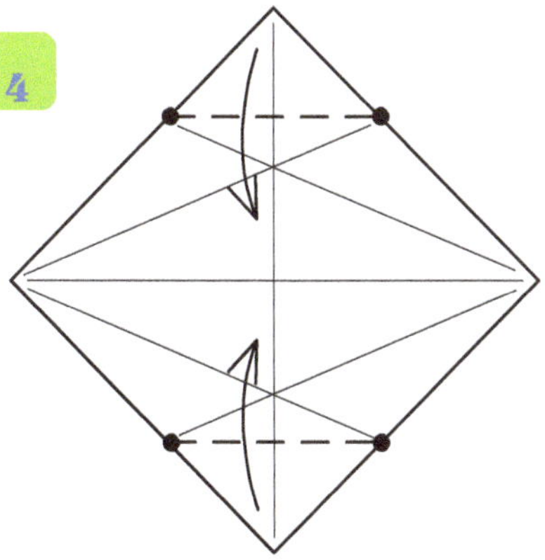

4.

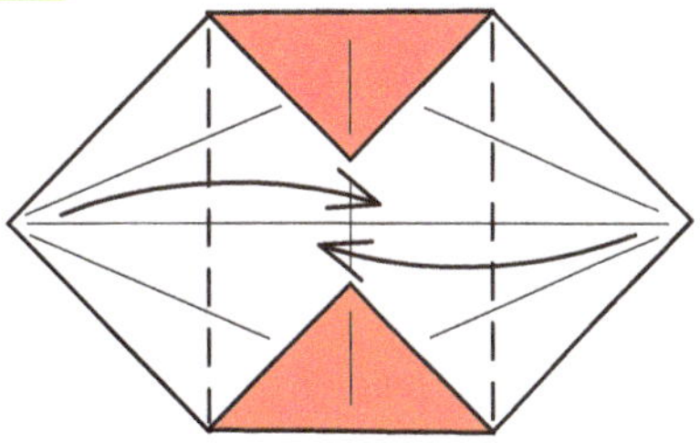

5. Rotate 90°.

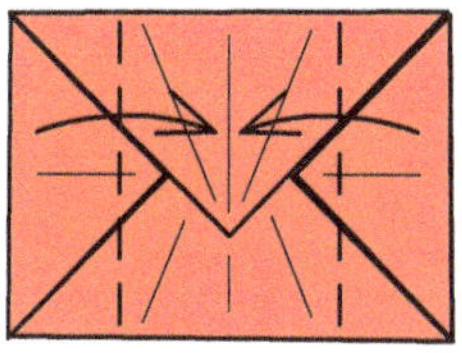

6. Fold to the center.

Vervet Monkey **107**

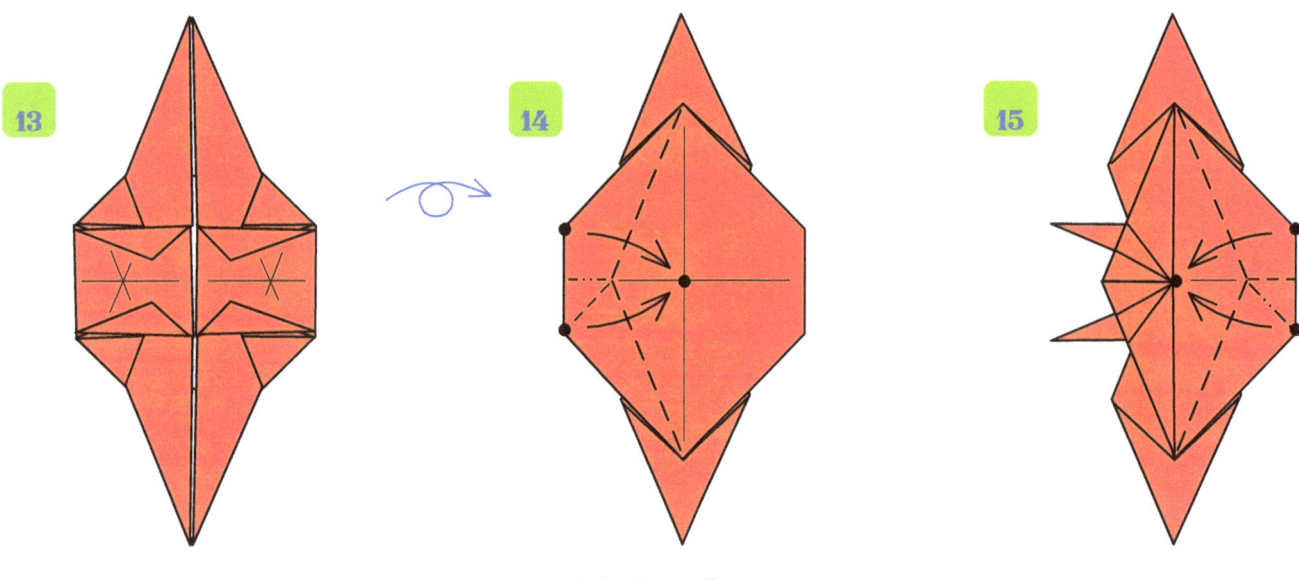

7. Make squash folds.
8. Pull out the hidden corner.
9. Squash-fold.
10. Petal-fold.
11. Make rabbit ears. Rotate 180°.
12. Repeat steps 7–11.
13.
14. The dots will meet.
15.

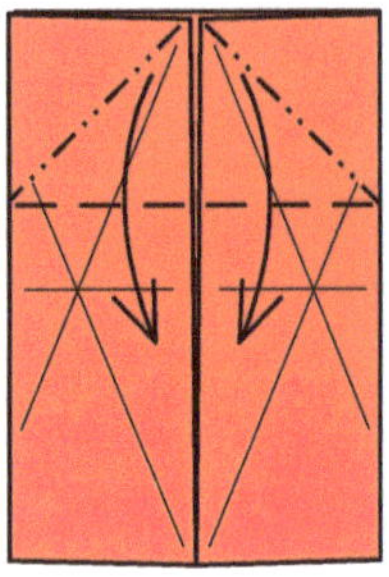

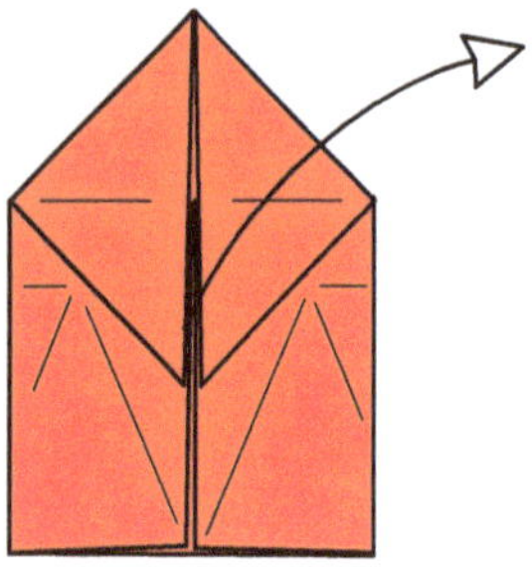

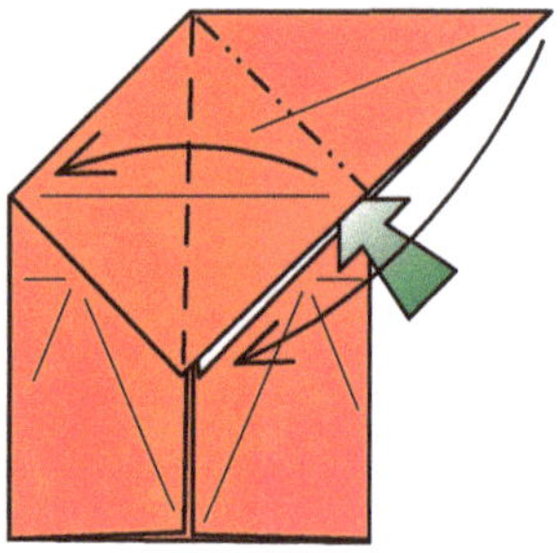

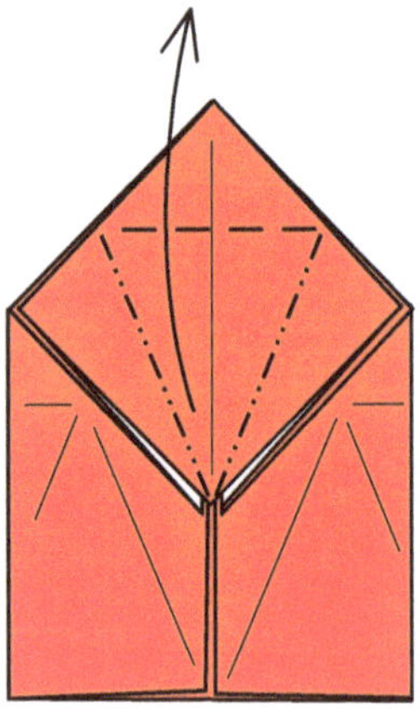

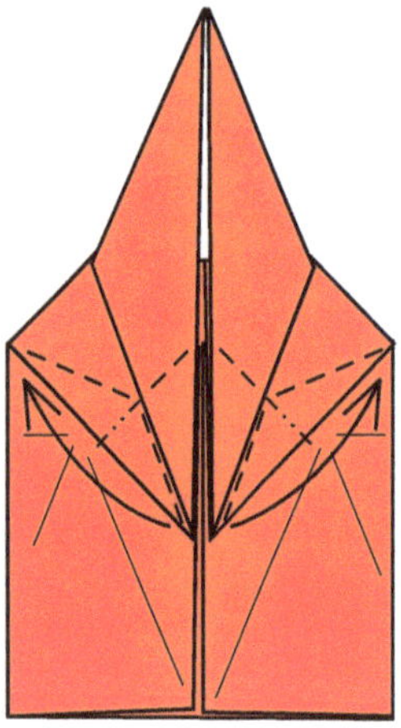

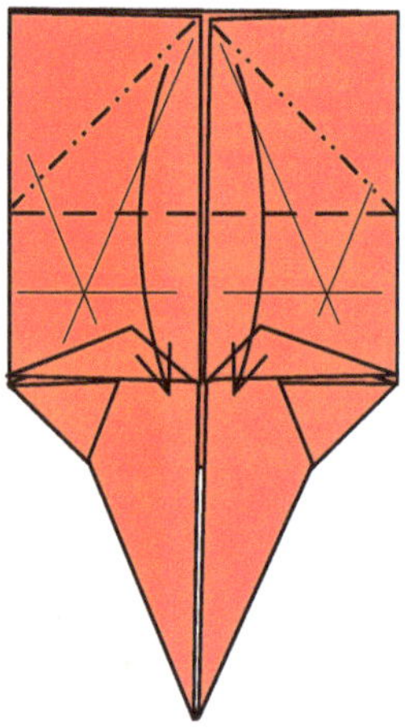

108 *Origami Symphony No. 7*

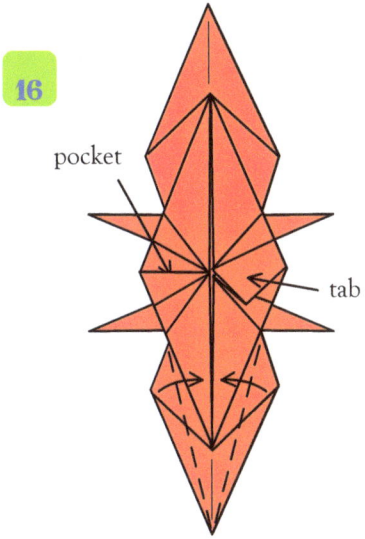

Note the tab and pocket.

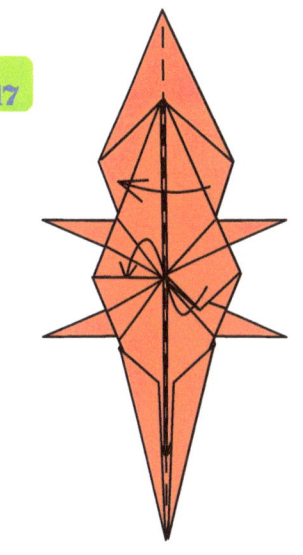

Fold in half and tuck the tab inside the pocket.

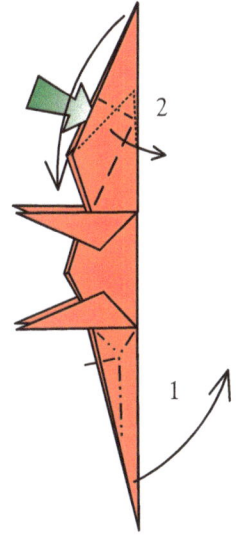

1. Double-rabbit-ear.
2. Squash-fold.
Rotate.

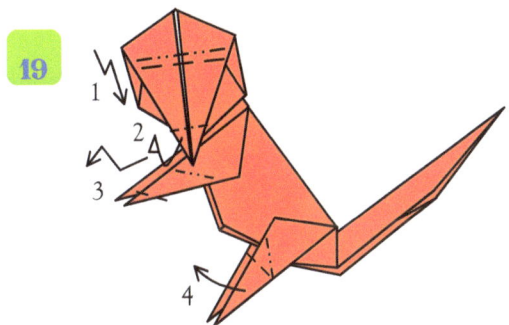

1. Pleat-fold.
2. Fold inside.
3. Make reverse folds, repeat behind.
4. Crimp-fold, repeat behind.

1. Make reverse folds.
2. Fold behind.
3. Make pleat folds.

Vervet Monkey

Vervet Monkey **109**

Proboscis Monkey

The older males of the proboscis monkeys have the large noses, used for attracting females. The large nose aids in amplifying their calls. They live on the island of Borneo in Southeastern Asia. They are very social and spend much of their time in trees along coastal mangrove swamps. Of all the monkeys, they are the best swimmers and have webbed feet. Jumping from trees, these monkeys will bellyflop in the water below. They feed on leaves, unripe fruit, and insects. They need to eat large amount of leaves and have bulging stomachs to manage it.

1. Fold and unfold.

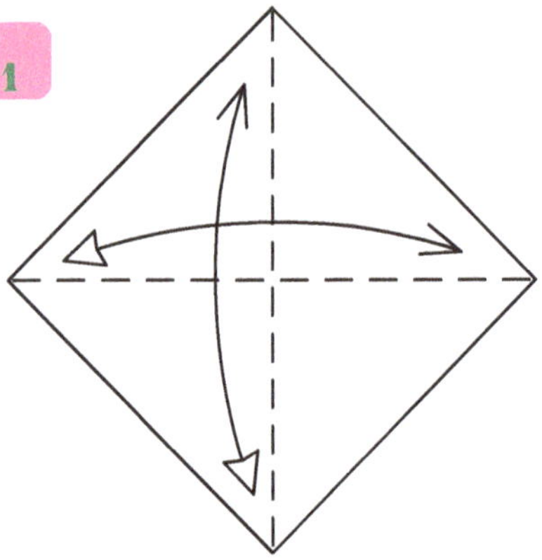

2. Fold and unfold on the edges.

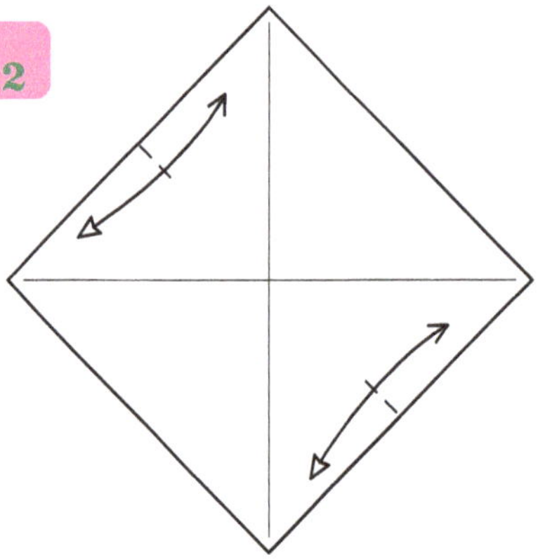

3. Fold and unfold on the edges.

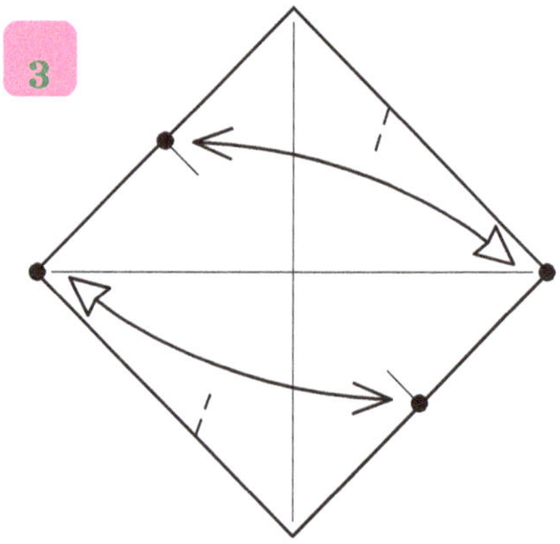

4.

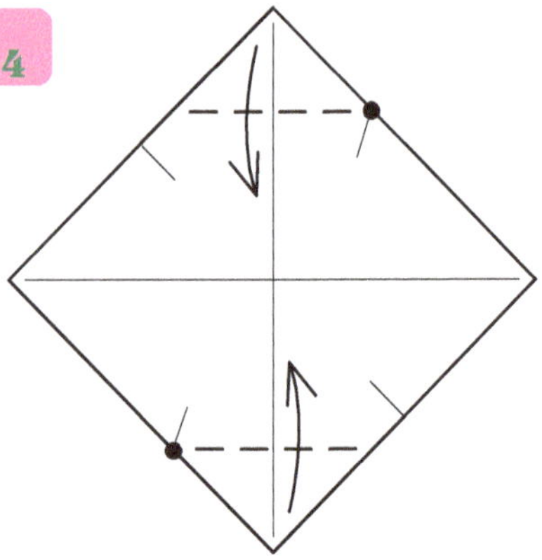

5. 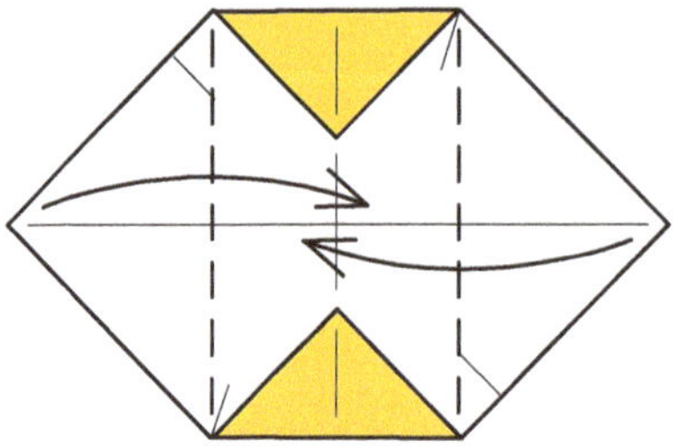 Rotate 90°.

6. Fold to the center.

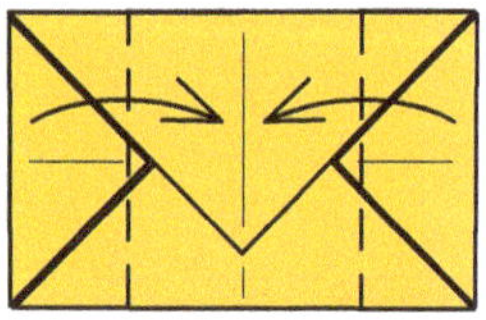

110　Origami Symphony No. 7

7 Make squash folds.

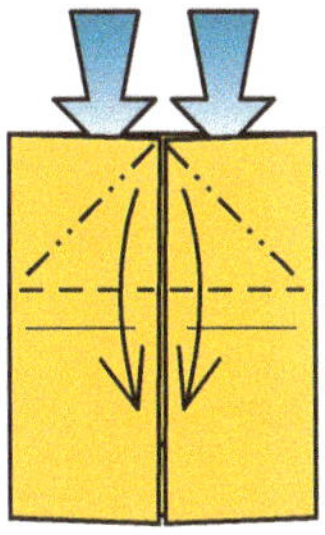

8 Pull out the hidden corner.

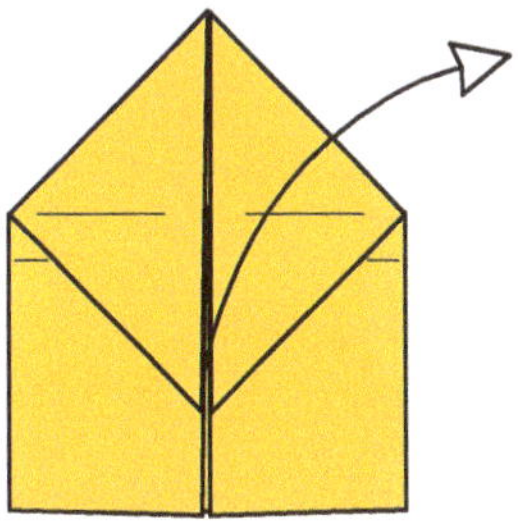

9 Squash-fold.

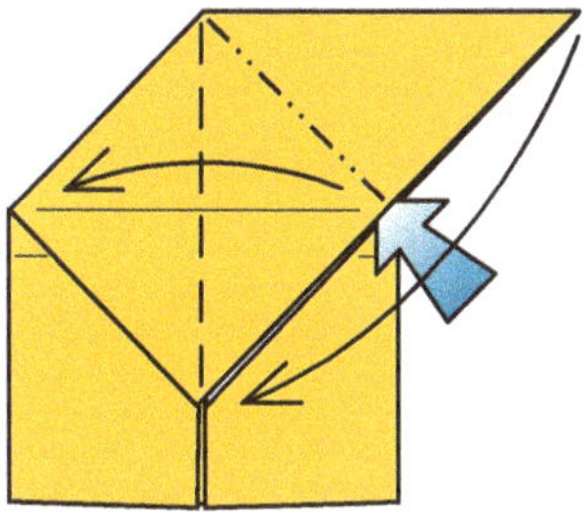

10 Fold to the center and unfold.

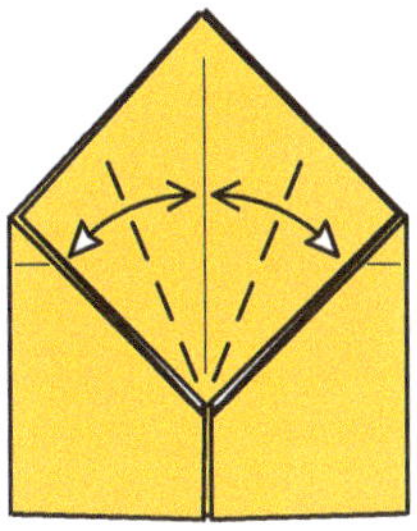

11 Petal-fold.

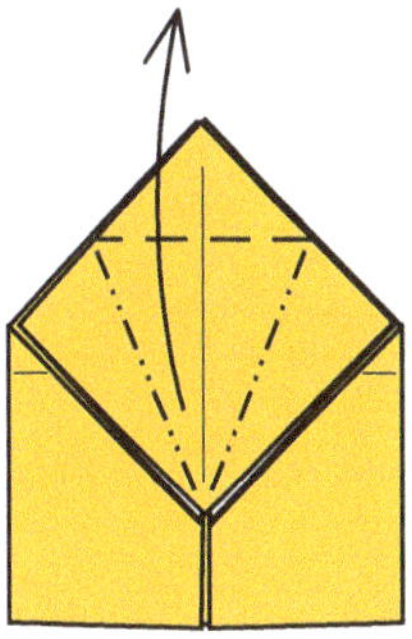

12

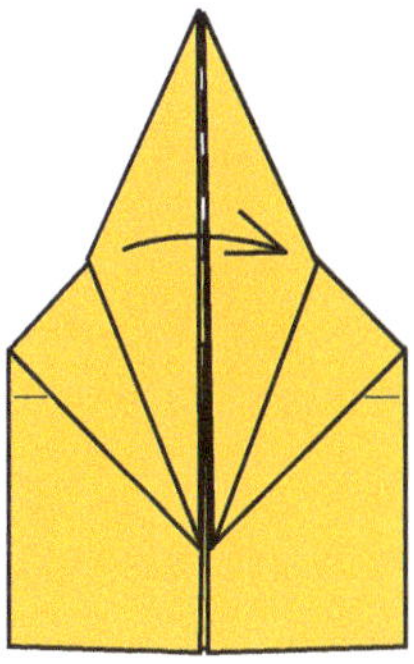

13 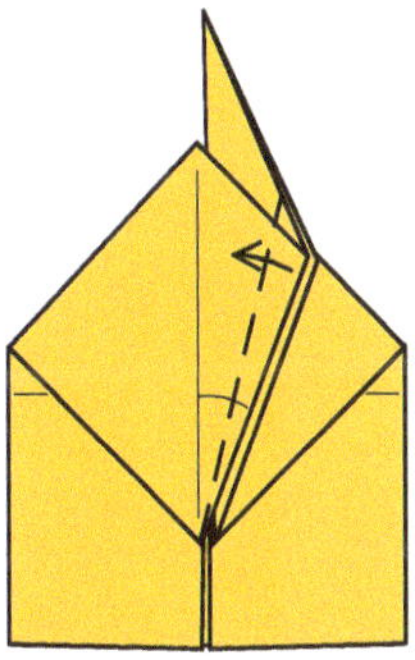 Fold at an angle of one-third.

14

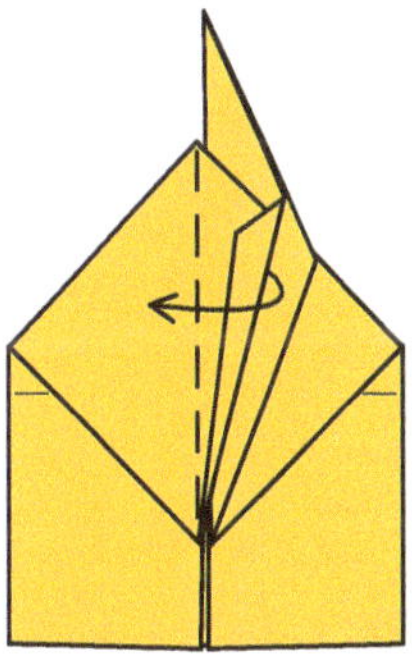

15 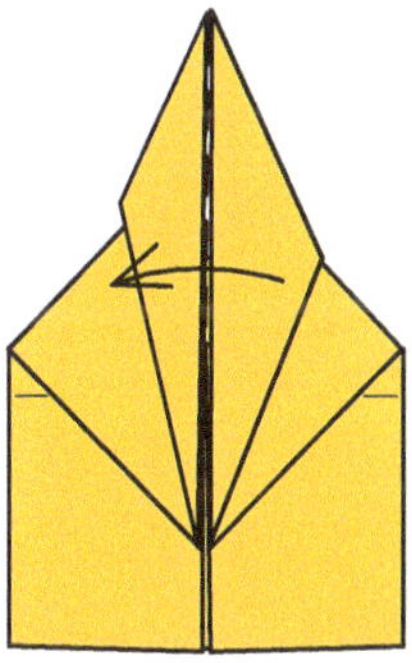 Repeat steps 12–14 in the opposite direction.

16 Rotate 180°.

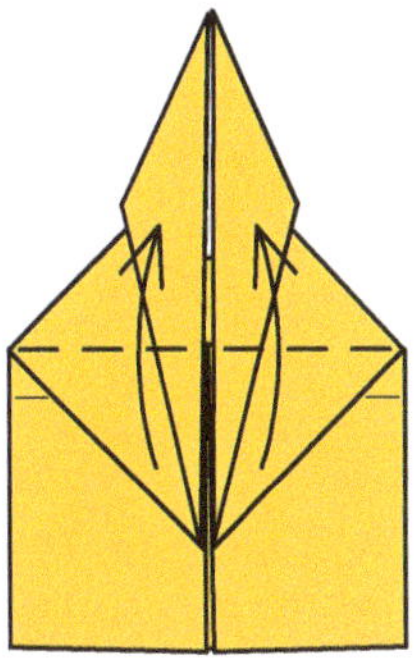

17 Repeat steps 7–16.

18

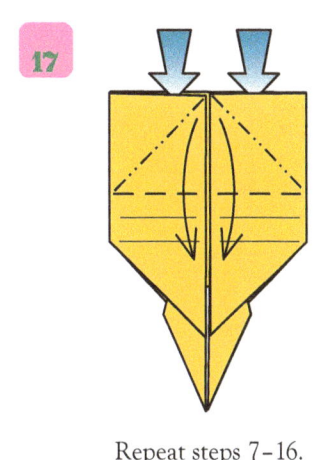
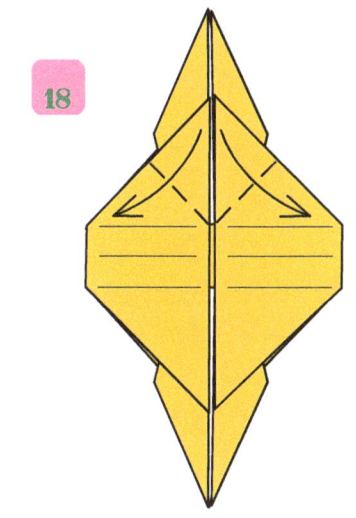

Proboscis Monkey **111**

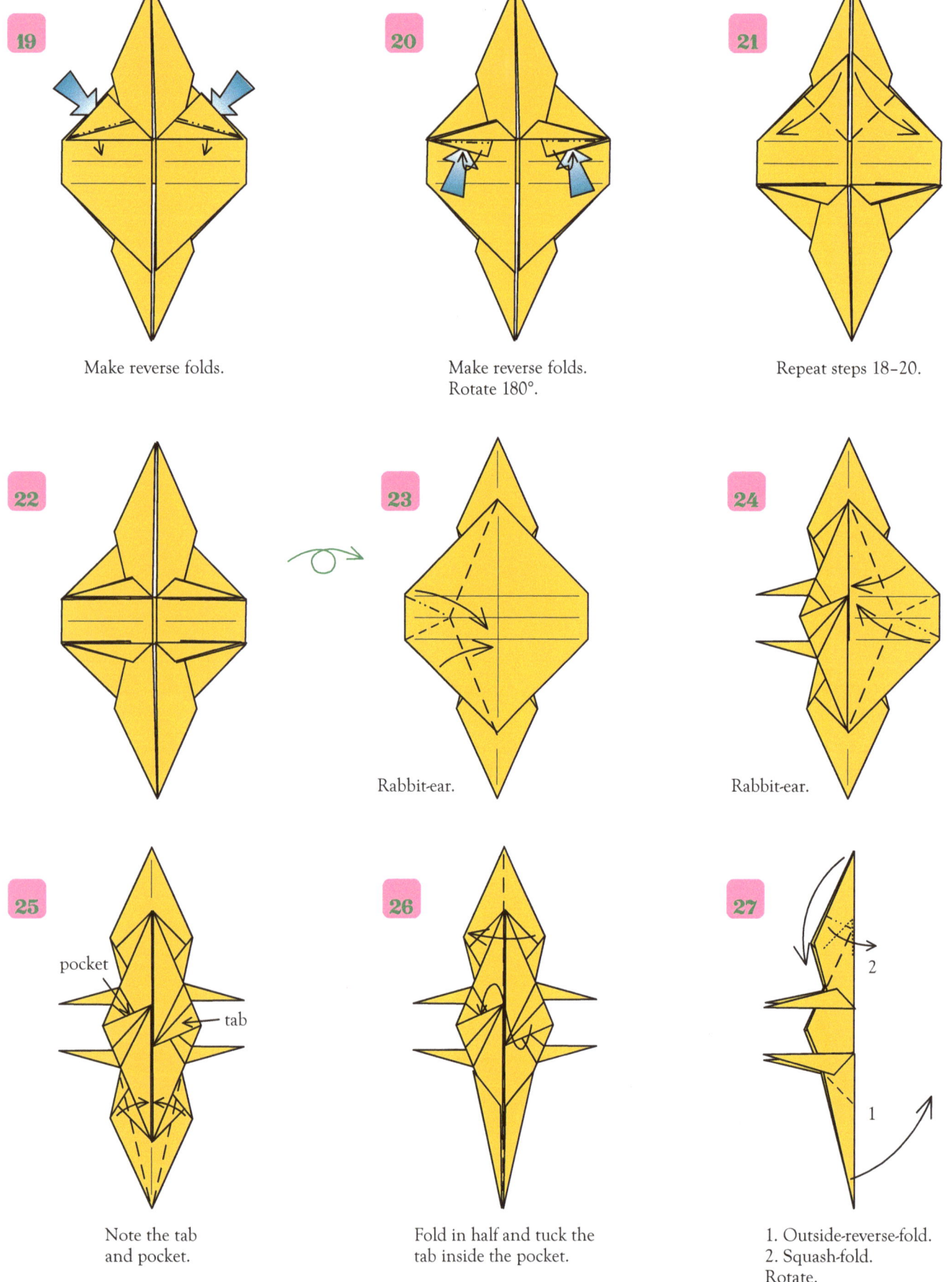

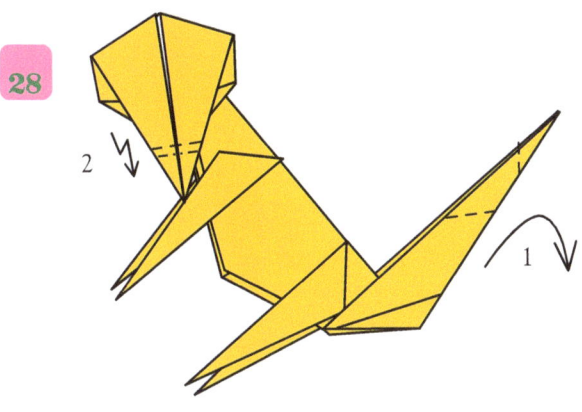

1. Make reverse folds.
2. Pleat-fold.

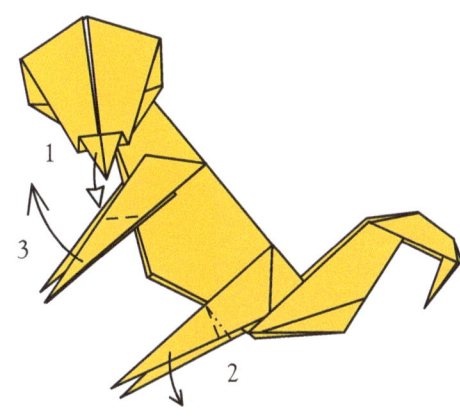

1. Unfold.
2. Crimp-fold, repeat behind.
3. Outside-reverse-fold, repeat behind.

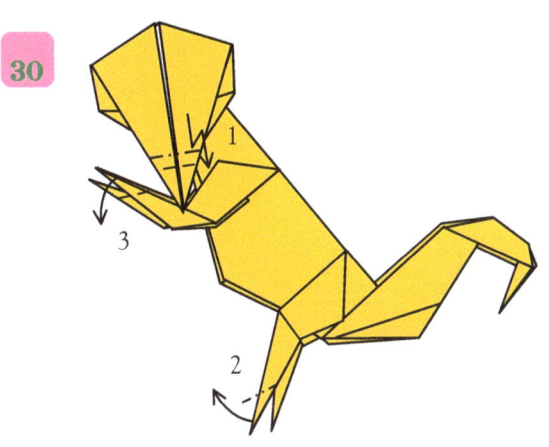

1. Fold inside with reverse folds.
2. Crimp-fold, repeat behind.
3. Outside-reverse-fold, repeat behind.

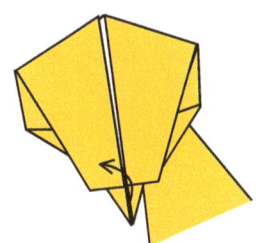

Lift up and spread the nose.

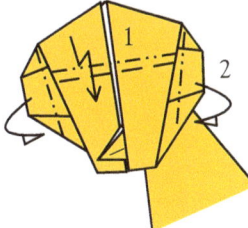

1. Pleat-fold.
2. Fold behind.

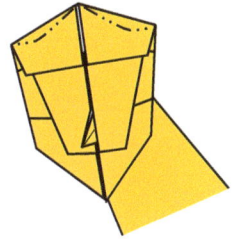

Shape the head.

Proboscis Monkey

Stacked Monkeys

This monkey can cling to a tree and link to duplicates of itself. How many monkeys can you link?

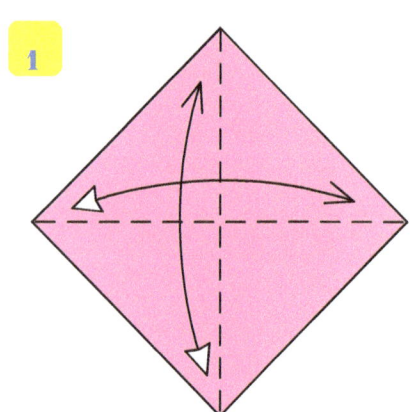

Fold and unfold.

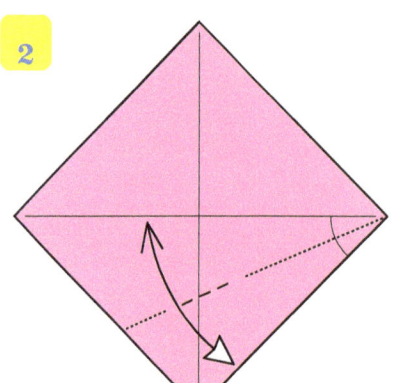

Fold and unfold along the diagonal.

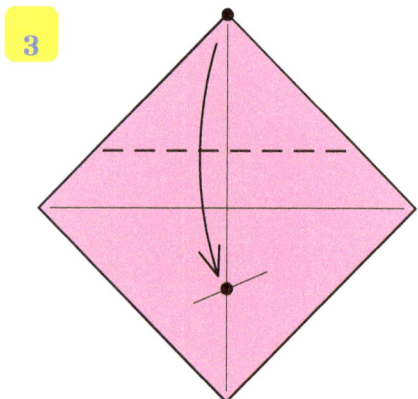

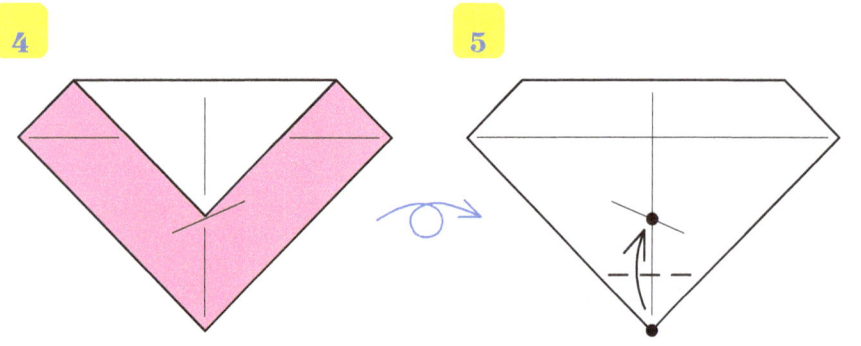

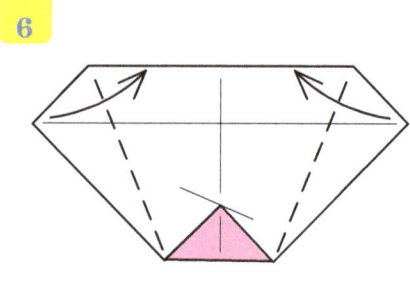

114   *Origami Symphony No. 7*

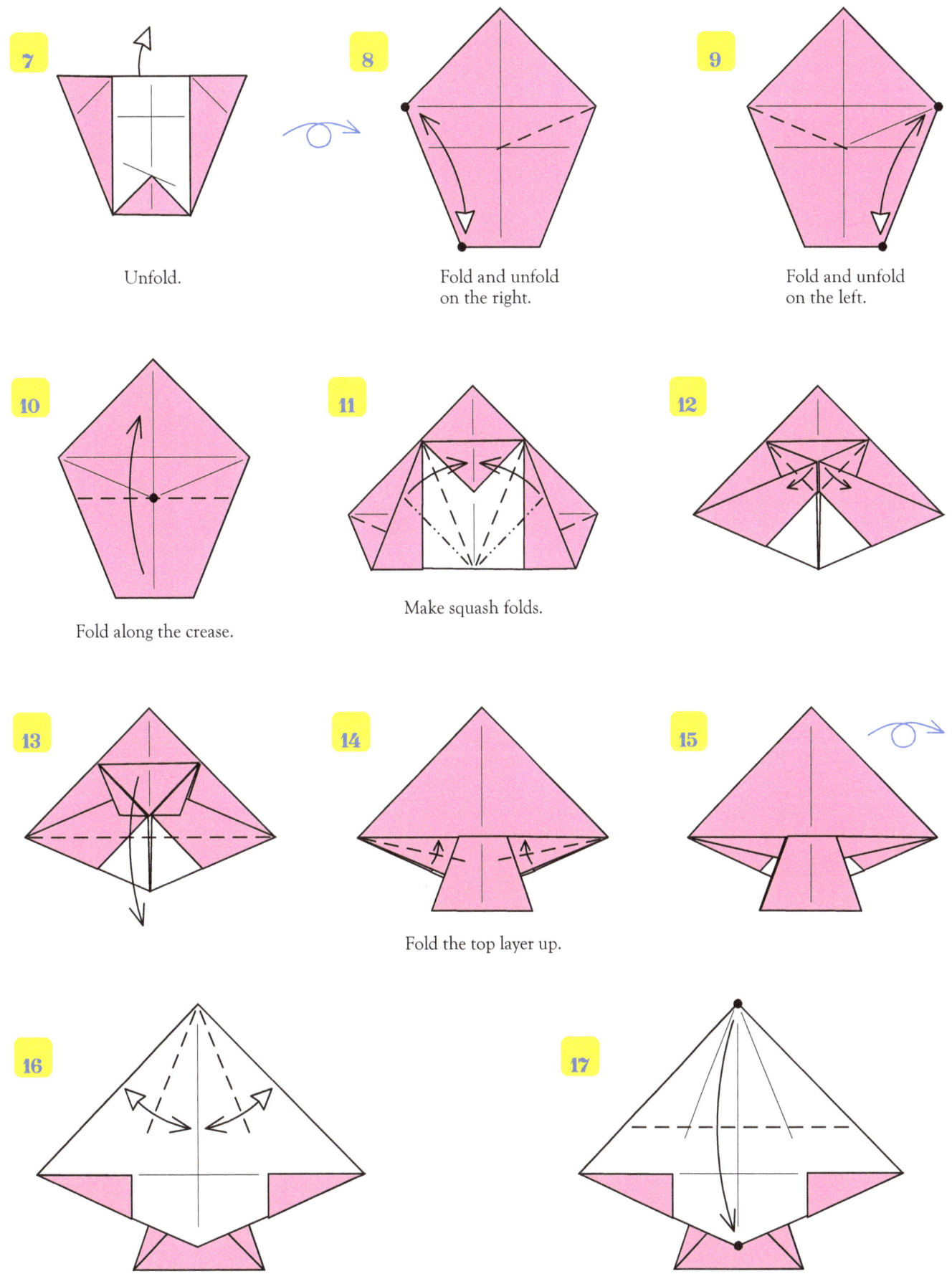

Stacked Monkeys

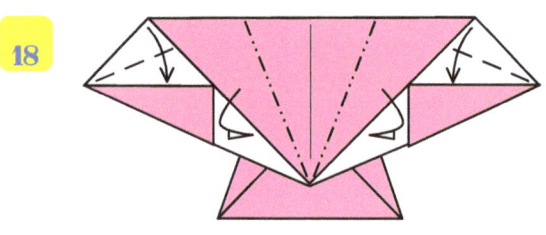

Mountain-fold along the creases.

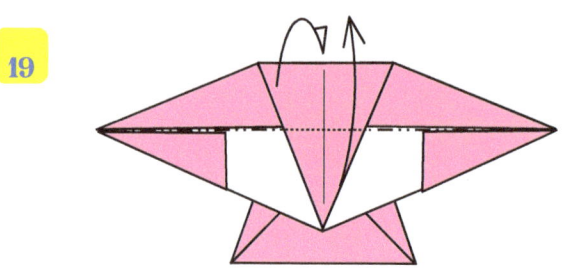

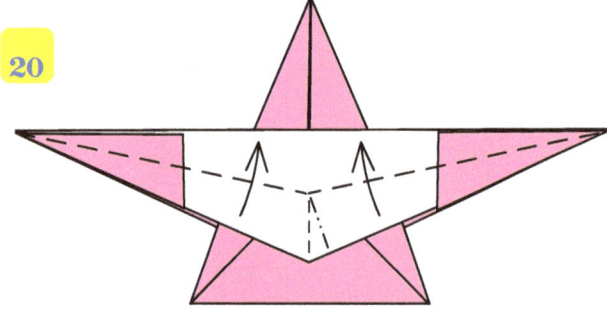

Rabbit-ear.

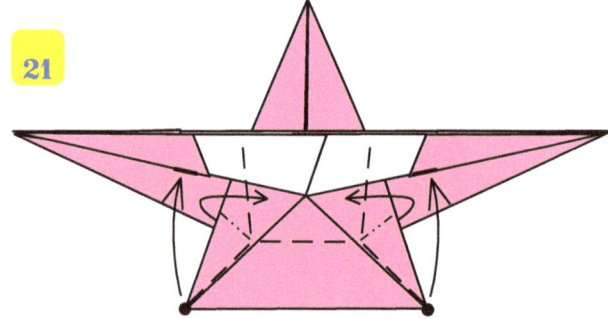

Push in on both sides while folding up.

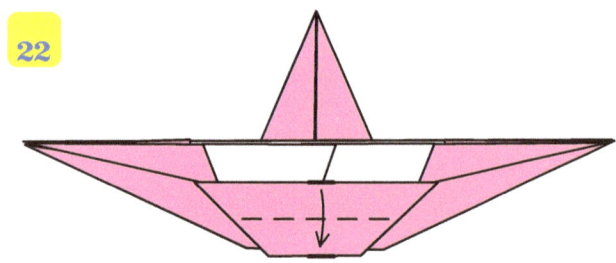

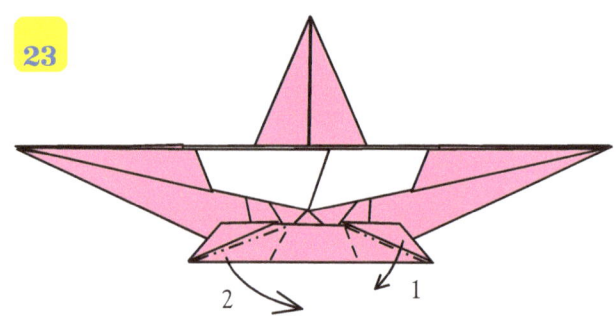

1. Squash-fold.
2. Stretch the flap.

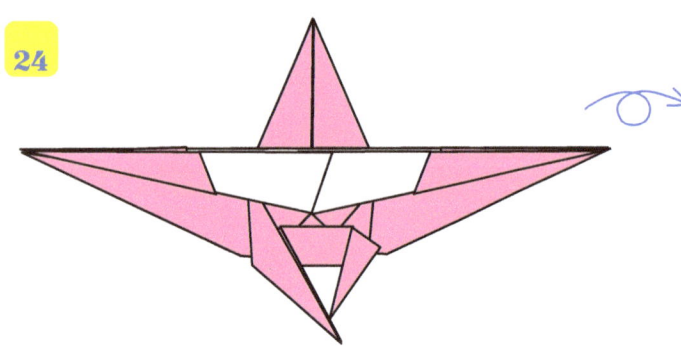

1. Rabbit-ear.
2. Make squash folds.

Tuck inside.

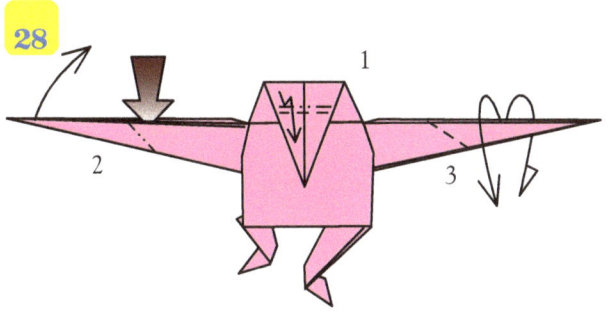

1. Pleat-fold.
2. Place your finder between the second and third layers for this reverse fold.
3. Outside-reverse-fold.

1. Fold behind.
2. Make squash folds.

Stacked Monkeys

Baboon

Bamboos are among the largest of the Old World monkeys, weighing between 30 to 80 pounds. Living in Africa and Arabia, they are found in open savannas and woodlands. During the day, they stay on the ground most of the time, walking on all four legs, in social troops of 50 or more. They will hang out in trees to eat and watch over the area, and sleep in the trees at night. The young baboons are playful. Baboons feed on grasses, fruit, insects, birds, rodents, and other mammals. They communicate with over 30 distinct vocal sounds.

1. Fold and unfold.

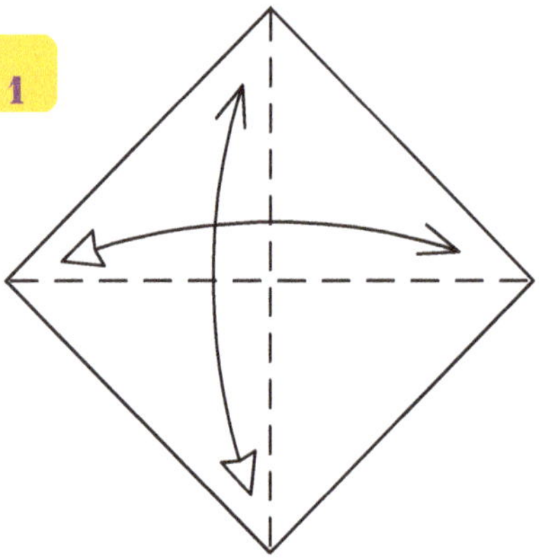

2. Fold to the center and unfold.

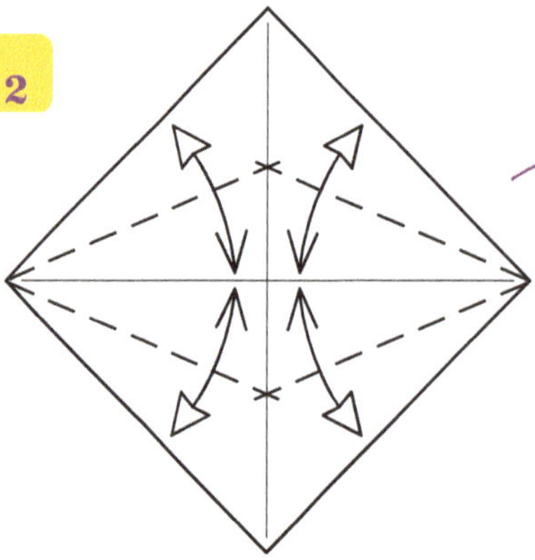

3. Fold and unfold.

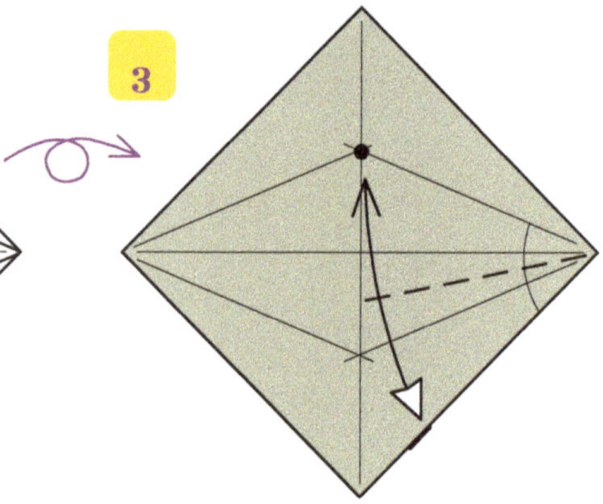

4. Repeat step 3 three times.

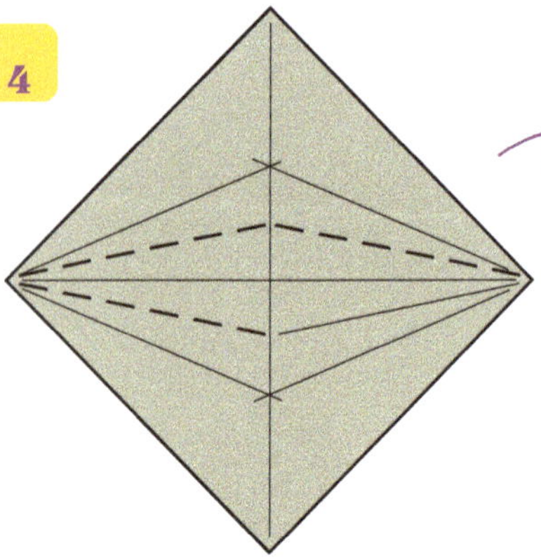

5.

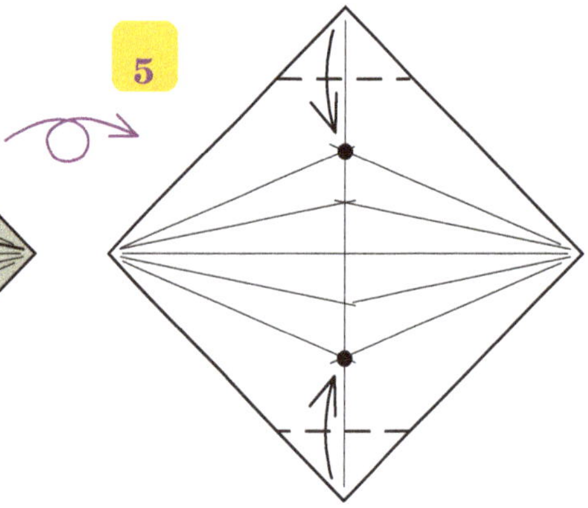

6. 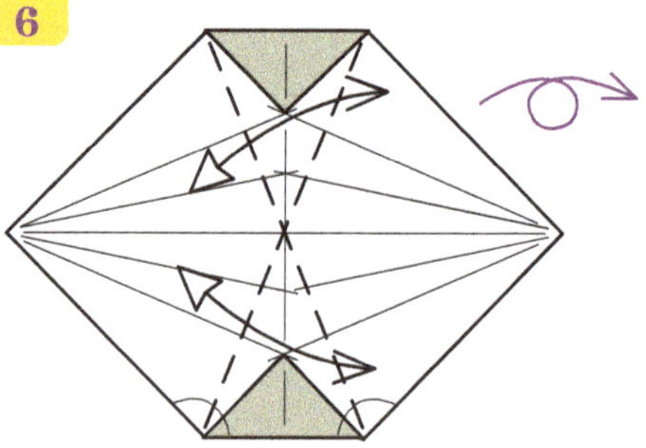 Fold and unfold.

118 Origami Symphony No. 7

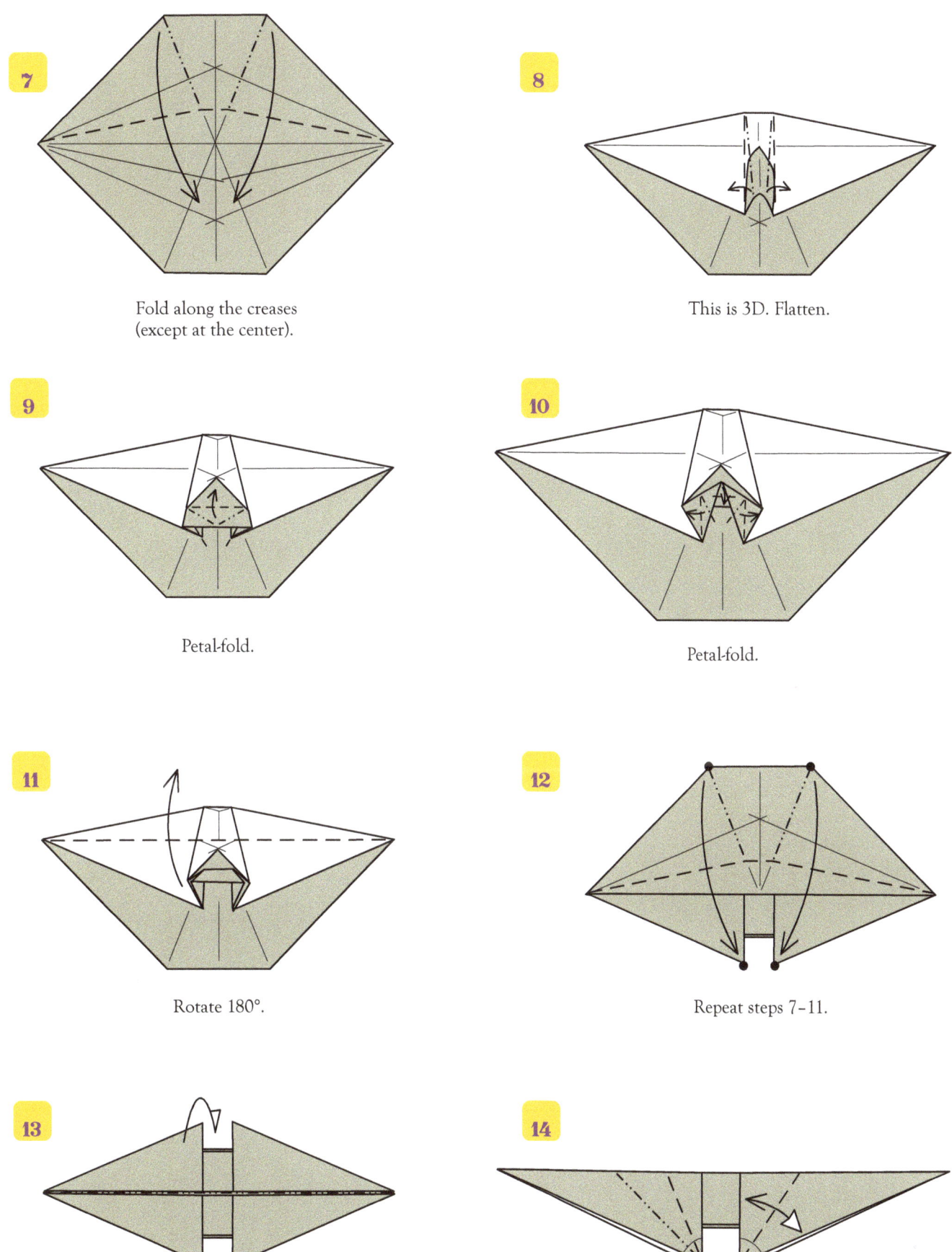

7 Fold along the creases (except at the center).

8 This is 3D. Flatten.

9 Petal-fold.

10 Petal-fold.

11 Rotate 180°.

12 Repeat steps 7–11.

13

14
1. Fold and unfold.
2. Fold and unfold in thirds.

Baboon 119

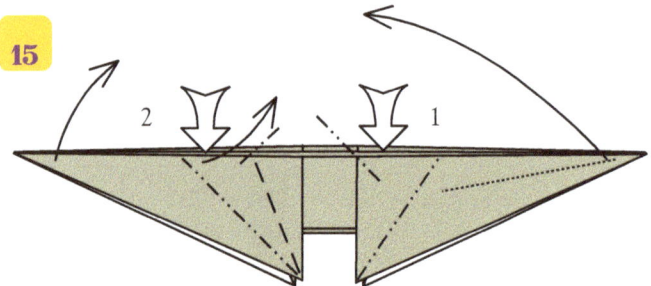

Push in at the top for these folds.
1. This is similar to a reverse fold.
2. Squash-fold.

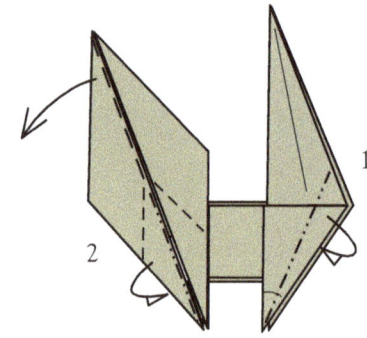

1. Fold inside at an angle of 1/3. Repeat behind.
2. This is similar to an outside reverse fold.

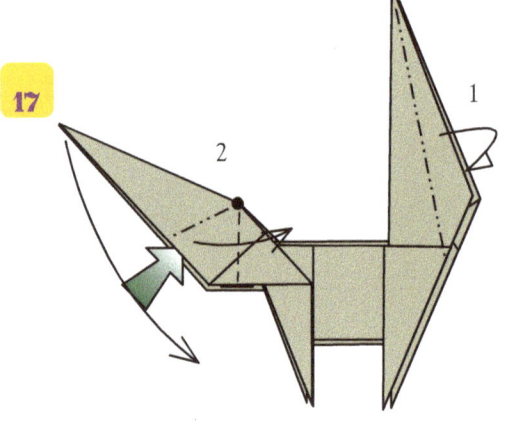

Note the horizontal bold line.
1. Fold inside along the crease, repeat behind.
2. Squash-fold.

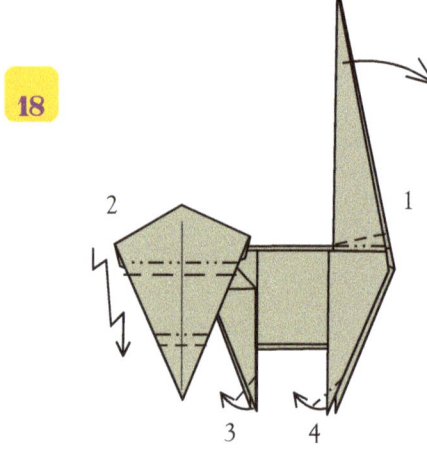

1. Crimp-fold.
2. Make pleat folds.
3. Outside-reverse-fold, repeat behind.
4. Reverse-fold, repeat behind.

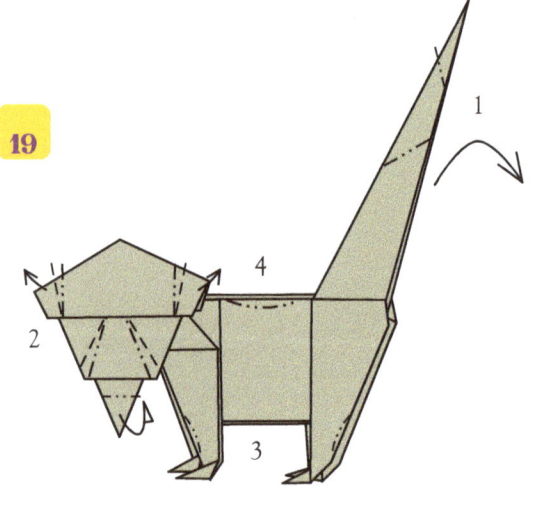

1. Make reverse folds.
2. Shape the head with pleat folds.
3. Shape the legs, repeat behind.
4. Shape the back.

Baboon

Angolan Black and White Colobus Monkey

The colobus is a small, black and white Old World monkey, weighing 20 to 30 pounds. Found in forests of Africa by the equator, they prefer to stay in trees. They are the most arboreal of the African monkeys and swing through trees by bouncing off branches for greater jumps. They live in troops of 8 to 18 monkeys. The babies are born white and taken care of by the mother and others in the troop. The colobus monkey eats leaves, fruit, bark, and flowers and can even eat plants which are toxic to other monkeys.

1. Fold and unfold.

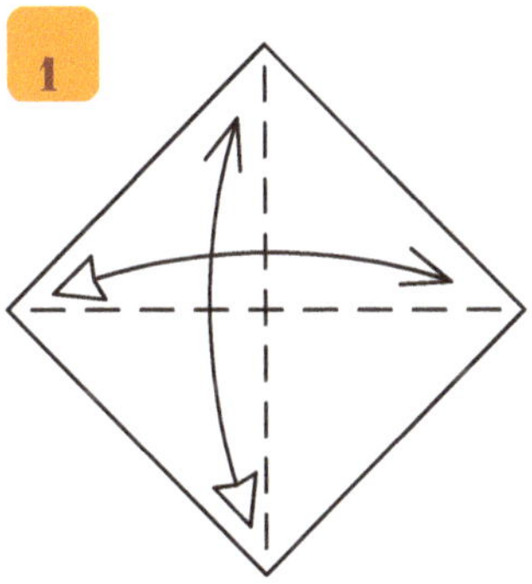

2. Fold to the center and unfold.

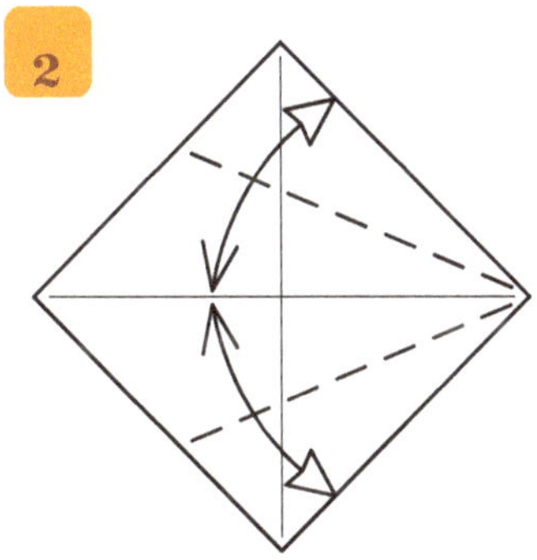

3. Fold and unfold at 1, 2, and 3.

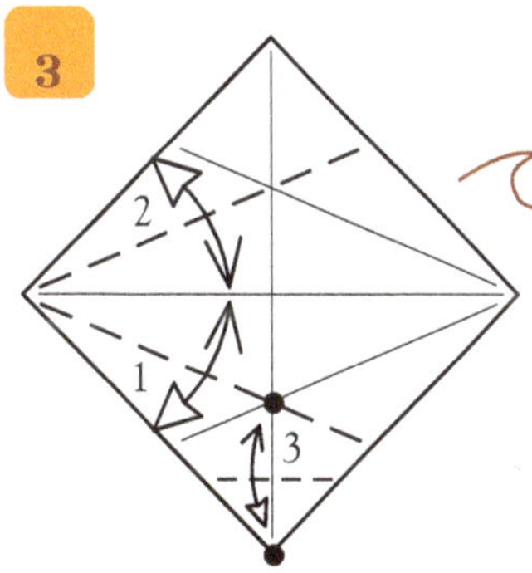

4. Fold and unfold.

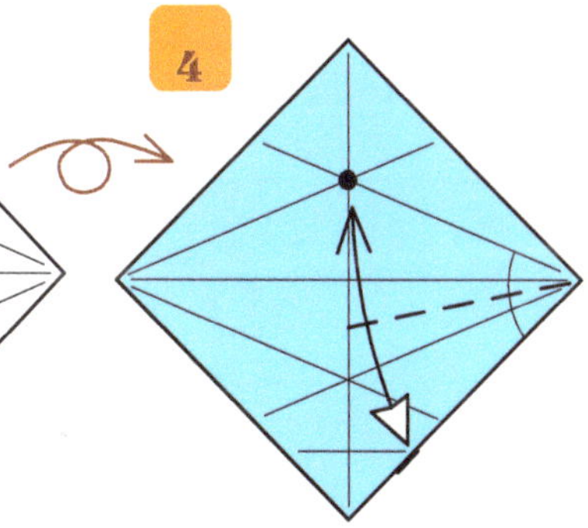

5. Repeat step 4 three times.

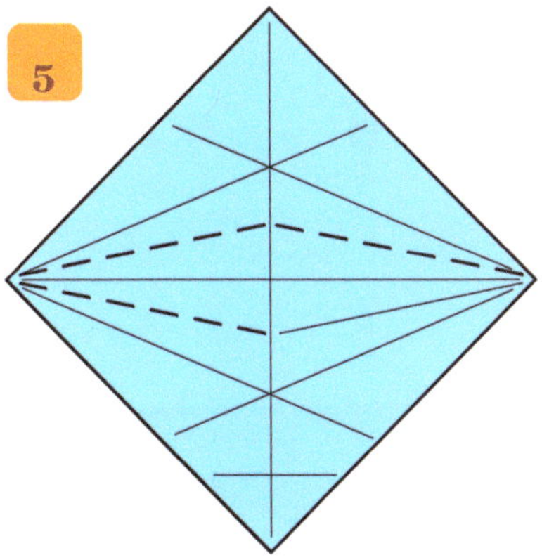

6. Fold and unfold.

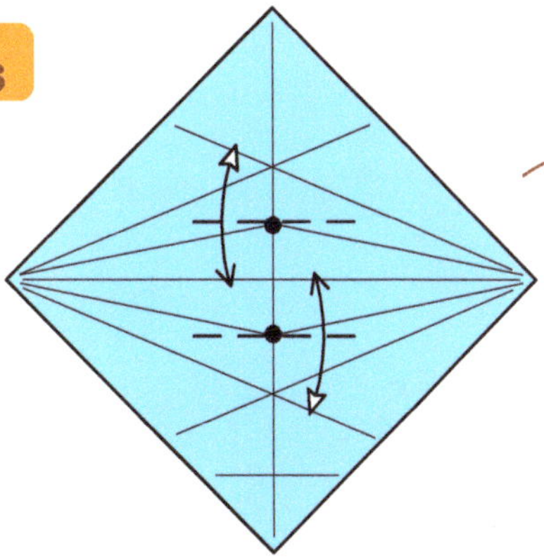

7. 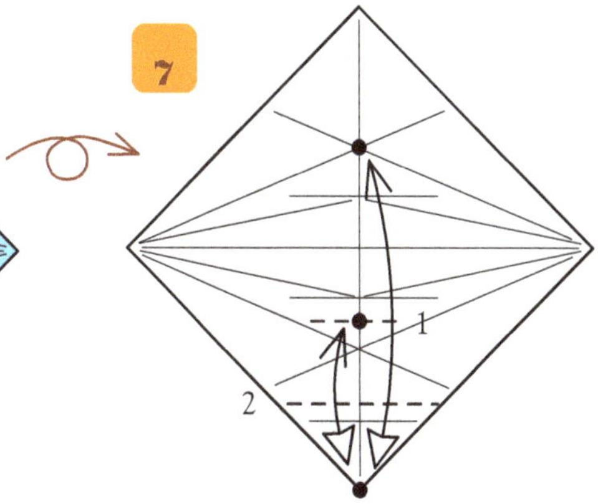
   1. Fold and unfold in the center.
   2. Fold and unfold.

Colobus Monkey 121

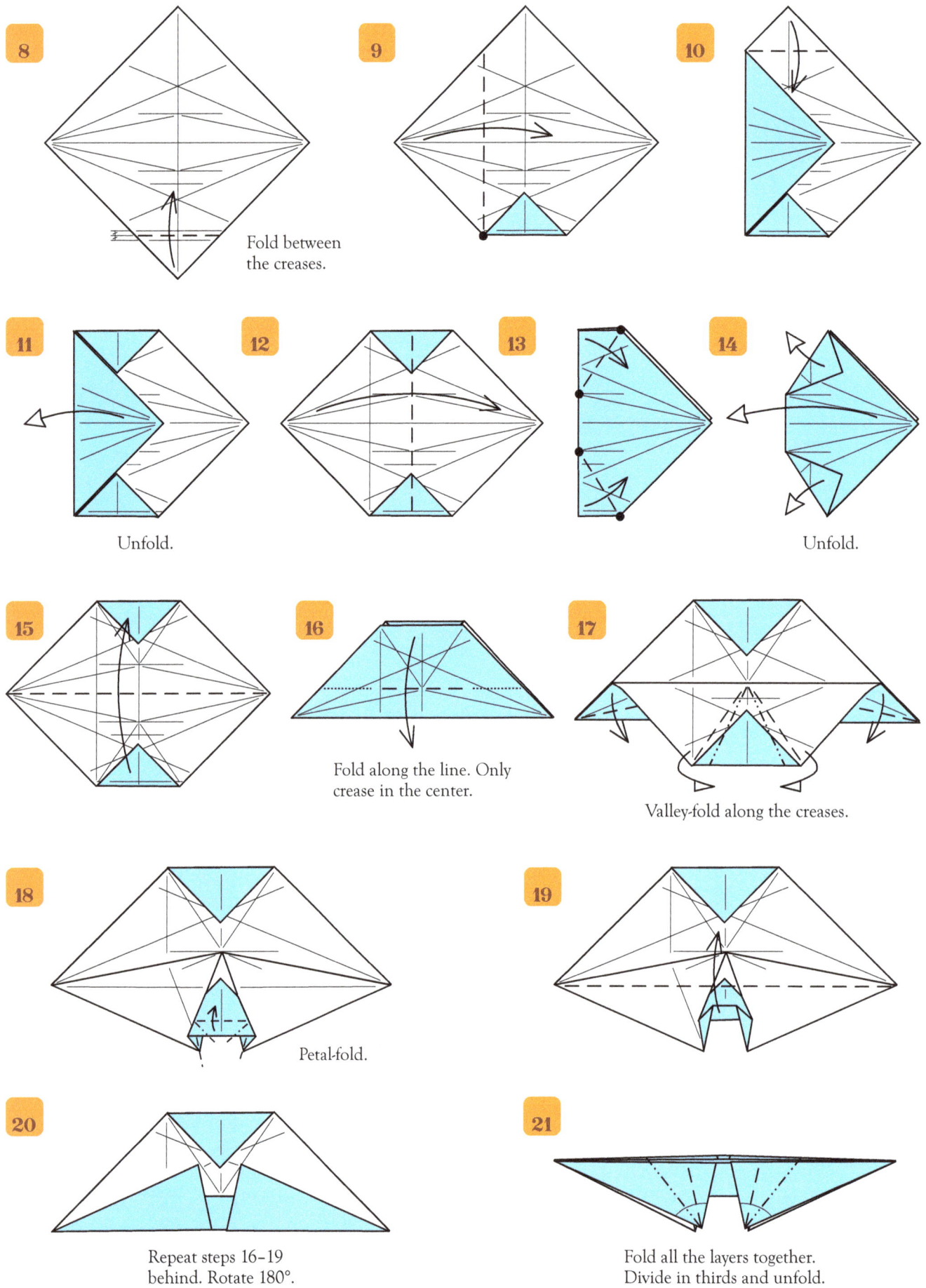

122 *Origami Symphony No. 7*

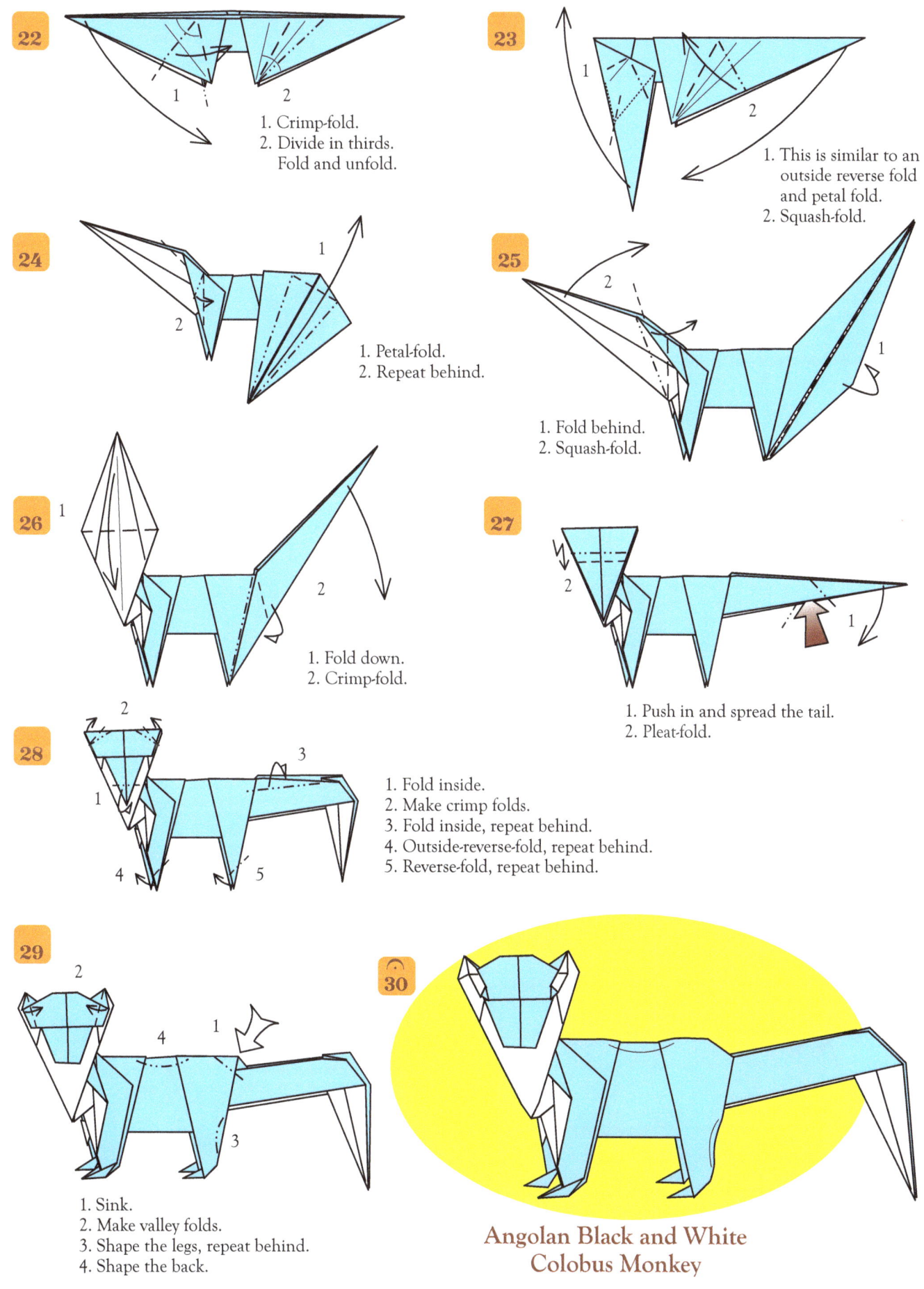

Mandrill

Similar to the baboon, the mandrill is distinct by its colorful face and rear. Mandrills live by the equator in Western Africa. Found in rainforests and thick bush, they feed on plants and small animals such as fruit, fungi, seeds, insects, worms, snakes, lizards, and small mammals. The males forage on the ground while the females and young forage in trees. Huge canine teeth are seen when the mandrill opens its mouth. They have large cheek pouches for storing food. They can travel at speeds of up to 25 miles per hour.

1. Fold and unfold.

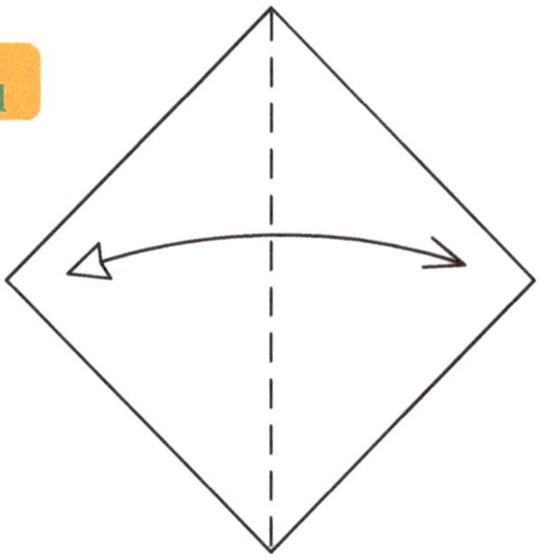

2.

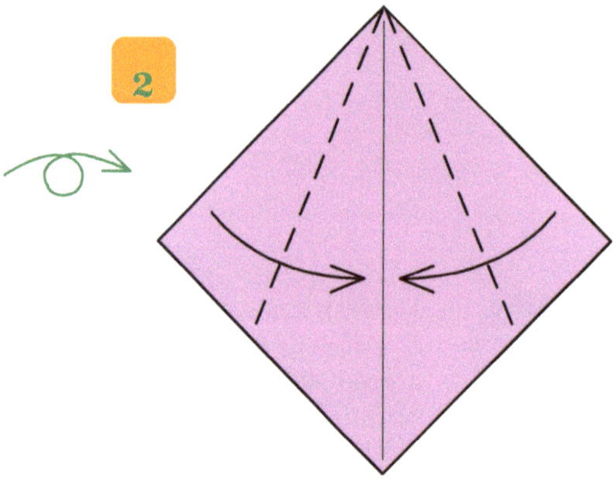

3.

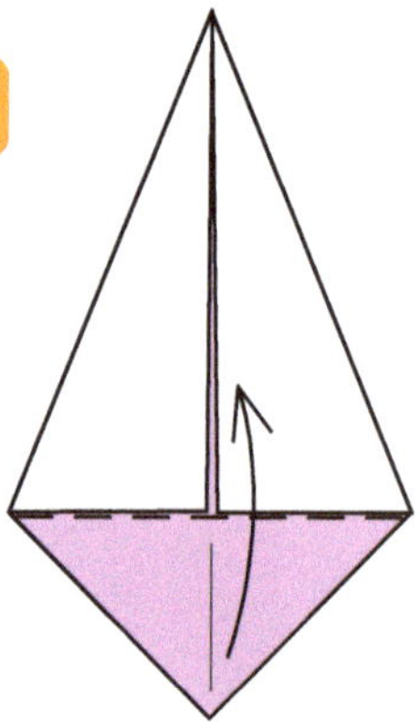

4.  Unfold.

5. Pleat-fold to the center.

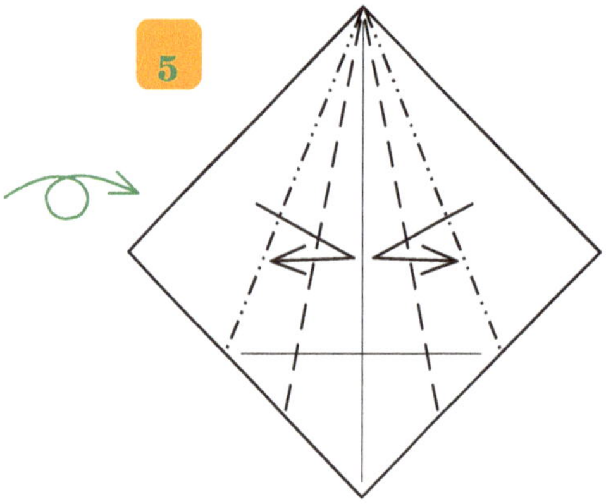

6. Unfold.

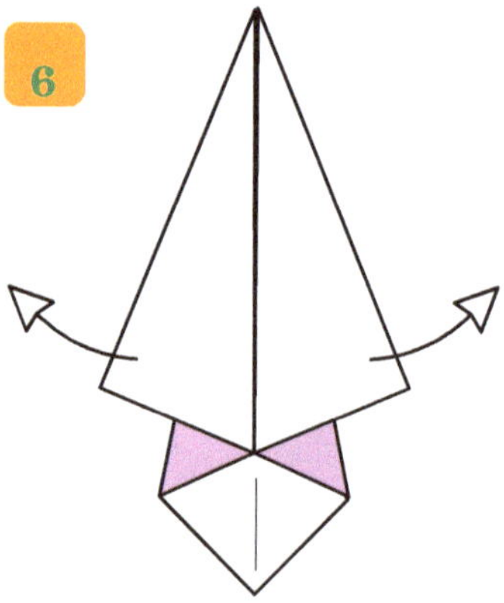

124 *Origami Symphony No. 7*

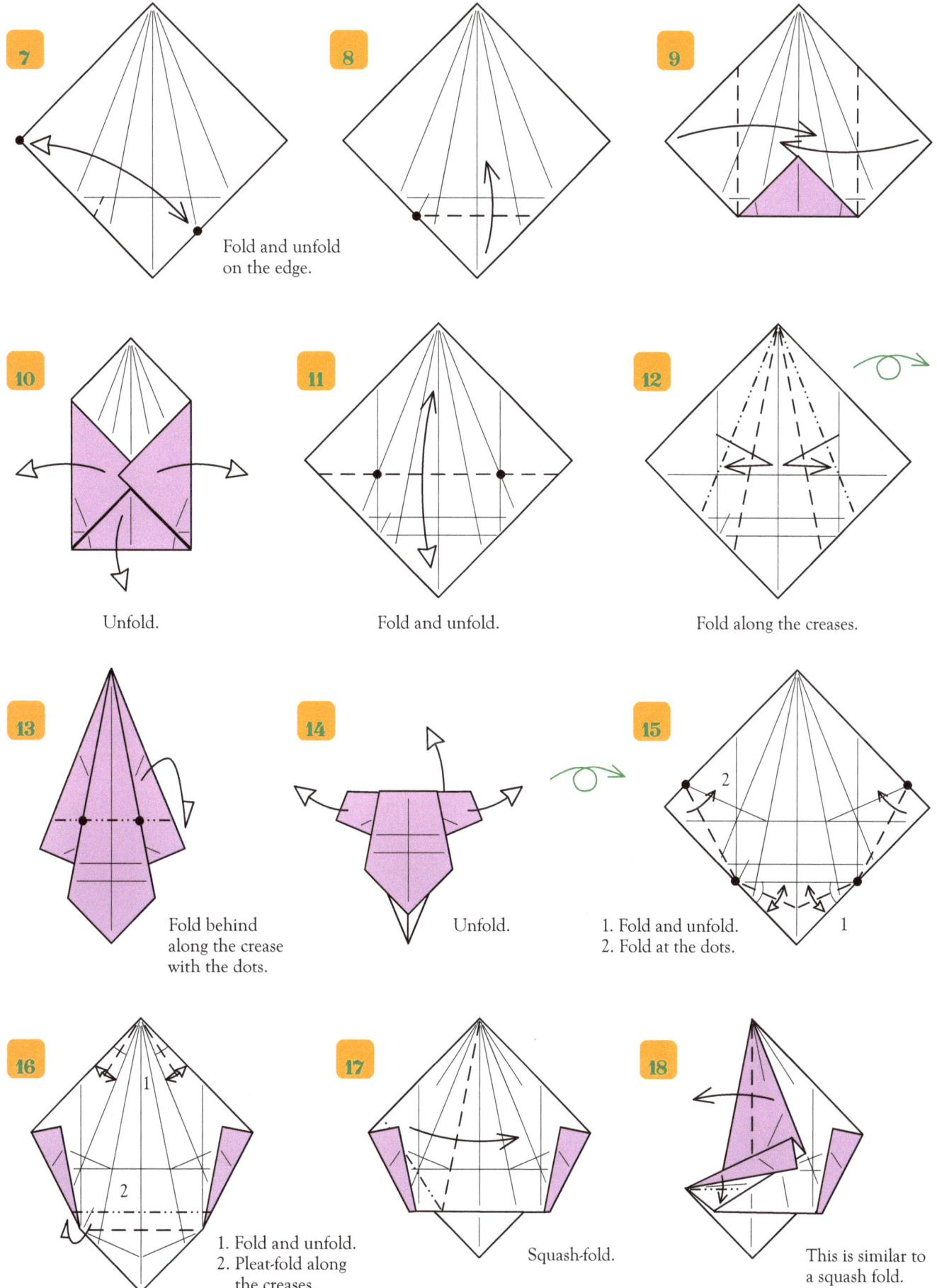

Mandrill 125

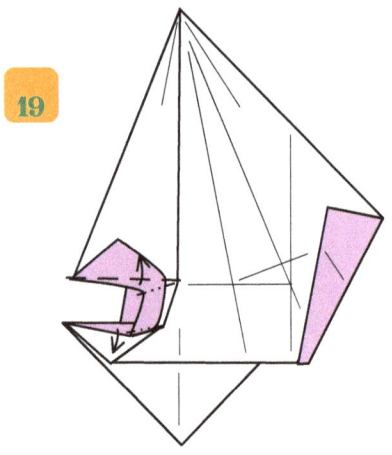

This is 3D. Flatten.

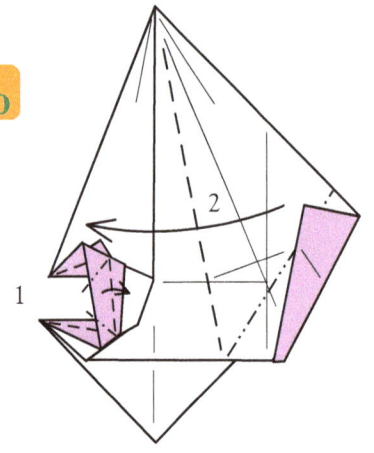

1. Petal-fold.
2. Repeat steps 17–20 on the right.

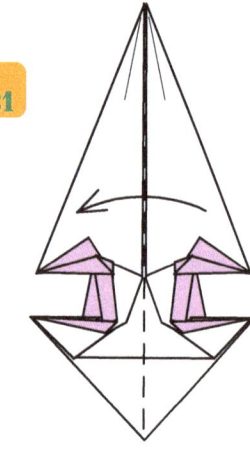

Fold in half and rotate 90°.

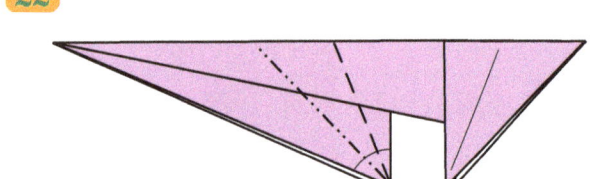

Fold and unfold in thirds.

Squash-fold.

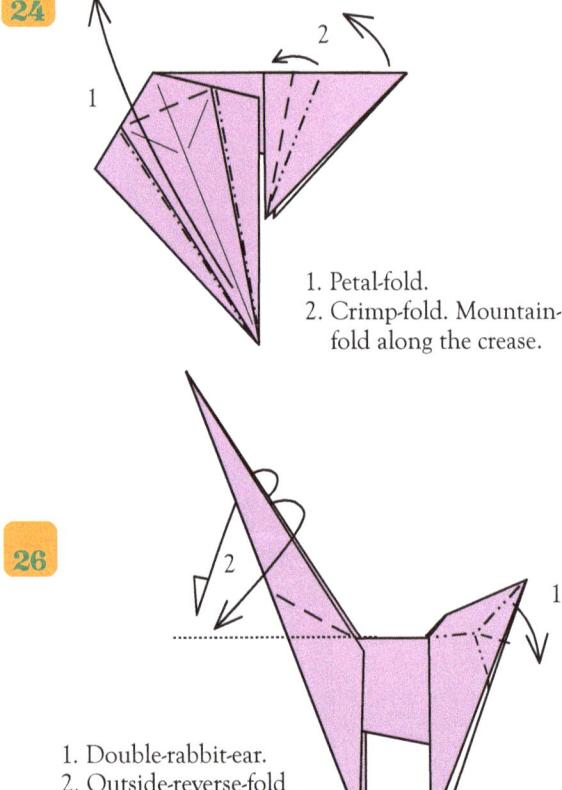

1. Petal-fold.
2. Crimp-fold. Mountain-fold along the crease.

1. Double-rabbit-ear.
2. Outside-reverse-fold to the line.

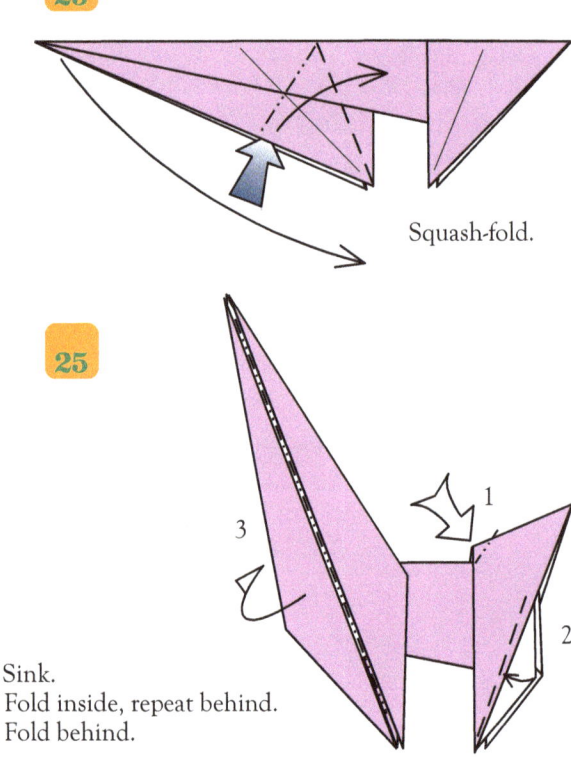

1. Sink.
2. Fold inside, repeat behind.
3. Fold behind.

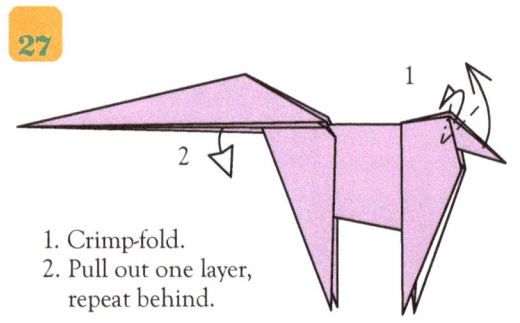

1. Crimp-fold.
2. Pull out one layer, repeat behind.

126 *Origami Symphony No. 7*

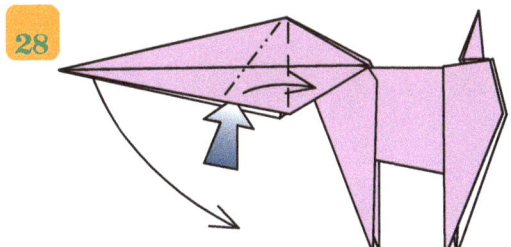

Squash-fold.

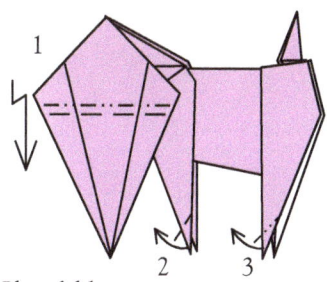

1. Pleat-fold.
2. Outside-reverse-fold, repeat behind.
3. Reverse-fold, repeat behind.

Spread the paper.

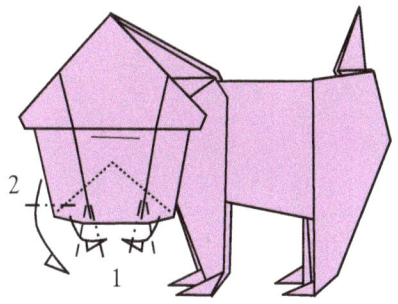

1. Refold along the creases.
2. Fold the hidden flap down.

1. Pleat-fold the inner layers.
2. Fold behind.

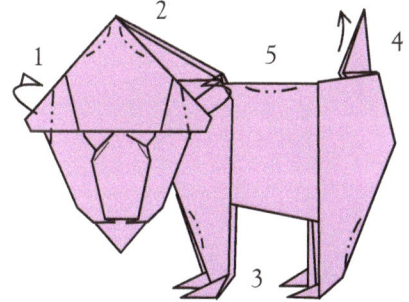

1. Fold behind.
2, 3, 4, 5. Shape the head, legs, tail, and body. Repeat behind.

Mandrill

Mandrill **127**